...BELIEVE IN MAGIC
HEAVENLY
HEAVENLY
HEAVENLY
...BELIEVE IN MAGIC
E IN MAGIC
...BELIEVE IN MAGIC

This book is dedicated to the memories
of two dear friends of Heavenly.

Andrew Weatherall
(1963–2020)
'Fail we may, sail we must.'

and

Peter James Lusty
(1970–2020)
'Are you scared of success?'

...BELIEVE IN MAGIC

HEAVENLY
RECORDINGS

THE FIRST 30 YEARS

WHITE
RABBIT

First published in Great Britain in 2020 by White Rabbit,
an imprint of The Orion Publishing Group Ltd
Carmelite House, 50 Victoria Embankment
London EC4Y 0DZ

An Hachette UK Company

1 3 5 7 9 10 8 6 4 2

A CIP catalogue record for this book is
available from the British Library.

ISBN (Hardback) 978 1 4746 1650 8
ISBN (eBook) 978 1 4746 1651 5

Designed by Paul Kelly
Typeset by Lora Findlay
Heavenly logo created by Paul Cannell
Printed in Italy

www.whiterabbitbooks.co.uk
www.orionbooks.co.uk

CONTENTS

S.O.S

In Residence

✓) OBEDIENCE TO THE LAW IS FREE DESIRE
UNDER CURFEW from SHARP NEON BARBED WIRE

WASTING AWAY THIS COUNTRY
WEARING LIKE A BORN DEAD
FREE HEROIN SHOTS FOR THOSE WHO
WILL NO LONGER BEG

CH) SPECTATERS of SUICIDE
EXPLODING IN SOCIETIES EYES
SPITING GLASS FROM OUR MOUTH
DYING LIKE YESTERDAY

✓²) THE ONLY FREE CHOICE IS THE REFUSAL TO PAY
LIFE REDUCED TO SUICIDE OR COMFORT PAIN

CIGARETTE DEAD LIPS SUCK RED
CHOCKED ON THE SAME LIES
THAT WEVE ALL SAID

100%

1c Portland Place, Regent Street, London W1B 1JA
T 44 (0) 20 7636 1000 F 44 (0) 20 7323 2340
langhamhotels.com

I've always believed that, as an artist, if you have a strong sense of your own aesthetics you have a much better chance of communicating to an audience.

Right from the start Heavenly seemed to have a real sense of itself and its mission. Stylistically, it may have looked chaotic and disconnected to the outside world, but that was the point. The sheer difference of the artists was its strength.

In some ways, as a rock band from Wales with an obsession with Guns N' Roses, we were the biggest risk of all, but then that was the maverick spirit of Heavenly. Over the years, that spirit has remained and grown and grown. I feel very grateful and properly proud to have played a small part in this incredible story.

MAGIC–FAITH–AESTHETICS. To me, that's what Heavenly stands for.

Nicky Wire
March 2020

In mid-May 1990 Bob Stanley handed me a piece of paper. We were on a press junket in Sweden, arranged by Stone Roses PR Philip Hall: I'd just finished working on *England's Dreaming*, and this was my first journalistic assignment after two years in a room. We saw the group play in Stockholm and sort of hung around them, not to much avail. There was a lot of spare time, and I bonded with Bob, who was then working for the *Melody Maker*. He told me about his group Saint Etienne and several other people that I should check out.

The paper mentioned The High ('Box Set Go'), Northside ('Moody Places'), and The Charlatans ('The Only One I Know'). 'Never heard of them,' I said. 'Where do I get them?' Bob pointed me in the direction of someone called Jeff Barrett who had an office in Panther House, near the huge Post Office building in Mount Pleasant. So I went up to Capersville, to be greeted by a man with very long ginger hair, who was presiding benignly over an office full of mad kids. 'Oh well,' I thought, 'this is the future and it looks like fun.'

In short order, I got pulled into the Heavenly orbit, seeing early London shows by the Manic Street Preachers, Flowered Up and Fabulous – whose best moment was when they came on stage and announced, in a voice dripping with sarcasm, 'Hullo. We're fabulous.' Apart from some great records by Saint Etienne and the Manic Street Preachers, the high spot of this early phase was the infamous Flowered Up squatted party in a plush Dulwich mansion owned by a criminal on the run: several days of mayhem in the secluded street where Kelvin MacKenzie then lived.

The friendship continued over the next decade, as Heavenly pursued its course with Saint Etienne, Doves and Beth Orton. Sometime in 2004 I bumped into Jeff just off Kensington High Street and handed him a CDR I'd burnt of songs from the turn of the sixties into the seventies. Jeff had the foresight and generosity to say, 'Why don't we do a compilation?'

Our connection has continued to the end of the twenty-first century's second decade: I've joined the Heavenly people for appearances at the Caught by the River stage at Festival N°6 in Portmeirion, Port Eliot and the Good Life Festival in North Wales. Nearly thirty years of meeting and music: here's to many more.

February 2020

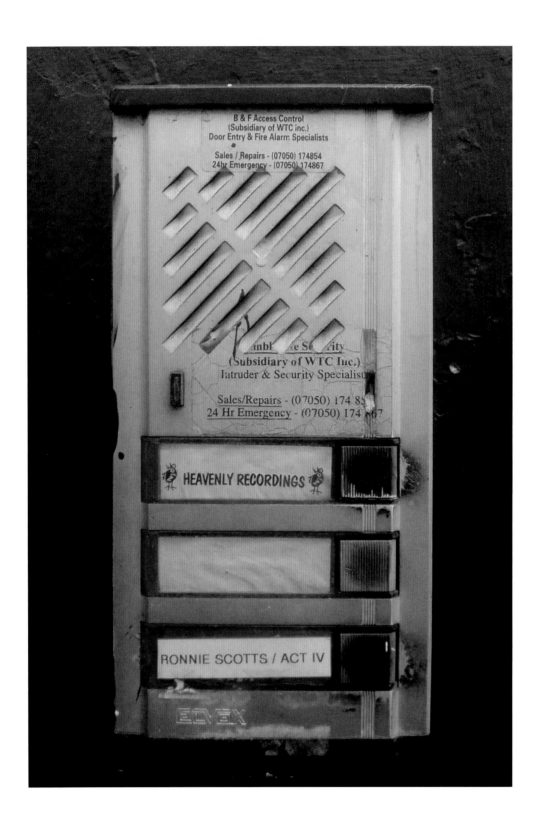

It's late. You can tell that from the way the streetlights blur everything inside the room. That's your excuse for not seeing straight anyway. Nothing to do with the fact that you've been here a while, possibly half the day. Certainly the best part of it.

You've definitely had a few. Some in the pub, quite a few more since. A glance around the room and it seems like you're in good company. A constantly swinging door brings in a succession of increasingly loose people with carrier bags full of cans of Red Stripe, packets of Marlboro Lights and bonhomie to spare. Over the course of the evening, the room has filled with musicians and writers, band managers, deep thinkers and professional drinkers. The conversations that are taking place – the ones you can make out over the noise anyway – espouse the kind of philosophy you only ever hear in perfectly formed song lyrics. '. . . *Send me a sign to save my life/ Cos at this moment in time there is nothing certain in these days of mine*', '. . . *but thinking young and growing older is no sin/And I can play the game of life to win*', '. . . *as we walk, hand and hand/Sisters, brothers, we'll make it to the promised lands*', '. . . *awopbopaloobop alopbamboom*'.

Someone tells you this place is actually an office and that he's the office hairdresser ('. . . *I'm just a boy with a new haircut/And that's a pretty nice haircut*'). He tells you it's the only office in the world where more work gets done when the boss isn't there. You can't stop wondering what kind of work would ever go on in these two and a half rooms. It feels more like the woozy, slow-motion bar scene near the start of Mean Streets ('. . . *But it's all right now, in fact, it's a gas*'). The only interior lighting is a giant neon bird bent out of blue and red, a beacon so bright it could act as a summons to some kind of hard-partying Batman three cities away. Actually, if he's coming, tell him to get some green Rizlas, and maybe another bottle of vodka ('. . . *My oh my oh my I've had a few*').

Then there's the music.

Said boss is up and dancing, lost in music ('. . . *no turning back*'). There's one Technics deck and a CD player, both working overtime – like a jukebox programmed by Apollo himself, the music keeps coming in relentless and irresistible waves, each loud enough and good enough to turn heads and sink cities. A perfect, logical flow of early Chicago house, lovers rock, frantic Aussie garage, five-string serenades, freakbeat, breakbeats, power pop, slouching grooves and celestial folk. It's an endless mixtape spooling onwards, a Dansette relentlessly dropping 7-inches one after another, an all-back-to-mine DJ set that never stops exploring around the next corner, and the next ('*Today on this program you will hear gospel/And rhythm and blues, and jazz/All those are just labels/We know that music is music . . .*'). It is a relentless, dynamite sound and you're sat inside it.

When things finally wind down – why do nights like this always have to stop? – someone reminds you it's a Monday night and calls you a taxi ('. . . *cos Monday sure does hurt*'). By the time you get in, you have no idea if the digits on display in the front of the cab are the time or the price that's clocked up while the driver's waited for you. It'll puzzle you all the way down the road, as you turn onto Shaftsbury Avenue, head out of Soho and eventually out of the centre of London. Eventually, as you turn the key in your front door, you find yourself wondering, 'Did that just actually happen?' And if you told anyone about it, would they even believe you? '*I'll tell you about the magic, and it'll free your soul/But it's like trying to tell a stranger 'bout rock and roll.*'

Anyone who ever spent a night in the Heavenly office on Frith Street will remember a night somewhere along those lines. Or maybe not; maybe they'll have a mental fog and a nagging feeling that they had the time of their lives before they had to deal with a weapons-grade hangover. That version of the Heavenly office was situated above Ronnie Scott's and opposite Bar Italia on Frith Street. It sat on a wonky trans-time ley line that connected the 2i's, the Astoria, the YMCA and the End. As much as it was a working environment, it was also a makeshift disco and an egalitarian meeting place – think a Quaker meeting house with religion replaced by *Raw Power*, *Bummed* and an armful of Strictly Rhythm 12-inches.

At that office, congregations met regularly, particularly on Mondays. For some, those Monday nights were the last gasp of the weekend, for many others they represented the early start of the next one. There were countless occasions when people would randomly turn up around 10 p.m. on the assumption that there would be a party on. Nine times out of ten, they were right. Strangely, no matter how many crazed Monday nights came and went and rocked the rest of the week like a thermonuclear blast, the legions of police refuelling outside Bar Italia never knocked on the door despite the fact that you could hear the music from nearby Charing Cross Road. Maybe they had bigger fish to fry. Maybe they just liked what they were hearing. The one time Westminster Council turned up to accuse Heavenly of opening an illicit drinking den, someone managed to convince them it was actually a respectable place of work.

On each of those Mondays (and Tuesdays and Wednesdays, Thursdays and occasional Fridays) the Frith Street office was a bricks and mortar embodiment of what Heavenly stood for. Much more than a mechanism for releasing music, 47 Frith Street was a warm and welcoming home from home (half the time there was someone asleep on the sofa trying to make it their actual home); it was where you heard the best music and met people who'd go on to become friends, comrades, work buddies. Ideas and crazed plans were welcome, encouraged, even. Bands could form there, career paths could radically change on the basis of a conversation with a stranger. Many of the ideas that have propelled and energised the label over the past thirty years happened after hours in the office.

There was a 'top down approach' that meant it was invariably Heavenly founder Jeff Barrett who cranked up the volume on the stereo sometime around 5 p.m. before switching the glowing neon sign on. Elsewhere in the same industry, anyone at their desks beyond 7 p.m. was frantically working late, trying to make sense of the rapidly changing landscape, or waiting for a call from the States. Here, the volume of the music made that kind of industrious behaviour impossible. The fridge full of cans didn't help much either. It would be reasonable to assume that this kind of hedonism would end up creating an unsustainable business model, and that insolvency, madness or death would be the logical conclusion. But Heavenly has always thrived off the kind of behaviour that encouraged the caper to continue. Bands could end up getting signed after pub conversations or exuberant tips from wild-eyed, worse-for-wear mates. Single choices might be made after reading the room at 2 a.m. and seeing if a particular song could make battered and flattened revellers get back onto their feet.

From the very beginning, Heavenly aspired to be more than just a label. The name was meant to encapsulate a feeling rather than just act as another machine for putting out singles and albums. It meant that over the years that feeling could manifest as a book, a gig, a festival, an exhibition, a night in the office or a plastic toy. And as a ceiling-high stack of great records. It helped that Paul Cannell's bird logo – originally cut into a pencil eraser – could be transferred to, and look brilliant on, pretty much any surface.

I'm writing in the past tense as I no longer work at Heavenly. I used to. They're in a different office now, one a few yards down the road that is no less creative – arguably more so now than in my day. It's still imbued with the same spirit of adventure as the one I left nine years ago. I started working at Heavenly in January 1994. At that point the office was two desks, one phone and a pedal-powered computer two floors above Wardour Street. You'd find it up a steep staircase above a newsagent called the Hobbit where, if your timing was spot on, you might be lucky enough to bump into a supremely lusty Tom Baker buying his daily newspaper. Over the road, London's premier heavy metal pub the Intrepid Fox and a Formica and frothy coffee caff called Bar Bruno. Most days, you'd see Jeffrey Bernard loudly berating some poor sod who'd been tasked with pushing his wheelchair from his flat on Berwick Street to the Coach and Horses on Greek Street. He'd had his right leg removed by this point, and really didn't look happy about it.

Soho in the mid-1990s was gloriously grimy and still partially off-limits. There were knocking shops everywhere, after-hours dive bars that served warm cans of Hofmeister, and streets you didn't want to walk down after dark, no matter how badly you needed a pee. Most major record companies were out west (Sony being the exception); lots of pubs closed up in the afternoon, and staff in specialist record shops still looked at you like you were pond life. It should go without saying that it was fantastic, and it suited Heavenly down to the ground.

Heavenly back then was Jeff Barrett, Martin Kelly, Tasha Lee, myself and Robert Linney – the poor accountant who had the job of trying to keep the office solvent, and would later go on to very successfully manage The Chemical Brothers. Although I'd later self-describe as Office Bez, at that point I was working in Heavenly's press office, where I learnt the job from Jeff, who remains to this day one of the greatest PR men in the game – a man who, according to former *NME* and *Melody Maker* writer (and one third of Saint Etienne) Bob Stanley, could 'convince you that you liked a record that he would admit himself he didn't even like'. The press office often worked independently to

the label, taking on records by artists we all loved. The first records I worked on were Underworld's *Dubnobasswithmyheadman*, Primal Scream's *Give Out But Don't Give Up* and Saint Etienne's *Tiger Bay*. That year wasn't the label's busiest time release-wise. Heavenly was between distributors and the sum total of releases was a series of four one-off singles grouped together as the Heavenly 7-inches. Frustration soon dictated that we start a club in a pub on a Sunday night. This was back before things like that derailed your relationship or got you sacked for being permanently hung-over at work (actually, thinking about it now, I did manage to completely derail my long-term relationship).

As a label and as a workplace, Heavenly was unconventional to say the least. Imagine that an office could also be like a clubhouse, one where your workmates were the people you went to the pub with at lunchtime and then again after work. One where all of the bands associated with the label and the press office were more like friends than clients. This design was entirely down to Jeff and the way he ran things. He'd never worked in a conventional office – none of us had – so why would he end up creating something that acted like one? On any given day, you might answer the door to Throb from Primal Scream, who'd be in need of a 'Berwick stop' between Covent Garden and Oxford Circus, or Paolo Hewitt and Paul Weller, who'd end up heading a football round the office for half an hour. If that sounds like a brag, imagine trying to get actual work done under those circumstances.

Unconventionality ran through every aspect of Heavenly, where day-to-day decisions were often driven by passion and the ability to make you smile rather than ideas of saleability. Why not start a hedonistic club night on a Sunday? Why not put out a soundtrack album to an imaginary island and make a plastic toy to go with it? Why not sign a bunch of Welsh punks when everyone was deep in their Balearic phase? Why not assign a catalogue number (HVN13) to an artwork made out of a bag that had once contained a toasted cheese sandwich that had been eaten by Bobby Gillespie?

It was there right from the start when the first Heavenly recording was released in the spring of 1990. HVN1 was an Andrew Weatherall-produced swirling Balearic throb named 'The World According to Sly & Lovechild'. Thirty years on, as I write this intro, that record is enjoying something of an unexpected second life thanks to inclusion on a Peggy Gou mix album. We could read that as a testament to a long-sighted view of how music works or a tribute to the passing of one of the world's greatest DJ talents but, really, it's just a sign of a label that's always been run by people with a great ears.

Heavenly's first year happened amidst a whole lot of chaos and a lot of gleeful press coverage that followed in its wake. The speed at which it blew up seems scarcely believable now – it's a masterclass in following instinct rather than trend. It's a period that ran from that Weatherall mix of Sly & Lovechild to Richey Edwards carving '4 Real' into his left forearm with a razor blade on a Wednesday night in Norwich Arts Centre; one that featured killer pop singles by Saint Etienne, Manic Street Preachers, East Village and Flowered Up as well as numerous parties in London and abroad. Heavenly and its associated acts quickly began to write their own stories, each one perfectly suited and massively appealing to the (then vibrant) weekly music press.

Heavenly's releases prior to the Manics speedball manifesto 'Motown Junk' might have given the impression that it was a London label that had sprung up in the wake of the acid house explosion, or a southern response to Factory's northern powerhouse. It was possibly a fair assumption: Flowered Up wore their Camden roots like tarnished suits of armour; Saint Etienne hailed from fringes of the city and arrived at Victoria Station with a sense of wonder and a unquenchable desire to eulogise the unsung corners and characters of the capital; while label associates like Weatherall were busy providing the soundtrack to wild Friday and Saturday nights in smoky basement rooms all over town. Even the one-off single release by the West Country's

finest naked hippie septet The Moonflowers remains a great piece of gonzo dancefloor swag.

In reality Heavenly was, and still is, a magnet for like-minded souls: the meeting point for so many people who'd been magnetically drawn to London from the sticks, entranced by Tin Pan Alley and Harry Beck's tube map, by Immediate Records and magazines that hailed from King's Reach Tower SE1; by 'West End Girls', the Wag and the Shoom; by BBC broadcasts from White City and the Pistols, The Clash and the Roxy. London was where the party was at that point, and the people who ran Heavenly happened to be there having the most fun. But London wasn't the reason for the label, it was just a catalyst – something it would continue to be though successive offices and their nearby pubs and, eventually, Heavenly's sister bar (the Social in Fitzrovia). Over the years, the label's gaze has variously moved north to Manchester, east to Holland, south to Australia and west to old South Wales. Wherever they're looking, what they're on the search for remains consistent: unique talent with an ear for a good story and a solid belief in the transcendent, magical powers of a perfect pop song.

It's been three decades since that initial flawless run of singles. Since then, Heavenly has steadfastly followed its own nose. Very little has been off limits, be it book publishing, running clubs up and down the length of Britain, signing a country and western band at the height of grunge, or allowing and encouraging King Gizzard and the Lizard Wizard to release five full-length albums in the space of a year. Heavenly's most stupidly limited release remains the sole single by the mysterious Ooh Ooh Ah Aah Band – the musical guise of former Heavenly employee and East Village drummer Spencer Smith. Only one hundred copies of 'Show Me the Way to Sasparella' – a track memorably described by Jon Savage as being the sound of 'a gay nervous breakdown' – were ever pressed to mark the occasion of Spence leaving the label. All were sold at Rough Trade on Talbot Road. Once heard, never forgotten.

Not everything has been easy, or even fun. Distribution deals have come and gone, often coinciding with regime changes at the sister company and ushering in hand-to-mouth periods of thinking on one's feet. Over the years, Heavenly records have been funded by Revolver (RIP), Columbia, Deconstruction and EMI. Where those labels do still exist today, they are unrecognisable from the days when Heavenly was part of their roster. Different bosses, different ideologies. Happily, Heavenly's most recent distribution relationship – with European giant [PIAS] – is the label's longest and most fruitful to date.

The Heavenly office is now back at the heart of things after spending a few years out of Soho on Portobello Road. It sits three floors up on Old Compton Street, halfway between the old sites on Wardour Street and Frith Street. Many of the faces have changed in there – take a bow Danny, Andrew, Katherine, Daisy, Diva and Sonny – but the ethos is the same. Jeff still gives the stereo a beating on a regular basis, the office hairdresser is still the same brilliant guy giving the same brilliant haircuts, and anyone with a good soul and an open mind is still welcome inside. Mondays especially.

Believe in Magic isn't a complete history of Heavenly. It focuses on thirty releases from those thirty years (apologies to anyone whose story has been lost in the creation of this book) and is an attempt to document one of the country's most consistently brilliant record labels – a label as innovative, as creative and as singular as Factory or Warp or Island in their early days. Only always with a better-stocked fridge.

Pictures on our wall: Robin Turner in the Frith Street office, sometime in 1996.

*Autumn 1981, Jeff Barrett got the job behind
the counter in a record shop that he'd dreamt
of since childhood . . .*

I was born in 1962 and grew up in Beeston,
Nottingham. Straight after leaving school at
sixteen, I went to work as a storeman at MBS
Bearings. It was a horrible, depressing job.
Depressing because I knew I didn't want to be
there. I didn't mind working because it paid for
records and gigs and clothes – I just didn't want
to work there. It was my own fault; I'd fucked up
at school. I left with zero qualifications and a shit
reference, which basically said 'unemployable'.
I knew that was a lie – I'd always worked and I'd
had jobs since I was twelve. Paper boy, errand
boy for the local Co-op, delivering pork pies to
pensioners on a big heavy bike.

I'd been a naughty kid at school. A mischievous
little fucker who liked smashing windows and
setting off fire alarms and wearing things that
weren't approved uniform and drawing cock and
balls on teachers' white lab coats in felt-tip pen.
At school I met like-minded people who were
also into similar things . . . drawing cock and
balls, that kind of thing. My best mate Pete was
a big Bowie nut. We all loved Bowie. Soul was
big in Nottingham; northern soul was a big part
of the soundtrack of youth-club discos. I went to
a grammar school, which was a surprise; I don't
think I was expected to pass my eleven-plus.
What an opportunity! I took it as an opportunity
to have a massive laugh.

So I failed everything. They brought these career
advisers in to ask what we all wanted to do.
Some kid who was good at maths was told to get
a job in a bank. They asked me if I'd ever thought
about the pit. The nearest pit was an hour away
from my house, but these people took one look
at me and thought I was only suitable for a
hardcore labouring job. I just wanted to work in a
record shop. Those places were windows onto an
exotic world and I'd grown up in a very un-exotic
way. My parents were quite boring. They were
lovely, and they were good parents, but they were
boring. They had no friends. There was never any

social interaction in my house. There was never
any music, just a couple of soundtrack albums
– *Carousel* and *West Side Story*. Both of which
I really liked. This sounds really disrespectful,
but everything I've ever done has been anti
my parents. I loved them both to bits but they
didn't drink, they didn't smoke. They'd never
have thought of getting high. I'd have been an
embarrassment to them if they had known how
I'd actually behaved. My lifestyle has been a
response to them in many ways.

At sixteen, I was full-time in a bearings business
and it was not where I wanted to be. I couldn't get
a job behind the counter in a record shop. Record
shops were inspiring and educational. They were
places of cultural significance, places I used to
hang out even before punk. Walking down to the
football across the Meadows estate, there was
a shop called Selectadisc and I was obsessed
with the window displays. To me, record shops
represented music in every way. I would never
have thought about the mechanics of how things
worked back then, of how a record was made
or how it got to the shops. How people wrote
about them or got to hear them. It was quite a
while later when I started thinking, 'How does a
gig happen? How do the people at the *NME* get
to hear music? How do the records get into the
window of Selectadisc?'

My obsession with music started at a really young
age. It was the early 1960s and I had an elder
brother and an elder sister who were both well
into music so I caught that same bug very early
on. Any music playing in the house was down
to them. My brother especially would go out of
his way to discover new music, he'd dance on
different dancefloors. He was obsessed with
r 'n' b and jazz. One of my earliest memories is
being in my bedroom, and my sister across the
hallway doing her hair in the bathroom with 'A
Hard Day's Night' blasting out of the radio. The
first record I bought was 'Looking Through the
Windows', a single by The Jackson 5; I bought it
from Boots with a record voucher I'd been given
for Christmas. Record vouchers were big currency
when I was a kid and, thankfully, people used to

give me them as presents all the time. 'Oh, he likes music, give him a voucher.'

My brother Stephen was a huge influence on my life. He's fifteen years older than me and was a hip kid. Everything about him raised questions when I was growing up, the first of which was, 'Where is he?' He officially lived at home but he was never, ever there. There were a few traces – a bit of fishing tackle (he was a keen angler), a few records, a Bakelite lighter and a ciggy-rolling machine. But he was out a lot; every night he'd be out dancing. I got that that freaked my parents out a bit. It's when I came to understand that the generation gap was huge. My siblings were part of the first post-war generation. My dad had been in the war at a very young age, my mum had worked in the NAAFI, in the ordnance depot. Then, before you know it, along came the teenagers who wanted to dress differently and act differently. And that was my brother.

I vividly remember one very significant event, when this lesser-seen brother decided to reappear on a Saturday night. On Saturdays we'd have tea between 5 and 5.30. We'd have it in the kitchen, and quite often it was kippers – always smoked fish, possibly a herring. Around that point, some bloke would come down the road ringing a bell selling the *Football Post*. My dad would religiously wait for this guy. Anyway, my brother re-emerged into this Saturday night scene and my dad started accusing him, 'You think this is a hotel, do you?' And then it kicked off and turned into something loud with my dad shouting something about 'wasting your bloody money on that rubbish'. My brother stormed out one way and Dad the other. I gingerly picked up this rubbish – a newspaper called *Melody Maker*. I'd have been about four or five. This *Melody Maker*, this item that had sparked a five-minute war in our kitchen on kippers night – that's always stayed with me. This was a music paper and it was a totem of rebellion.

Not long after that, Stephen moved west to Cornwall where he learnt to cook and worked in restaurants. And he stayed in Cornwall. When I

was eleven, I remember my sister coming round to tell us Stephen had called – we didn't have a telephone in the house – and he was getting married in St Ives. And she's French. We were all invited. On the day before the wedding, I remember talking to my brother, who asked if I was still into music. There was a little record shop on Fore Street back then and he took me there and bought me a few records. I chose 'Born to Be With You' by Dave Edmunds and 'Give Me Love, Give Me Peace on Earth' by George Harrison. I was overjoyed that this older person who I didn't really know was actually talking to me about music in a way that wasn't condescending.

Stephen and Brigitte (his fiancée) worked at a restaurant called Noni's Bistro. I genuinely didn't know what the fuck that meant. The menu was on a blackboard and I didn't know what the fuck that meant either. We were well and truly out of our comfort zones having entered this world of weird. It really unsettled our mum and dad but me, I was just beginning to learn a new language here.

Her family turned up at the wedding; they were very sophisticated. My brother was wearing double denim and a Mickey Mouse print shirt; she was wearing all white, with clogs and a floppy hat. There were hippies there, and post-hippies; flamboyant people that Stephen had met along the way. This wedding was incredible, a total gas. I drank champagne for the first time; a naked woman came running through the room giggling before getting locked in a wardrobe. She was probably only twenty; she was a waitress at Stephen's place.

In the kitchen there was a crew of pot washers – some cockneys, some Aussies – and they were blasting out The Faces the whole time. I sat on the steps outside listening to the music and passively smoking pot. My mum and dad went home but my brother asked if I'd like stay a little longer. I ended up staying for a few weeks. I used to bomb around the arcades and the beaches, it was a whole new world. From then on, I'd spend a large chunk of my summer holidays down there. Later, my sister-in-law turned me on to American literature, American cigarettes, gin. Those summers really opened my mind right up. You could always rely on the dishwashers to have great taste in music. They were adults to me, even though really they were twenty years old and not long out of school themselves.

Things moved on and Stephen moved to Plymouth to set up a restaurant with a load of cash from a wealthy local solicitor. By the summer of 1979, I'd been in that job at MBS Bearings for over a year. I was genuinely depressed. I had a good bunch of mates to have a laugh with but I was getting stuck in this job. The worst thing was, I was actually getting good at it, and I really didn't want to get good. I got offered a mad promotion in the same place and it scared the shit out of me. I didn't want to live on the estate I'd grown up on. I knew how easy it would be for me to just fall into humdrum. What my brother had taught me, and what music had taught me, was that there was something else out there. I just wanted to taste that. Reading music papers and seeing tour dates made me want to travel. What was Eric's in Liverpool like? They put on the same groups I watched at the Sandpiper in Nottingham. Those adverts had sent me up to Manchester to watch bands at the Factory; they had made me more curious about the rest of the country than anything I'd ever been taught in school.

My mum spotted that I was scared of getting stuck in the place I'd been born in, so she wrote to my brother asking if he'd have me. My parents were knocking on a bit by then; they didn't know what to do with me. I went down in the autumn of 1979 but wasn't prepared for a big move, came back and got a job in a burger joint that was owned by two gay guys who also owned a nightclub called Shades. I'd been in there once to see a punk band called Raped. Debut single 'Pretty Paedophiles'. Terrible band. Anyway, we'd go to Shades after work. Although we talk about those years as being 'punk years', I've always dug disco. Music has always been mashed up for me. It still is. I loved sixties rock – the Stones,

The Kinks, the Small Faces – but I was never a rock kid. People would be trying to tell me Bad Company were amazing; I preferred The Chi-Lites.

After a while, I'd saved some money and I went back to Plymouth. My brother got me to work. Dishwasher, waiter, I did everything apart from chef(fing). I was signing on and getting my rent paid and getting paid cash, buying records and clothes. I was happy. I was reading every music paper going – Sounds, Melody Maker, NME and Record Mirror. The Face started around then too. I became known in the record shops mainly because I was the first person in to buy music on new release day. Eventually I got a letter back from a job application I'd sent to HMV and went in for an interview. It was a classic interview. The guy was in the pub when I got there. When he came back stinking of booze, he made himself a spliff, put his feet on the desk and said, 'You've got the job.'

Within a month of starting, I became the shop's singles buyer. That meant I was on top of buying independent releases as well as stocking up on Shakin' Stevens and Bucks Fizz. We sold a lot of Shaky. We were a chart return shop so the bulk of what was sold was Top 10 music. The reps used to give us free copies of crap to sell on in exchange for putting the numbers through the chart return book. Pretty quickly I started stocking lots of young, independent stuff. I bought from a company in Bristol called Revolver, who were a distribution company aligned to the independent network called the Cartel. They were based in Bristol, servicing Wales and the south-west. I built up good custom for their records in the shop.

Through the job I started meeting a lot of like-minded people. You'd get some kid walking in in their lunch break saying, 'I don't suppose you've got 'Procession' by New Order, have you?' Two or three times after you've said, 'Yes, and have you heard this?' you've made a mate. And he tells his mate, who tells his mate, and suddenly you were the shop. I'd make it my business to be the shop that always had whatever record the music papers were losing it over. The first Pale

Fountains single, '(There's Always) Something on My Mind', on Les Disques du Crépuscule was a big record for us. There were quite a few clubs in town – soul clubs and funk clubs – so I'd get whatever was on Larry Levan's chart that week on import. It meant hearing a whole load of brilliant music across loads of genres.

The most significant record I ever stocked was 'Hand in Glove' by The Smiths. Each week, buying records involved dealing with Revolver, who would call up to go through a list of what we wanted. This would take place weekly for records that would arrive two weeks later. When 'Hand in Glove' came up, I asked for ten. They spluttered as if I'd gone mad. I asked, 'Do you think that's a bit light?' They thought I'd be sending copies back. I said, 'I tell you what – I bet I order another ten the next day. Because in my world that group is going to be massive.' You knew through the music press and through John Peel that the band was going to be huge. The day that box of records arrived I opened it with the same kind of enthusiasm that I'd dive into the *NME* with. The box arrived around midday as the lunchtime crowd were coming in, I played 'Hand in Glove' then I flipped it. Then I played it again and flipped it again. And people came over asking, 'Is this it? Give us one!' I sold ten within an hour, including my own copy. I ordered twenty-five more for delivery the next day. Revolver were mind-blown. In their part of the world, this was unique and it was in a branch of HMV in Plymouth. But I knew my customers, and I knew my music.

Not long afterwards, I got offered a job in the record shop attached to Revolver distribution in Bristol. I was still incredibly happy in my job in Plymouth, everything was great, but I'd got a call off a guy called Lloyd Harris who ran the distribution arm. They had a tiny shop that was situated up a staircase. It had no windows and was without a doubt the most intimidating shop of all time. Mike Chadwick had been the shop manager there and he was leaving to go into distribution. The shop had a massive clientele that covered local reggae soundsystems, indie

kids at the university and the likes of Nellee Hooper and the Wild Bunch who were demanding the latest electro records. Lloyd called me up and asked if I wanted Mike's old job. I consider that phone call to be the first break anyone ever gave me. The HMV job I should have had years before. I got this job on the merits of having bought thirty-five copies of 'Hand in Glove' within forty-eight hours of release.

So I went and it was really, really good. I stayed there for a year. It was very intense. Intense learning, intense work. But I never quite settled in Bristol. I'd had to relinquish the regular DJ gig I'd built up in town, I had a girlfriend back in Plymouth and I wanted to be back there. As soon as I'd cashed up on Saturday I'd be on the first train back to Plymouth before heading back to open up on Monday morning. That year at Revolver coincided with a pretty amazing year for music. Aztec Camera's first album came out, the Cocteau Twins were on the rise, electro was getting big, Studio One were reissuing some truly great music.

While I was at Revolver, I took advantage of the fact that they had the distribution arm behind the shop. They would get things in way before release, and their access to white labels and promos was something else. I loved it. It felt a bit elitist, it was great.

One label I'd had an eye on through their early promos was Creation. They were up to maybe five releases. Sounds had reviewed Creation founder Alan McGee's club night, the Living Room, which was happening in pubs across central London. Reading about a night of garage rock in some shitty pub . . . I really liked the sound of it. I would get sent test pressings of their singles by bands with brilliant, bonkers names like the Jasmine Minks, Biff Bang Pow! and The Revolving Paint Dream. They were all bad-sounding garage records but I loved them. Production wasn't an issue, they were properly DIY. It wasn't just the sound of the records I liked. The sales notes that came with each one had a load of crazy ranting written by Alan –

rants that might as well have said, 'I don't give a fuck if you buy this record or not.'

All the time I was in Bristol, I was being headhunted by HMV. They were offering me assistant manager jobs and things like that. In some ways, that job felt as institutionalised as the bearings warehouse, but I went back and used it as a stepping stone. I didn't see it as a smart move, more an opportunity to make a move on some of the things people had offered in the time I was away. When I went back to HMV there was a new manager called Nick. I was renting his basement room off him and within a week of being there, I'd convinced him that we had to leave HMV and open a market stall of our own selling records. He was a bit put out by this, but I convinced him. The stall was called Rhythm.

Even though I'd been gone for a year, I knew I still had a customer base in Plymouth that no one had filled since. My relationship with Revolver was good enough for them to give us an account so we could stock new releases. We bought dead stock from shops around Exeter and Dartmouth and put some of our own stuff we were happy to get rid of up there too. We found a market pitch between a carpet-remnants lorry and an out-of-date cake stall, and we sold Crass records and Fall records and psychobilly stuff. What kept us going initially, though, was Frankie Goes to Hollywood. Over the summer, the market did this thing called the Summer Run, where it moved every day to different towns – Looe, Padstow, Teignmouth, Dawlish; straight places full of tourists who weren't there for *Live at the Witch Trails*. We sold Frankie t-shirts hand over fist.

A mate of my brother's had a club called Ziggy's where I started putting on nights. It was just off Union Street which back then was a red-light street. Plymouth was still a full-on naval town, awash with Americans, Russians and squaddies. Union Street was all fried chicken, fried hookers and fried faces. Puke everywhere, military police all over the place. Ziggy's was tucked away enough to avoid the most hardcore punters, which was lucky as we weren't playing chart

music. Or sailors' music. I ran a few nights there – one playing punk rock, alternative and current Creation stuff, and another night where I played a lot of psychobilly stuff. 'Human Chicken' by The Dancing Did was a very big number. After a while, I started putting on groups. The first show was Pink Industry, a band from Liverpool that featured Jayne Casey. Slightly industrial, a bit electronic. We put them on one week and the Factory group Stockholm Monsters the next. To pay for those nights, we put on a big Sisters of Mercy gig at the Top Rank.

Before I'd left Revolver I'd rung Alan McGee using the number printed on the bottom of the Creation sales sheets. This was the first time I'd actually tried to speak to anyone 'in the industry'. Up until then the processes beyond the bit I was involved in were completely obscured, and I'm not even sure I'd ever really thought about what they were. I was nervous calling this label that I'd fallen for and I definitely didn't expect the main guy behind the label to answer the phone, but he did. I told him I'd really enjoyed the records he'd put out and I really liked the sound of his club nights and I'd like to book some of his groups. And he stopped me and said, 'Are you taking the fucking piss?' He could not believe I'd want to promote his groups in Plymouth. He said, 'I put those groups on in London and nae cunt comes.' And that was the start of a really good friendship. I did go back to Plymouth and I did book his groups. Some of the time, nae cunt came; other times loads of people came.

I left the market stall after being approached by a local kid I'd always known as Ferdie who had legally changed his name to James Williamson after the guitarist from The Stooges. He'd inherited some money and wanted to open a shop. And he wanted to call it Meat Whiplash after a song by The Fire Engines. When we opened it, it was a weird little shop situated between a bootleg Halfords and somewhere that sold dirty books. It was all painted pink with Velvets, Elevators, Big Star, Stooges and Cramps sleeves stuck on the wall. It seemed to intimidate people who were trying to decide whether to come in or not.

Every Saturday morning at Meat Whiplash, we'd be in there, hung-over. We'd be lying with our heads on the counter hoping no one wanted to buy records that day; at least until the pub opened and we could begin to get rid of the hangovers. We were there, feeling like shit, and this guy came in the shop. His name was James Endeacott. He had strawberry-blonde curls and it was obvious from his body language that he had just chanced upon somewhere he had had no idea about ten minutes beforehand. He walked in, stood there and looked around at this place with pink walls and record sleeves slapped on over the top. We had a Birthday Party section that also had records by the band Nick Cave and Roland Howard had before them, The Boys Next Door. We had an Australian section with The Triffids albums on import. He turned round, caught me looking at him, and said, 'What the fucking hell is this place doing here?' He genuinely couldn't believe it. He pointed at a Jesus and Mary Chain poster on the wall and said, 'Now you're really taking the piss.'

That poster James saw was for a show I was putting on in early '85 at Ziggy's. The Mary Chain were just blowing up in the press so I made a very big deal out of it. In a lot of ways, it was a precursor to me becoming a publicist. In other ways, it was a continuation of how I'd behaved at school. The tabloid papers had cottoned on to early gigs that had ended in rucks and they'd christened them a 'blasphemous rock band'. With that in mind, I called up BBC South-West as a concerned, outraged punter saying, 'Have you heard this blasphemous riot band are coming to town?' I added 'riot' just to up the ante. A couple of days later, my brother told me he'd had some of the local licensing cops in his restaurant for an after-hours drink, and they were a bit concerned. I asked why and he said that they'd asked him why his brother was promoting a gig by a blasphemous riot band. He found the whole thing hilarious.

Alan McGee came down for the gig, which was totally sold out. The local press had gone overboard, as hoped: there were tons of people desperate to get in and a policeman on horseback turned up to try to control the crowd. It was mental. I remember standing on the corner of Union Street with McGee looking back at the madness outside the venue and him saying, 'Barrett, what the fuck are you doing living in Plymouth?' And then he offered me a job at Creation.

I took a few months to get it together but in that time I went up to stay with Alan a few times. Alan was living in a flat in Tottenham and I went up to go see the Mary Chain at the Three Johns in Angel. The gig itself had its own community; there were fanzine sellers and kids all buzzing about music. It's where I first met Kevin Pearce, who had a great zine called *Hungry Beat*. This was pre-*C86*, before that real explosion of independent music, back when it was a real buzz. The Mary Chain gig was a revelation. It was written up in *Sounds* by Jane Suck and I felt privileged to have been invited.

I never dreamt that I'd get offered a job by Alan McGee when I first called that number on the sales sheet back at Revolver. It was fucking nuts. I was Creation's first employee. I moved to London in the summer of 1985 and went to work in the office at 83 Clerkenwell Road. They'd been in a tiny one-desk, one-seat office; when I arrived they moved into a corner room that became a home for me for a long time. Nothing was defined in there, there were no clear roles. There was Alan who was just a force of nature; and his partner, Dick Green, a calmer, lovely guy. Ed Ball was around too. He had the group, The Times. Alan was a massive fan. Again, he didn't have a defined role, he was just moving in their orbit.

The first job Alan gave me was tour managing The Jesus and Mary Chain around Europe. I didn't have a passport, I don't drive, I'd never been abroad and I don't think I'd ever heard the words 'tour' and 'manager' used in the same sentence before. We headed out to play some shows in the

The Jesus and Mary Chain
soundchecking at Ziggy's in Plymouth.

Clockwise from top left: Jim Reid; Bobby Gillespie and
Jeff Barrett; Jim Reid and Douglas Hart with manager
Alan McGee.

Benelux countries – I'm pretty sure I didn't know what a Benelux was either. I was ridiculously ill equipped for the job but I was buoyed along by the fact that I was seeing every night what I consider at that point to be the greatest rock 'n' roll band in the world. Every set was fifteen minutes long and ended in ear-splitting cacophony. Unfortunately, no one had told any of the promoters.

As a fan it was insane. I was shit at the job but being in a van with a group was a fucking revelation. It gave me a real insight into how groups worked. You know, two of them hated each other, some liked speed, some didn't drink. It wasn't without incident. The ludicrous thing was that when I got back, Alan said, 'Have you done the accounts?' What accounts? 'Have you got the receipts?' What receipts? 'You were the fucking tour manager!' 'Alan, I don't know what one is.' Needless to say, I wasn't asked to do that again.

Creation was an education in how everything worked. I was suddenly part of the process. The bands signed to the label were always in the office. I was given a job of 'doing everything'. I was told to take records to radio or to press. Doing press appealed to me as I'd been such an avid reader of it. I loved getting let into the offices of the *NME* and *Melody Maker*, first when they were in New Oxford Street, then in King's Reach Tower. And because I had an encyclopaedic knowledge of those papers, I knew who'd like what records, so I'd only give certain things to certain writers. I didn't bother scatter-gunning. I didn't realise at the time but, in press terms, that that was something of a valuable skill.

Alan put me on this thing called the Enterprise Allowance Scheme. Back then you could be a benefits cheat without feeling guilty. It was much easier to sign on and get your rent paid, and then be in a band or work at a small record label earning cash in hand. That's hard to imagine now in a time when most groups have to have jobs to get by. Alan signed me up to that scheme saying, 'I'm going to put £2000 in your bank account, you're going to give me it back in two months'

time. You're going to say you're a consultant in the music industry, main client Creation Records.' All new to me, all great. They paid you £25 a week and you got your rent paid. I don't think he paid me much more on top of that, so I started putting on groups in the room above a pub on Royal College Street in Camden.

I'd spent a lot of time looking in *Time Out* to try to work out what the antithesis of the Bull and Gate was. At that point, the Bull and Gate was a pay-to-play gig. It was mostly horrible, you'd get a good gig once in a blue moon. I wanted every night to be a good gig, even if it wasn't necessarily a group I liked that much. I didn't charge anyone to play, which meant I couldn't always pay everybody, but we'd split the door. I wanted it to echo what I'd witnessed at the Three Johns, creating a community where fanzine writers could gather to sell stuff and to hang out. Writers like Bob Stanley, Kevin Pearce, Simon Bereznik used to turn up a lot; garage bands would hang out. The Black Horse was a great working-class boozer. We put nights on three times a week under the name the Backdoor to Babylon and created a venue within a pub. It meant you might have a band playing upstairs and some people might not give a fuck, or might not get in, but they'd come and hang out and drink. There was no stage and it held about sixty people. We put on early Happy Mondays shows and the House of Love broke out of there, going from being first on a three-band bill to signed to Creation and headlining. Lots of the neighbours complained vehemently about the racket but the landlord liked the money it was bringing in. For me, it wasn't about making a load of money, it was about making friends. I hadn't been in London that long, it was a good way to meet people.

It was through promoting at the Black Horse that I met East Village. There was a kid called Richard who told me about a band from High Wycombe, then called Episode 4. He gave me a cassette which was the best-looking demo I'd ever been given, fully realised, a clear sense of who and what the band was. I remember going back to my flat and playing that cassette over and over again.

I stayed up all night until it was an acceptable time to ring the number on the tape the next day. Paul Kelly answered the phone a bit bewildered that this speeding madman was raving about their demo tape. I told him about the Black Horse and that I loved his band's songs and asked if they wanted to support McCarthy the next weekend. They said yes and a few days later, I was watching one of my favourite gigs of all-time, even to this day. I put someone on the door so I could watch them and then magic happened. Little did any of us know that we'd end up as lifelong friends, working and partying together from that night onwards.

Back on the street the neighbours eventually won the volume war so we had to move out. Stuck for somewhere to put on a bunch of shows I had booked, I wandered across to the Falcon which was just over the road. It might have later become a legendary music venue but back then it was just a crappy, empty boozer. I walked in on a Friday lunchtime. It was open but there was nobody in there apart from a grumpy old fucker called Pat who was stood behind the bar. I ordered a pint and introduced myself as the guy who was doing the gigs over the road and asked if I could see the back room. It was a total shit hole but it was ready to go. Peeling wallpaper, a pool table in the middle of the room, only ever used by the occasional stripper. No music ever. It was almost purpose-built; it had a stage which the Black Horse hadn't. Baxter, the landlord, had seen what we were doing over the road and he wanted it, he was practically chucking the pool table out the minute I walked in. The back room at the Falcon became Babylon Revisited and then the Phil Kaufman Club in tribute to Gram Parsons' tour manager, the man who fulfilled Gram's last wishes and took his body to Joshua Tree and burnt it. The gigs carried on.

Back at Creation, without tour-management responsibilities, I was building an understanding of how press worked. I got very good at that part of it, something that Alan spotted, as did Dave Harper, who was the press guy at Out Promotions which was in the office above us.

They looked after Factory, a lot of Mute records and big independent labels like Rhythm King. He knew I was a massive Factory fan and adored Happy Mondays, who were still making people at the music papers scratch their heads in bewilderment. Dave came down one day to tell me he was going to be head of press at RCA. It was such a weird thing to tell me – why would you go and work there? It wasn't a cool label. At that point I didn't understand that he might be motivated by money, job security, the kinds of things I've never really thought about, then or now. But, as a result, he offered me the Factory job, which was another pinch-yourself moment. The first record I worked on was *Bummed* by the Mondays. It was pretty well known all over town that I was their biggest fan. I'd promoted shows and got them on tours. I'd been a cheerleader ever since I'd first heard them. And off it went, I became their press guy.

My role at Creation had changed radically and I started my own company which I called Capersville. It was a name that had stuck with me since I was a fifteen-year-old in Nottingham. I used to see these older kids – punks, but not stereotypical – who had this amazing look. They'd wear boy-scout scarves turned the other way round, like a bandana with the woggle at the back. I looked up to them, wanted to know what they listened to, where they went, what they read. I once plucked up the courage to say, 'Are you a group?' One of them said, 'We're called Capersville,' and, flicking their scarves, 'And these are our capers.' They did one gig – their farewell show – and I couldn't go. It was probably complete bullshit, but as an idea it was just amazing. I just thought of a caper as an adventure, a mischief. It's why I chose that name – a homage to those kids and an indication of what I wanted the company to be. It felt like a fanzine name in a fanzine world. It was me, it was the luck I'd had. It was all a caper.

When we set the company up, we chose our groups well. I did a deal with Alan where I moved into this little annexe and did press for some of his groups in lieu of rent. We looked after lots of

Previous page: Happy Mondays with Phil Saxe (then manager) and Dave Harper (then PR) in the back of a van outside the Black Horse, Camden, 1987. This was taken before their first headline gig in the capital, promoted by Jeff Barrett.

Right: Jeff Barrett photographed in 1987.

Factory stuff and a load of Creation records. I was doing press for the House of Love. They weren't a band I loved, but I knew exactly who would love that band. It was a classic case of me knowing how to do my job right. I let the *Melody Maker* get carried away with them and then the *NME*, to the point where I got the covers of both papers in the same week, which wasn't a popular move within that world. Outside of that world, it was huge, and we got offered loads of work off the back of it. I hadn't engineered it . . . but I didn't stop it happening either. Both magazines went to print on a Monday and I knew I'd get a phone call shortly after they'd hit the presses. Two phone calls, actually. And I knew the word 'cunt' would be involved, possibly multiple times. I just thought the whole thing was funny. I worked on My Bloody Valentine, starting with *You Made Me Realise*. That record was an incredible, incredible piece of work by a group who had transitioned into something significantly different from where they'd started. They were properly phenomenal live, unlike anything else around, a complete game-changer.

From the Capersville office, I started up two small labels – first Head, then Sub Aqua. Neither were career moves, they were more a natural progression from groupie-dom and fanzine culture. I ran Head with Bill Prince, whose band The Wishing Stones were signed there. They featured a fucking funny guy called John Niven who joined the band, came down from Scotland and stayed in Bill's flat for a bit and never really went back. The other band on the label was The Servants, a *C86* band, Go-Betweens acolytes.

From being out at gigs, I met this kid called Josh Hampson. We were both into early Pop Will Eat Itself, used to go to gigs. He told me he was starting a band called Loop. I liked them a lot. It was Josh, his girlfriend and their mate. They sounded like Spacemen 3 and I really loved the roots of where it all came from. I started putting out Loop's records. Pretty quickly they started getting a lot of coverage. That guy I'd met many years before in Meat Whiplash – James Endeacott – joined the band and they started going somewhere.

While I still enjoyed doing gigs, I'd usually just stand on the door and get shitfaced and have a laugh. I wasn't really that arsed about watching the bands any more.

Sleeve artwork for Loop's 1987 album Heaven's End. *Photos by Steve Pyke.*

One day, a chap called Richard Norris came by. I knew Richard as a fanzine kid, he had a great one called *Strange Things are Happening* and he used to come to the office to blag records. I thought that magazine was brilliant, it was a door to a very different world. One night at the Falcon – I think it was an Inspiral Carpets gig – he came by and said, 'What are you doing? We're going to Clink Street for an acid house party.' I'd heard of acid house but wasn't really sure what it was, it hadn't seeped right into culture by this point. 'Trust me, you'll love it. There's this great drug called ecstasy and this incredible music . . . a bit disco and then this other sound.' I didn't follow him down that night but he did set a thought process in motion which soon became all-consuming. Shortly afterwards I knocked the Falcon on the head and became pretty much a full-time raver.

Although I was used to working with more traditional bands, I know if I'd have lived in London when the Wag and the Beat Route were the heart of the action, I'd have gone there. As it was, I lived in Plymouth and we tried to do our versions of those nights, albeit with the occasional drift into Dancing Did records. Acid house arrived at the perfect time for me. And Richard Norris not only encouraged me to check those clubs out and to explore further, he also introduced me to Andrew Weatherall, saying, 'There's a guy on that scene who I know you're going to get on with.'

Something had happened early on in 1988 that I wasn't privy to, but I made sure I made up for lost time. It was a meeting of minds, a collision of previously disparate tribes. Tribes were a very big thing in the eighties – before acid house, different tribes might be looking at what Soul II Soul and Norman Jay were doing and what, say, Mutoid Waste were up to or what Coldcut were playing on KISS FM. The indie scene I was part of, it was a bit boring, a bit closed shop. It was easy to see where the derogatory tag of 'students' came from. I liked to think I was never as black and white as that. It wasn't a cynical

The Wishing Stones.
(L–R): Stewart Garden, John Niven, Bill Prince, Andy Kerr.

move to get off my nut and dance to disco, it wasn't an odd thing. What was odd was the community of people I was doing it with, people who would never have mixed together before the right drugs and the right music connected them. I was meeting people from different musical backgrounds. That was a mutual thing.

Richard Norris saying I'd get on with Andrew wasn't that odd. I don't think there was ever really anything cynical about any of the things that led to Heavenly; there was no networking or social climbing. It's always been a fellow-traveller thing. You spot people along the way who you have an affinity with and you form a bond. I think it's how we've always worked over the years, in every aspect of what we do – from records to clubs and books. Nights down the pub even.

Andrew was an incredible DJ even then, and a *Boy's Own* writer who had made an impression on the *NME*. They were trying to get their heads around this new scene but their writers were

mostly stuck at the bar in the Falcon. I was having a terrible time trying to get press on the second Primal Scream album. I knew at the time it wasn't a great record. Helen Mead, the reviews editor at *NME* at the time, had this great idea of getting Andrew to review the Scream live. She was very kindly trying to save my job – McGee had told me if I didn't get any press on that record, I was out. She'd noticed that Andrew had said nice things about the album after he'd come round the office and I'd given him a copy. It ended up in the Uppers and Downers list in *Boy's Own* magazine. 'Uppers – the ballads off the new Primal Scream record.' Correct. That one line was the most significant piece of press that record got anywhere, ever.

Andrew, Chris Clunn and I got the train to Exeter to review a Scream gig. Andrew filed it under the name Audrey Witherspoon. It was Helen's idea and I'll always love her for that. Me giving him that record that day opened the door to what came next, though he was the one who ran through it. Some people have kindly given

Right: Bobby Gillespie, Robert Young and Jeff, backstage in Tokyo, 1994. Snapped by Pennie Smith.

Title spread: Jeff Barrett and Andrew Innes at Robert Young's wedding in Brighton. Also by Pennie Smith.

me a lot more credit for helping Primal Scream along but I just gave Andrew that record and took Andrew Innes to Future at the Sound Shaft where Weatherall was playing. Innes made 'Loaded' with Weatherall, I was just the catalyst. Which is possibly what I've always been? Anyway, Alan still sacked me from the Scream press job, in a Pizza Hut at the top of Tottenham Court Road at lunchtime.

As I was still working for Factory, I was in Manchester a lot so I knew a lot of people up there and often ended up at the Haçienda. Friends would hold my hand and take me to the promised land; it was amazing. Doors were opened, as were minds. Conversations all seemed like opportunities. I was as on the frontline as can be at that point when I got a call from Mike Chadwick back at Revolver. They wanted to set up an in-house label and he asked if I was up for starting one with him. I could A&R it, name it, run it. Being where they were in Bristol, there was a lot of music being punted to them. I think I just was the first person Mike thought of calling that day when thinking about an outlet for all the music that he was being given. He had no idea that I was at the centre of this creative storm where things were constantly coming my way, and I was ready. Heavenly was already a state of mind. Seemed like the right time to make it something really special.

If there's a continuous theme that runs through all of this, I think it's that everything comes down to conversations with people about music. It might seem like it all starts with someone on one side of the counter who is selling you something, or someone writing excitedly in a magazine telling you about a band you need to hear, but I don't think I've ever really seen things as one-way transactions. It's more an ongoing dialogue, one that never really stops and helps to build up this growing soundtrack to our lives, something that's passed from one person to another. That's really the ever-present thread. That's why we still believe in magic.

SLY AND LO
THE WORLD
ACCO
LY
CHILD
Soul of Europe Mix by Andrew Weatherall
Soul of Europe Mix
DING TO SLY & LOVE
CHILD

45 RPM
A

SLY AND LOVECHILD –
THE WORLD ACCORDING TO SLY & LOVECHILD
(Soul Of Europe Mix)
Remixed by Andrew Weatherall
Written by Elliot Gannon.
© and ℗ 1990 HEAVENLY
Made in France. HVN 112-1A
45 rpm.

The first Heavenly release felt different to records I'd released before. It felt like it was part of the zeitgeist and a record absolutely of its time. With Sub Aqua and Head, I'd put out music that I loved because I could. If you look back at those releases, you could feel musical history in the sounds of the bands, whether it was Loop who harked back to the Velvets, East Village who were deeply influenced by The Beatles and The Byrds, or Laugh who sometimes sounded like a bonkers freakbeat band and at others, almost like Prince. 'The World According to Sly & Lovechild' was very much where it was at in the summer of 1990. The day it was released, it was hip and hot and now. I was energised in a whole different way when Heavenly started. It felt like we were tuned into the times and part of a very real scene.

I'd met Andrew Weatherall because of that scene. He was a fellow traveller and a kindred spirit and someone I looked up to. He was immensely talented, he was cool and smart, a great DJ and very good company. And he was important, you could sense that. Getting Andrew involved in it was just totally, totally obvious. He had the imagination to do something brilliant. And I could ask him. I didn't have to think, 'Wouldn't it be amazing to get Andrew Weatherall to remix this?' I could just say, 'Andrew, listen to this.'

'This is all right.'

'Will you do additional production and a remix on it?'

'Yeah, all right.'

It was kind of easy, but it was new to all of us. It hadn't been like that before. Andrew hadn't been asked that question many times – making music wasn't something that he'd seen coming. We were all deeply immersed in music that we loved. None of us could believe our fucking luck, really.
Jeff Barrett

Title spread: A message to the world: HVN1, the first Heavenly recording.
Right: Andrew Weatherall.

Below: The West Country's finest naked hippie sextet, Moonflowers, 1990.

June the fourth 1989.
Primrose Hill, Staten Island, Chalk Farm,
Massif Central, Gospel Oak, São Paulo,
Boston Manor, Costa Rica, Arnos Grove,
San Clemente, Tufnell Park, Gracetown, York Way,
Videoton, Clerkenwell, Portobello, Maida Vale,
Old Ford, Valencia, Kennington, Galveston,
Holland Park, Studamer, Dollis Hill, Fougères,
London Fields, Bratislava, Haggerston,
Lavinia, Canonbury, Alice Springs,
Tooting Graveney, Baffin Island, Pollards Hill,
Winnipeg, Plumstead Common,
Hyderabad, Silvertown, Buffalo.

Foxbase Alpha is a record that dreams of supersonic flight and the glamour of the jet age; a record that evokes both luxury lifestyles and low-end theories. The Foxbase itself was a place where points on a map can be collected together to make poetry; where Phil Spector and Derrick May help form a girl group who cover songs by The Fall. It's a record that points towards a possible future where a perfect 7-inch single can – and should – be as respected as any work hanging in the Tate.

The debut album by Saint Etienne – a forever future-facing group who cherry-picked curiosities from the past to create perfect pop music for now – *Foxbase Alpha* was released in the same month as Primal Scream's *Screamadelica*, Nirvana's *Nevermind* and Talk Talk's *Laughing Stock*. It more than holds its own against them. *Foxbase Alpha* made Saint Etienne a band, cementing a relationship between lifelong friends Bob Stanley and Pete Wiggs, and singer Sarah Cracknell.

Three decades on from their first single (HVN2, 'Only Love Can Break Your Heart' – the record that properly set Heavenly Recordings on its journey) Saint Etienne remain one of Britain's most consistently brilliant pop groups, a band who believe in their art form and continue to produce music that joyously backs up that belief.
Robin Turner

BOB STANLEY

In the first six months of 1990 a lot of records were lumped together as sounding Balearic.

'Floatation' by The Grid, 'World in Motion', Movement 98, the first Bocca Juniors single, records by Sheer Taft and Primal Scream. Post-Soul II Soul, it was the first year that people in Britain were making those kinds of records. The tempo hadn't changed much from the early acid house records – a lot of those early acid records were quite slow, they just sounded a lot more noisy. Acid house came and went very quickly, it was pretty much over by the time Bros got an acid remix done (for their single 'I Quit'). The original scene had split. You had people wanting harder and faster music, which gave birth to clubs like Rage that took place at Heaven and clubs like the Labyrinth in Dalston. Elsewhere, the people who'd been associated with Boy's Own were making and playing slower, mellower-sounding music like the things people were hearing out in Ibiza.

I'd been thinking for a while that whatever was going to follow 'baggy' wasn't going to be more guitars. You'd go and see Happy Mondays or The Stone Roses at the point they were properly breaking and they'd just have a DJ before them who would be playing Balearic-sounding records. The two things made sense together but they weren't remotely the same thing. I thought if you could make sample-based music that joined the two things together it would do pretty well. It was one of the very few times in my life where I've recognised an opportunity and acted on it.

'Only Love Can Break Your Heart' and 'Kiss and Make Up' were the first things we'd recorded in a studio that worked out. Previously, Pete and I had borrowed a Roland 303 off Richard Norris and tried to make an acid house record with it in 1988, but people had always said those things are notoriously difficult to control and we didn't manage to get anything usable out of it. Those first two successful recordings were done in January 1990 at Ian Catt's studio, which was in his old bedroom in his parents' house on a former prefab estate in Mitcham. Back then we were recording onto reel-to-reel, splicing tape. The backwards bit on 'Only Love . . .' is the sound of actual tape spooling back. The sessions happened in the evenings as Pete still had a full-time job then as a computer trouble-fixer. I think the whole thing cost us around £200.

We had an ambition to make music but we weren't expecting anyone to put it out. We hadn't written anything, we just had the idea to do a couple of cover versions – one Neil Young song and one song by The Field Mice, who Ian had done a lot of work with. The vocals on 'Only Love Can Break Your Heart' were by Moira Lambert who was a band from Croydon called Faith Over Reason; the singer on 'Kiss and Make Up' was Donna Savage from a New Zealand band called Dead Famous People. She was on the same label as Debsey from Dolly Mixture; we'd tried to track her down initially but hadn't had any luck so we asked her label mate instead.

We wanted Jeff to be the first person to hear the tracks. He was someone we trusted; I knew him as a press officer and a promoter. He had great ears and was a brilliant raconteur. I'd met him when I moved to London in 1986 through gigs he put on at Bay 63 in Ladbroke Grove and then at the Black Horse and the Falcon. When I started writing for the *NME* he was doing press for Factory and Creation, some early KLF stuff – lots of really exciting music. He was also a really good source of inspirational records; his taste would really influence what Pete and I listened to. He used to play me loads of reggae records, things on Greensleeves and Trojan that eventually seeped into what we were doing with Ian in the studio.

Pete and I went to meet him one evening in the Bush Ranger on Goldhawk Road. We asked him to listen to a couple of tracks and see if he thought they were any good. He sat there listening to 'Only Love . . .' on my Walkman, hands over the headphones, nodding. When it finished, he said, 'I'm starting a record label. Can I put this out?' There was never any question of doing it with anyone else after that. He said he was going to call the label Heavenly, then a few weeks later he ended up pretty angry with me because there was a post-Talulah Gosh band with the same name and he knew I'd have known that. I hadn't

mentioned it because I genuinely hadn't wanted to put him off calling the label that – it felt like such a great name that could stick around for a long time.

Having Heavenly put the record out was exciting in itself. The two labels Jeff had done previously hadn't really taken off, but it felt like if he had someone backing him and he could take time out from PR it would go. I can't imagine a band like The House of Love would have got anywhere like as far as they did without him as their press officer. He was just incredibly convincing. He could get you to like a record that you wouldn't normally like that he didn't even like. The House of Love's loss would hopefully be a big gain for us.

Once the record started going out to people, we were convinced we were going to get caught out and revealed as somehow fraudulent. The whole thing was hilarious. We weren't musicians, we'd borrowed a singer from another band. When Andrew Weatherall said he wanted to remix it, it seemed absolutely ridiculous to us. He'd laughingly told us he was really pissed off when he heard about the record at first as he wanted to start a band and use a football-related name and we'd had the best one, hence why they ended up as Bocca Juniors. It all just seemed like madness.

After 'Kiss and Make Up' came out Jeff told us to get on with recording an album. We still hadn't written one proper song of our own. We'd recorded a couple of instrumentals that had helped make our initial live shows at bit longer. If he hadn't have told us to get on with it I don't know whether we would ever have bothered. The first thing we wrote with lyrics was 'Nothing Can Stop Us'. The structure was lifted from 'Eye Know' by De La Soul, which had an instrumental chorus that's a sample. I still think we got very lucky in the studio. We never spent more than three days working on tracks back then, so it would have come together very quickly. When it came to playing it to Heavenly, we were even more nervous than when we'd first played 'Only Love Can Break Your Heart'.

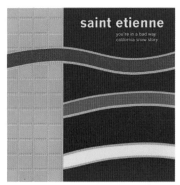

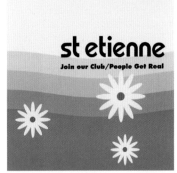

Foxbase Alpha was recorded over a year. We kept going back to the studio until we had enough tracks that we liked that would sort of fit together as an album. It was only when we put the football sample at the start and 'Dilworth's Theme' at the end that it actually felt like a proper record – up until then it had all felt very disparate. We knew we wanted the album to feel like a manifesto. Everything was supposed to reflect our world view, from the artwork to the samples to the sleeve notes. It was very much an announcement of 'who we are' twinned with an underlying thought that we probably wouldn't get to make another album. I don't suppose many bands starting off think beyond the record they're working on at that point; in our case it was a chance to pile our entire personalities, our loves and our senses of humour into something.

We worked with Sarah [Cracknell] on 'Nothing Can Stop Us' and all got on really well. Up until meeting her, we thought we'd work with different singers on each track, like Soul II Soul had done. They were an unlikely role-model band for us. Sarah's voice suited what we doing and, by the time the album came out, she'd recorded half a dozen songs and we were a three-piece.

Prior to the album, we reissued 'Only Love Can Break Your Heart' as a double a-side with 'Filthy', which became our first Top 40 single. Jeff, Pete and I were really against the idea; Alan McGee was managing us at the time and convinced us to do it. It felt like a slightly unpleasant commercial move whereas, in general, we were allowed pretty much free rein to do things the way we wanted to do them. That meant being able to do handwritten adverts in the music papers that looked like pages torn from fanzines. Even doing those, we were sure that someone would rumble us and say, 'They're just ripping off The Fall' or 'You nicked that off The Monkees'.

By the time *Foxbase Alpha* came out we'd started doing proper gigs, which was something I'd never wanted to do. The first thing we ever did was a PA at Rage. Everything played before us was 150bpm then we came on and did 'Only Love

Can Break Your Heart'. We didn't even tell our friends we were doing it. Once Sarah joined the band, we became more like an actual live band. I'd never thought of us evolving that way, I've always been much happier in the studio than on stage then and now.

The two shows we did with all the other Heavenly bands (London and Paris) were both great – really good fun where everyone was so supportive of each other. Before those shows we did a tiny gig just with the Manics in Birmingham. Pete and I got blouses and spray-painted them: one said '48 Crash' and the other said 'Ballroom Blitz'. We thought they'd be really pleased but they thought we were taking the piss out of them. I'm pretty sure they always thought we were taking the piss.

Those early days of Heavenly genuinely felt like being part of a family. It was incredibly exciting albeit for a brief period. It felt like all of the people involved were helping to push everyone else forward. It's what any great record label should feel like. It was disappointing when the Manics and Flowered Up left Heavenly, because it felt like the label was beginning to splinter. Everyone got on so well; it felt like there was a shared purpose. Obviously the Manics had the ambition to be on a major label and sell sixteen million copies of their first album, and it felt like Flowered Up couldn't last at that pace they were going, but naively I really did think that Jeff would get the backing to keep those bands and keep the family together.

Title spread: Join our club: Bob Stanley, Pete Wiggs and Celina Nash on Parliament Hill.

Previous page: Early publicity shot of Pete, Sarah Cracknell and Bob.

Opposite: A selection of early Saint Etienne single sleeves.

NICKY: 'We'll never write a love song. Ever. Full stop.'

RICHEY: 'Or a ballad. Or a trip-out.'

NICKY: 'We'll be dead before we have to do that.' *Snub TV, January 1991*

Manic Street Preachers would have seemed like an anomaly wherever they came from. The band arrived from Blackwood, South Wales, fuelled by a fierce, uptight and righteous self-belief totally at odds with the loose-limbed and loved-up shrug of 'baggy', a sound very much the flavour of the month with the music press in 1990. Here were four kids in tight white jeans and spray-painted Miss Selfridge blouses citing Public Enemy and Guns N' Roses while making a noise that sounded like the first Clash album joyriding the Welsh Valleys at pub kicking-out time. Here was a band completely out of step with the zeitgeist.

Yet, when they signed to Heavenly and released their first single, they drew a line in the sand. You're either with us or against us. Interviews were wild and confrontational, kicking against anyone and everyone. In their world, they expected to sell sixteen million copies of their debut album and split up, Slowdive were worse than Hitler and youth culture was just another invented product. They, and they alone, were 4 Real. It was addictive and intoxicating, catnip for music writers desperate for something quotable and also for a growing tribe of fans who quickly adopted aspects of the band's look when manning the barriers at the front of the stage.

The Manics' Heavenly output is minimal – two scorch-mark singles and a handful of b-sides. Those tracks propelled the band from bottom of the bill at the Camden Underworld to the cover of the *NME*, in the process becoming one of the UK's most consistently brilliant and perpetually confrontational rock 'n' roll bands. *Robin Turner*

We'd heard about the Manics through Bob Stanley and Kevin Pearce's excitable testimonials but we hadn't seen them play live. Philip [Hall,

Manic Street Preachers' manager] got in touch with Jeff saying, 'I really want you to come and see my band.' Their next London gig was at the Rock Garden [in August 1990]. It wasn't the kind of venue you usually saw up-and-coming bands in and was known as a pay-to-play gig. The bill on the night was really odd – four random bands that really didn't fit together. We went in and it was pretty empty. We were at the back of the hall and there weren't more than a few bodies dotted around the rest of the room. That didn't stop the Manics walking on with the kind of confidence you'd expect from a band headlining Wembley Arena. And when they played, boy did they mean it. They were burning. I don't think I've ever seen a band that's performed like that in such a tiny, sparsely populated venue.

My first reaction was to laugh. It wasn't laughing at them, it was like a physical reaction to their sincerity, which seemed so mad and out of place. I think Jeff and I were just thrown by how on fire they were. Our laughter quickly turned to us saying, 'Fuck, they're amazing!' The gig ended with Nicky Wire completely trashing his bass on stage, which is no mean feat. It seemed like such a bold – some might say crazed – gesture in front of so few people. They really were for real.

We quickly started talking about how we had to sign them, but each of us questioned how that was possible. Heavenly was perceived as a dance label, each of the releases up to that point had been born out of this new club culture, whether it was Sly & Lovechild, Saint Etienne or Flowered Up. The lightbulb moment was the realisation that that was exactly why we should sign them. If acid house had done one thing, it had torn down barriers and made anything seem possible. Why not sign a Welsh punk rock band?

After the gig we headed backstage, although the venue didn't really have a dressing room. There was just a corridor with bright, horrible strip-lighting and what looked like cupboard doors that you had to step up into to get onto the stage. That space just made their ferocity on stage all the more incredible. They were all back there, looking pretty dejected when Jeff uttered the immortal words, 'We'd really like to put your records out.' Sean [Moore] turned to us and immediately responded, 'Fuck off,' which was the prompt for us christening him Rude Kid after the *Viz* character. Nicky then said, 'Who are you? Fucking EMI?' James just sat there with his head down, quietly watching what was going on. There was a lot of animosity firing back at us, which was a bit unexpected. When we said we were from Heavenly, the mood visibly lightened. They knew Saint Etienne, and James and Richey had seen Flowered Up in Newport a few weeks before. From there, everything started rolling.

I don't think I've ever worked with a band that have polarised opinion in the way they did, and I don't think I ever will again. People either loved them or detested them. It felt like there were more haters at the start and that we had our work cut out winning people over. A lot of people thought we were mad. I remember Alan McGee telling me as much, but people like Andrew Weatherall and Jon Savage got it and began spreading the word on our behalf. It felt like you were fighting the band's corner. We got to love them as people very quickly, and it felt like we were on the same side, punching outwards.

When they went to Columbia, I felt really sad that they were leaving Heavenly. I knew it was part of their manifesto and I knew we didn't have the money to fulfil their ambitions – Revolver were backing out financially, so there was no way we could fund the kind of record they were determined to make. I would love to have heard a Manics album made in the way that they were recording for us, on the limited funds we'd worked with up to that point – but we all knew from the start that wasn't going to happen. Philip and the band were always really straight with us about their plans and, at the end of the day, they knew exactly what they were doing. *Martin Kelly*

JAMES DEAN BRADFIELD
We were aware of Heavenly before we met anyone there. We'd heard 'It's On' by Flowered Up and gone to see them when they played at

TJ's in Newport the week the single came out. Richey knew Jeff was this revered press officer from when he'd cropped up in mentions in music-paper gossip columns. We all assumed he'd be like your typical 'indie chap' – we were expecting cords and modish ephemera, and he was so far from that. Philip might have told us lots about him but he never mentioned the hair. It was a massive shock to us. We were all obsessed with the fact he had long curls like Robert Plant.

Phil absolutely loved Jeff. He thought he was part of a natural evolution of Soho music mavericks, cut from the same cloth as the people behind labels like Immediate and Stiff and a lot of points in between. He believed the foundation stones of the record industry should be laid by characters like that. It was probably Philip's idea to target Heavenly, but very quickly it became Nick and Richey's obsession. There wasn't any other option as far as he was concerned.

Up to that point, we'd done everything off our own backs. We pressed our first single ['Suicide Alley'] ourselves and we'd recorded an EP for punk label Damaged Goods ['New Art Riot']. From those records we'd got ourselves a few single reviews – Steven Wells gave us an 'alternative single of the week' in the *NME*. Before we'd even played London, Nick and Richey had made a lot of contacts with fanzine writers who Jeff admired. Richey has become pen pals with Bob Stanley and with Kevin Pearce who wrote *Something Beginning with O*. They had a pretty extensive list of people Jeff knew in that world, so Richey undertook these mad grassroots PR campaigns where he sent collaged pictures and manifestos made of cut-up letters to loads of people. Kevin booked us to play the Horse and Groom on Great Portland Street and Bob Stanley reviewed it for the *Melody Maker*. After the gig, one of the Jasmine Minks helped push-start our van so we could get home, which was a huge thing because I was a massive fan of theirs and also we wouldn't have got back to Wales without their help.

That combined effort got Philip and Martin [Hall, Philip's brother and the band's co-manager]

Manic Street Preachers: 'Motown Junk' (Heavenly)
Rock'n'roll 1991 style. Enough energy, attitude and violence to start a revolution?

MANIC STREET PREACHERS offer another alternative to the
dreadful spate of Sheep with Wah Wah guitars.

Live (these guys also played with Flowered Up recently)
they BURN. CONVICTION and TUNES. Possibly the first
"confrontational" U.K. band in years to actually combine having
something to say and looking cool.
MOTOWN JUNK sounds like a HIT. Where do they lie?
Think about The Clash,Public Enemy,Guns 'n' Roses,

Where do they fit?
We think they will turn heads,minds and wardrobes to their way
of thinking over the next few months........BELIEVE IT.
To support the single...............
A 20 date club tour commencing 18th January, a SNUB TV appearance
on the 21st January, the day of single release.
A Mark Goodier Radio Ohe session going out week commencing
28th January.
LOTS OF PRESS. NME has already seen the potential,(note name on th
cover a couple of weeks ago for a live review, and they were support
act.) and are giving them a two page colour feature,for issue
dated 19th January.
SOUNDS. NME,VOX,MM and NUMBER ONE all running features,also
expect live reviews from the tour.

So there you go,.........BE YOUNG,BE HIP and BE HEAVENLY.

to come and see us rehearsing in Newbridge comprehensive school. When we started working with them things quickly started segueing towards Heavenly.

We always knew we wanted to sign to a major label. That was a very clear position between all of us from the off. We were wildly, insanely ambitious and we wanted to reach as many people as possible. If a major label was good enough for Public Enemy and The Clash, it was good enough for us. Heavenly was the perfect bridge between what we'd done and that ambition.

We first properly met Jeff and Martin [Kelly] in the Bushranger on Goldhawk Road. They'd been to see us playing the Rock Garden in Covent Garden a few weeks before. The four of us sat drinking Coca-Cola and they were drinking bottles of Grolsch. It was obvious there was a brilliant dynamic between Jeff and Martin straight away. Think Brian Clough and Peter Taylor, they filled in the gaps for one another.

None of us had ever seen Grolsch bottles with the flip tops before; it looked properly exotic and opulent. We'd all order tuna melts and Richey would say things like, 'We fucking despise Bob Dylan' to cause a reaction. I remember Jeff saying, 'We know why you're saying that and we're going to let you get away with it.' We talked about how we thought 'Up the Hill and Down the Slope' by The Loft was where indie defined itself and became something – it was great to have a conversation with people who actually understood what we talking about and gave a shit about our opinions. At one point Martin turned to me and said, 'If you're going to play a Les Paul Custom, you'd better mean business.' They humoured us.

There were already rough and ready demos of 'Motown Junk', 'Spectators of Suicide', 'You Love Us' and 'Repeat', but after we signed with Heavenly the professional nature of our recordings went up immediately. We were sent to Power Plant studios in Willesden, north London,

SOUNDS
60p
JANUARY 26, 1991
HIPPY CHICKS
Fantastic
SOHO
poster inside
SEX, STYLE AND SUBVERSION FROM
MANIC STREET PREACHERS
GENERATION TERRORISTS
RETRO SPECIAL
THIN LIZZY
Man, they were cool, they were red hot. . .
BIRDLAND
Time to stop the bottle fights
CARTER (USM)
Can they survive a blessing from Jonathan King?
LIVE
The Cure
Happy Mondays
Ride
The Farm
NMA
MANIC STREET PREACHERS PHOTO BY STEVE DOUBLE. BIRDLAND PHOTO BY ALASTAIR INDGE. CARTER (USM) PHOTO BY MARTYN STRICKLAND
FULL S.O.R.

to work in the same room where 'Maggie May' was recorded. That blew our minds. It was not a box that we'd wanted to tick on our list of things to achieve; it was just amazing rock 'n' roll history for us. In the studio there was a galley control room above the live room. It was almost proprietary the way someone was above you. It wouldn't have been out of place in something like *Rock Follies*. For that whole session, we slept in the van parked on the street outside.

The producer, Robin Evans, was amazingly instinctive and intuitive. I don't think anyone could have done a better job on 'Motown Junk'. Without wanting to sound big-headed, I think it stands up as a perfect indie single. It's a bit like the alien in *The Thing*: it's bursting with something but you don't quite know what's going to come out of it. Same with the b-side tracks 'Sorrow 16' and 'We Her Majesty's Prisoners'. That session was the first time we worked with Dave Eringa who has subsequently worked on nearly all of our records and has become one of my best friends. On the first day in the studio he had a KISS buckle belt on and hair like Sebastian Bach from Skid Row. He looked like he'd walked straight out of the Valleys, so we got on with him straight away. Robin Evans was really encouraging of all my ideas for harmonies and guitar parts. At that point I didn't know anything about guitar effects. When we were recording 'We Her Majesty's Prisoners' I remember saying to him, 'I just want the guitar to sound like it's trying to escape the Earth because it's completely disgusted by what's going on.' He set up an effect that had been used all over *Dark Side of the Moon*. Sensing my initial shock, he reassured me by saying it wouldn't 'sound like any hippie-dippy shit, not the way you play'.

A month or two after recording, we played the Heavenly Christmas gig at the Camden Underworld. It was a month or so before 'Motown Junk' came out. East Village, Saint Etienne and Flowered Up all played. I remember Nick saying from the stage, 'The reason we're on first is because we're the fucking best.' It was a great night, but backstage was an eye-opener. We weren't naive to how life could be – I was working as a barman in the Memo in Newbridge at the time, I saw blood-curdling fights every week, I had to break up fights and got into them myself. Every week I saw lots of very heavy drinking and lots of post-hippie metal drugs. But backstage at that gig was a bit different. Flowered Up already had a reputation for living hard in a more urban way. Cocaine was flying round the room and I remember seeing a proper handgun sat on a table in there. I'd never seen a gun before – apart from those owned by the dads of mates who lived on farms up in Mynyddislwyn, who had shotguns. I remember thinking, 'Why is there a handgun here? And why are they trying to snort drugs through the barrel?' It was only the second time I'd ever seen anyone take coke – the first was when Steve Marriott played the Memo. I had to take the rider up to him. I opened the door and he said, 'All right, geez, put the Nuclear Brown (Newcastle Brown Ale) on the table!' All I could say was, 'Fucking hell, *Miami Vice*!' The second time was the Heavenly gig at the Underworld. God bless Stevie Marriott, but he wasn't snorting it through a pistol.

After we played, Sean got really drunk on champagne and tried to help me load our gear up afterwards, which involved him chucking the drums under the van. The next day he kept ranting, 'It's fucking rubbish, it's just affluent cider! It's fucking shit, I'll never drink it again.' It felt like a really good gig.

During those months on Heavenly we crammed so much in but it still felt like things were moving too slowly for us. We were so impatient, willing things to happen faster. We went in to record a second single a couple of months after and hit a crisis immediately when we were forced to use a different room in Power Plant that we didn't like as much. Despite a lot of effort, the Heavenly recording of 'You Love Us' just didn't sound as good, or as immediate as 'Motown Junk'. It was a problem for us because that was our biggest song at that point and we were pinning a lot of hope on it. It was mixed three or four times by Robin Evans in the studio. Jeff hadn't been happy with the first couple, then, when he heard the third one, he said it sounded like Thin Lizzy. It just wasn't right. In the end we settled on a mix in order to get the record out.

There was definitely a sense of us expanding our parameters around then. Nick and Richey were really happy, they could see things coming into focus and parts of a bigger picture emerging. Everything was in place – the sleeve artwork was amazing and they were each on fire, quote-wise. We'd been given all the tools to do the best job we could but sometimes things just don't come together in the studio. And 'You Love Us' – that version – just didn't. When we were leaving the studio, Robin Millar [owner of Power Plant Studio, producer of Sade's *Diamond Life*] said to Dave Eringa, 'That song is a hit . . . but not yet.' Dave bounded up to tell me straight away, the first of many, many such incidences in our friendship where he says exactly the wrong thing at the wrong time. But the seed was planted right there that if we ever did a major-label record we'd re-record it. As a band, you couldn't make too many mistakes early on, it was a high-stakes game. People forget how vicious the music press was back then – and all the better for it. The single reviews in the music papers were such a big thing for bands. If you didn't get single of the week or you weren't pulled out as an exceptional release, it rippled through the band, the managers. Those ripples could quickly feel like failure.

I've always wondered if there was a correlation between the recording of 'You Love Us' and the 4 Real incident. Steven Wells wrote, 'I just wish their records were as good as their interviews.' And that really hurt us. For me, as the musical backbone of the band, that was in my head day and night, day and night. After having been supportive, that felt like Swells saying that I was the one letting the band down. We knew that lots of journalists just thought we were cunts. To them we were a shit Welsh band. The subtext was pretty simple: 'Of course they're shit, they're Welsh.' In a lot of cases, it wasn't even a subtext, it was overt and upfront. So we punched hard

straight away. We were always trying to stay ahead, always there with a 'fuck you'.

The first time I'd ever left the country was for the Heavenly gig at the Locomotive in Paris. We were in a little two-star hotel in the city with Flowered Up. I remember it was a Sunday and I was walking around the city so fucked off that I couldn't get a Sunday dinner. I was that naive, I just assumed it was a global thing. On the day of the gig, I was in the hotel sleeping and I got woken by a fire alarm. There was some mad shouting in English and then some in French so I went downstairs to investigate, before a police van pulled up and six armed gendarmes piled out. When they started speaking and I said, 'Sorry, I'm British.' BAMM. I was slammed against the wall with a nightstick in my ribs, face against the wall. Flowered Up had set the alarms off and done something mental, so the hotel had called the police. I managed to convince them it was nothing to do with me, so they kicked me a couple of times and sent me off down the road.

The gig that evening felt like a moment. It was a really cool show in a venue that felt 'other'. It wasn't like any venue we'd played in before – it wasn't a dirty British pub, it was a famous French gig venue just near the Moulin Rouge. It felt like a significant outpost on our journey. For the gig, I wore one of my mum's gold blouses that she'd forbidden me from taking. I'd spray painted it; it looked brilliant. Nick was chucking his bass everywhere, Richey was hammered and Philip was more drunk than anyone else. He was still backstage holding court when Flowered Up went on. Jeff was visibly annoyed, I remember him saying, 'Are you going to come and watch my band, Phil?' It must have been the first time he'd had the tables turned on him in a decade.

By this point we'd met Rob Stringer at Columbia. We quickly found we really got on with him beyond initial questions of 'what bands do you like?' or 'what team do you support?' We'd had that with Jeff and Martin and we had it with Rob. He really knew his sport and he could quote every Clash b-side – two of the most significant

things for us back then. He was a massive Luton Town fan, which was such a badge of honour. It wasn't like so many people in the music industry claiming to be Arsenal fans the minute they moved to London.

Although there was an inevitability about us leaving the label, that Heavenly history is absolutely essential to us as a band. It's without a shadow of a doubt our foundation stone. If I had one regret about that time, it's that we didn't do a third single for them. If we'd have done one more – either 'Repeat' or 'Stay Beautiful' (called 'Generation Terrorists' at that point) – we could have released a perfect little mini-album. But we never committed to doing an album for them or even gave the impression we would. That was all out in the open and had everyone's blessing. If we had recorded an album for them, it would have been a very different beast to *Generation Terrorists*. I think Heavenly would have campaigned for the production to be different – definitely rawer – and it would have been shorter. It might have had a chance of being a classic indie debut album but we would never have written 'Motorcycle Emptiness' if we hadn't worked with Steve Brown, who helped to channel us in such a focused way. That's the trade-off.

Years later, they asked us if we would do the Forever Heavenly show at the Royal Festival Hall in 2008. It was as they were coming to the end of their deal with EMI and a crossroads point for a lot of the industry. It felt like a lot of questions were being asked of labels, about how they'd work in this new normal of downloads and streams and diminishing incomes. As soon as they asked us to play we said yes. We always feel like we owe a debt to Heavenly. You meet enough people in life who are total idiots, so when you meet the right people, you just know it. When you meet people who can help you and understand you and you get on with, it's really important. It's luck to meet people along your journey who are brilliant inspirational people, who are forces for getting things done. To get a brand-new label to the point where you're putting out records as strong as 'It's On', 'Nothing Can

Stop Us' and 'Motown Junk' in the space of six months . . . that's some achievement. That kind of streak wasn't an easy thing to do, then or now. The process of getting those things lined up was massively hard: shit-loads of phone calls and getting deals done; shit-loads of cashing in favours; shit-loads of calling up journalists and saying, 'Give this a chance . . .' Arguing with bands over artwork or what tracks are going on the record. It's all really clunky, nuts and bolts, day-to-day bullshit. You have to deal with all that stuff just to get to the point where a record is ready for release.

Very quickly after starting up, Heavenly got to a point where the succession of singles they put out really showed them as the best independent record company in Britain. Eclectic without being forced together. There was a line – a kind of rock 'n' roll symmetry – that ran between the releases. We got so lucky meeting Martin, Philip and Michael [Hall, third brother and also Manics' co-manager], we got so lucky meeting Terri and Lizzy [Philip's wife and her sister who worked for Hall or Nothing management] and we got so lucky meeting Jeff and Martin and subsequently Rob Stringer. So when you have a chance to say thank you, you've really just got to take it.

On the night train: Manic Street Preachers on stage at the Locomotive, Paris, March 1991.

ILFORD HP5 PLUS

ILFORD HP5 PLUS

Heavenly goes In Seine. The label's entire roster headed to Paris for an early showcase gig at the Locomotive on 1 March 1991.

This page: Paul Kelly (East Village); Stephanie Ansell (Saint Etienne).

Opposite (top): Nicky Wire (Manic Street Preachers); (bottom) Flowered Up.

As much a code of conduct as a band, Flowered Up were an unnatural high. A weed that grew through the pavement cracks of a north London council estate and transformed into the original full-petal racket, they went from club faces to cover stars and into total chaos within two short years. The five-headed embodiment of a post-acid-house club culture that had rewired brains the country over, Flowered Up were Heavenly's first bona fide 'band'. They also provided the nascent label with one of the first real lessons in how the industry worked: if you get enough people rabidly excited by something, someone with a bigger wallet is inevitably going to come and try to buy it off you.

After two killer 45s for Heavenly ('It's On' and 'Phobia') the band were poached by London Records for a deal rumoured to be worth in the region of six million pounds. Unfortunately, it took a while for the band to realise that the money wasn't all theirs. After one overproduced, underwhelming album and a drug-fuelled spending spree, the relationship with the label had soured. The delivery of an uneditable, twelve-minute-long single that somehow managed to perfectly encapsulate the anticipation, execution and aftermath of a night out was the final straw. The band returned to Heavenly with that track, 'Weekender', their glorious, immortal swan song.
Robin Turner

DES PENNEY *Flowered Up manager*
From the start of 1988, me and Liam [Maher, Flowered Up singer] were going out every night of the week. For a stretch of two solid years there wasn't a night that I wasn't out in London. Pilled-up every fucking night, lapping it up, living it and loving it. Acid house quickly encouraged people's desire to push and experiment. People wanted explore the opportunities that were clearly unfolding. More than just a music scene, there was a whole new economy emerging, one that provided a completely fresh starting point for a lot of people. All of a sudden the despair and monotony of the eighties fell away. Even if your life wasn't radically changed, the pills provided a colourful backdrop that made life more bearable.

Before acid house happened, I liked to go and see live bands. That was what drew me to places like the upstairs at Spectrum. There, people like Terry Farley and Pete Heller and Roger the Hippie played the music that was becoming known as Balearic. The music was a lot more diverse than in the main room, lots of different influences falling together. People obviously came to clubbing from different backgrounds – you'd party with mods, people from the soul scene, people who'd liked heavy rock. Everyone had come together in front of the speakers but people's previous musical tastes mostly remained intact; yet they were a lot more accepting of differences, not so uniform.

After a while, the parties started to wane. They were becoming repetitive and you started to get all this DJ worship going on. I wasn't into it. DJs had been an extension of the music and the dancefloor but as things got bigger, lots of people's egos were growing, whether they were playing records or putting on clubs. It felt like something else needed to happen. The buzz was fading and all the real fun seemed to be happening afterwards. Everyone was making new friends, yet personal communication wasn't a big thing when you were out in a club. You'd catch people's names but then rapidly forget them as information fused into the beats and melody. The most you'd remember afterwards would be a rosy-cheeked MDMA gurn. All the good ideas and deep bonds were made after the clubs and parties. Those small hours provided a fertile space where ideas were spoken, then heard and expanded upon. Or sometimes justifiably killed stone dead for being too bonkers. In my experience, those nights variously encouraged authors, fashionistas, songwriters, actors, designers of graphics, interiors and life, lawyers, accountants, artists, hairdressers, models, restaurateurs, carpenters, builders, black cabbies, drug dealers, bank robbers, junkies and whores.

One of those after-hours conversations began after seeing The Stone Roses at Dingwalls [May 1989]. I decided we had to form a band for

the people in the clubs, people that had been listening to rock 'n' roll just a couple of years before. The only live bands that had aligned themselves with the scene, drawn inspiration and given it back were New Order, the Mondays and the Roses, each of them having been together for five years or more. That Dingwalls show was one of the most amazing, inspirational gigs I've ever seen, before or since. It literally changed our lives.

My idea for the band was Liam singing, me managing and Liam's brother Joe and his mates Andy [Jackson, bass player] and John [O'Brien, the band's first drummer] playing the music. Liam initially said, 'I can't sing.' So I pointed to Strummer, Shaun Ryder, Lydon. They were singers we loved – not being able to sing hadn't done them any harm. He had it – whatever it is, he had it. All of that Balearic summer, people would come up to me and say, 'Liam would make an incredible frontman.' Including Jeff.

We'd met Jeff, Alan McGee and Bobby Gillespie at Spectrum. We used to sell them pills and we'd inevitably talk a lot – as you do when you're refreshed. We quickly found we had similar musical tastes. We really got on, especially with Jeff. He was someone you could talk to about music; his knowledge was boundless without ever being patronising. If you talked about a song, or a musician, he'd always have a story about that song, or that artist. It just opened a world up. He was a proper fan, an enthusiast. That was something I had never come across before. It was really inspiring.

Coming round to the idea, Liam came up with the name Flowered Up on the day we decided we'd actually get the band together. Around that point, people would say they were loved up or fucked up or whatever – the name was a variation on that. I didn't like it. I thought it sounded too sixties. But after mulling it over for a bit, it grew on me. I drew a logo that was based on the buddleia flower – the cone-shaped things that grow on building sites and railway sidings that are made up of hundreds of tiny four-petalled flowers. I picked one, pressed it and drew around the edges. There was the logo. The colours were perfect too. Buddleia is an urban weed that rises through the cracks. It felt like it was us.

Initially we wanted to write three songs and drop into a party as a live band. No one would announce it, the band would just come on and play. We talked Boy's Own into letting us do it before we even had a song written then we camped to my flat in Regent's Park where we spent four days and nights with a drum machine, a Portastudio and a notepad. By the end, we had three songs: 'Sunshine', 'Flapping' and 'Doris . . . is a Little Bit Partial'. We'd all mucked together and knocked them out. I'd written the drum patterns and some of the lyrics.

After an article on the band in *Boy's Own* and the successful execution of our three-songs-live performance idea at Kazoo – a friend's club night in Paddington – things went insane. Crazed gigs in clubs and at parties, mad phone calls from A&R men pretending to be council estate kids. We signed to Jeff's new label Heavenly and

THE PRETENDERS: 'PACKED!' LP REVIEW   MAY 19 1990 WEEKLY   55p

MELODY · MAKER

NWA
IS BRITAIN READY FOR THE LA OUTLAWS?

SIMPLE MINDS
LENNY KRAVITZ
TOM VERLAINE
BLUE AEROPLANES
PETE MURPHY
NED'S ATOMIC
DUSTBIN
MARK STEWART

FLOWERED UP
SOUTHERN SCALLIES FIGHT BACK!

A TRIBE CALLED QUEST

THE CHURCH

LIVE
WORLD PARTY
BILLY BRAGG
JOHN LENNON TRIBUTE
THE SHAMEN
THIN WHITE ROPE
MIDNIGHT OIL
SILVERFISH

ISSN 0025-9012

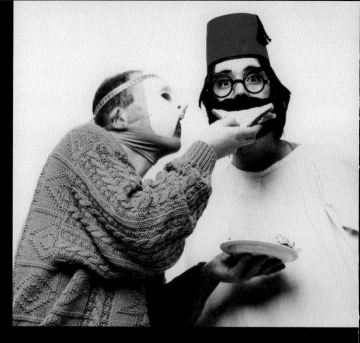

released two singles with them, got the cover of *Melody Maker* before the first one came out and the cover of *NME* the week it actually came out. Played gigs all over and signed to London Records for five albums. Partied harder than anyone else around, made a bad album and then found ourselves stuck.

The whole process of writing and recording the album was amateur. None of us had a clue what the fuck we were doing. We'd seen the band as a way out of our council-estate lifestyle and an extension of the party – of acid house itself – but we'd got ourselves into a drug-induced, near-coma state. We were scrambling around trying to learn a way to write, to find a formula to create new songs – while trying to keep control of a drug problem that was pulsing away at the heart of the band.

Some of us were full-on heroin addicts at that point, roaming around the streets of King's Cross looking to score. Everything was becoming more and more clouded in the narcotic fog that had descended around us. It's mental to think now of what we used to do to score in a pre-mobile phone age. An average day for me and Liam would involve waking up in the morning with horrendous drug hangovers and the full intention of getting on with things like going to meetings at London Records as previously arranged. By 1 p.m. we'd be in a crack house by way of a diversion, before not making the meetings at London. Most of the time the rest of the day was written off – some days I'd have to pretend I was still capable of acting like a manager. The crack houses we'd end up in were always tense and on edge, filthy and squalid with degradation peering out from the darkened corners offering a blow job for a speck of crack. There was a massive irony that we had left the loving, caring and inspirational friends who'd helped us on our way for this nightmare scenario. We had sacrificed Heavenly for this hell, and that absolute fuck-up couldn't be any more obvious. That said, I'd sometimes head to the Heavenly office after leaving one of those shitholes and hang out there as they were, thankfully, never judgemental.

Obviously, we were rapidly rinsing whatever money we had. How we got away with it I still don't know. Anyone running any business outside of the music industry would have taken one look at us and said, 'You know what, go enjoy your drugs but don't bother us any more.' But the music business allowed us – encouraged us, even – to get away with a lot more than we should have.

We'd ended up in the position we were in because we were quite clueless. Being young and naive, we'd ended up making a substandard record [*A Life with Brian*] with the wrong producer [Nigel Gilroy]. We'd tried to rescue the record, ending up spending a load more of our own money trying to fix it in the mixing stage. Sonically the record is shit, it doesn't stand up to any of the records we were inspired by, which was always the intention. And added to our inexperience, we were haemorrhaging money. We were paying out for a rehearsal room, trying to demo stuff, out of control on drugs.

The warning signs and alarm bells were all too apparent and our once-tight unit began to fragment and crack. One of the biggest problems for the band was that Liam would often not turn up. As much as I was missing meetings, he wasn't making it to rehearsals. I'd get a phone call from Tim [Dorney] asking if Liam was with me at 11 a.m. The rest of the band had got together for a day's work and the main person hadn't bothered to turn up. They'd get a call from him about 4 p.m. telling them he was on his way. He'd then turn up at 7 p.m. That was happening all the time in London. We'd tried sending Liam away on holiday to clean up and we'd tried to remove any of the pressures of being 'a pop star' or whatever it was that was going on in his head, but none of it worked. The only viable solution seemed to be to get the fuck out of London.

Out of desperation as much as anything else we booked a residential studio in Sussex called the House in the Woods. Being there gave us the ability to just concentrate on the music and try to make writing a new set of songs the band's main focus. The drug problem was still massive. Obviously, drugs travelled with us and there were always people who could scoot back and forth between there and London to pick up more gear. But, really, the only thing we needed to do day-to-day was to get people out of bed. It was pretty much impossible for them not to attend a session. It meant the band could spend time in the studio with their instruments, being a band. And that's how 'Weekender' came about.

The original jam that the twelve-minute version got arranged from was forty-five minutes long. It was a continuous play, an evolution that went through all of the different sections of the song and a few more. It was extended and it was all over the shop, but there was something there. Over the space of a couple of weeks, we worked on it solidly and ended up with a twenty-five minute version.

We weren't attempting to write a piece of music, or multiple pieces of music, that fitted into any particular style. It just came how it came, which is how songwriting had always worked for us. There was no formula, we weren't specifically writing for a reason other than to see if we could do it and what would come out. The first two singles on Heavenly were an extension of that experiment. It was only when we signed to London that we got given a very quick and very serious lesson in how the music business worked. It was a massive wake-up call that we weren't comfortable with. We didn't write songs to get played on the radio; we'd started with the intention of writing music that could blend into DJ sets in clubs. 'Weekender' was as much a nod to that original idea as it was a rebellion against the conventions and restrictions of the industry we'd found ourselves in. The formative influences of the band were brought very much to the fore. Joe, the guitarist, was obsessed with Pink Floyd, Hendrix and The Who – that's what he'd learnt to play along to. Jacko the bass player's favourite band was Rush. John, the drummer, was a mod; Tim knew electronic music, and acid house was still a massive thing for Liam and me. Lyrically, the song captured our disillusionment with that

scene. It had gone from being an underground thing to mainstream in a short space of time and there were weekenders everywhere – people who would go out on Friday and Saturday then be back in work on a Monday.

We still thought of ourselves as pretty hardcore – our two-year period where we were out every night was dedication as far as we were concerned. That element seemed to have gone, and it was never going to return. I was too young to have been a fully-fledged punk, but after getting to know [punk photographer] Dennis Morris, who'd toured with the Pistols, he'd talk about the weekenders of punk: people who'd go to punk clubs in a suit and come out of the toilet wearing a bin liner. I imagine it was the same in the 1950s and '60s. So it felt like every major culture shift had those early adopters who lived it as a lifestyle and then later those people who were happy to dip in and get out. With me and Liam – and I'm sure with the punks and the Teds and the rockers and the hippies too – it's only at the point where the something breaks big that you realise how special the underground was. Looking back, these things are always so short-lived.

Once we'd rehearsed and demoed the track, it was clear it wasn't going to be a three-minute record. It had a bigger story to tell. We knew it was a vast improvement and a huge move on from where we'd been, musically. When it came to recording it, the most bizarre idea – and the best one – came from the A&R man Paul McDonald, who suggested we work with Clive Langer. In our whole time at London, it was the only idea he came up with that actually helped. We were a bit ignorant about Clive's previous work apart from Madness, and possibly the suggestion was simply down to the fact that we were from the same part of London as them. We saw Clive as a bit too old, too establishment. When we met him, we connected in a way we never had with a producer before. It was first-class. He had no desire to muck about with the song, he just wanted to tighten the arrangement. And he is a Camden boy just like us.

It was evident very early on in the jamming process that we had something special. It was clearly some kind of beast that warranted our full attention. That's why there wasn't a batch of songs written at that time – all the attention was focused on getting this one track right. Also, as a piece, it's as long and as varied as an EP of songs would have been. The only other song written around that time was 'Better Life' [released posthumously as the Heavenly 7-inch, HVN38, in the summer of 1994], but that came about in down time in the studio while we were recording 'Weekender'.

Between the writing and recording of 'Weekender', Jacko left the band. He thought the drummer was too limited and he had had enough of the drug situation. John Tuvey was pretty restricted – he'd learnt playing along to mod records; he was tight but he didn't have any flare. When Jacko left, we lost a key ingredient. We didn't realise that until he'd gone, and by then it was too late. When that happened, I began to realise how much we'd been winging it with the initial writing process we had. We knew the fundamentals of writing a song, but who did it and where it came from, we didn't have a clue. We'd fumbled through to that point: 'Phobia' had been written by Liam and his girlfriend Tammy; 'Hysterically Blue' was all me; 'Take It' was a lyric we'd appropriated from a little song Joe Strummer plays on the piano in *Rude Boy*. After 'Weekender' all that seemed to have dried up. Liam was in the room but he wasn't contributing any more than he had to. Joe had dried up completely, he'd starting wacking power chords over everything and it just wasn't advancing the sound at all. Tim was becoming more and more frustrated with the lack of progress in any direction, which was totally understandable. That said, we all knew we had this beast of a track and we had a feeling that if we got it out, things would open up for us.

From the outside it might seem pretty incredible that we managed to get anything done at all, but there was an insane amount of enthusiasm coming back to us from people like Jeff, from

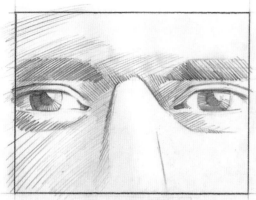

(1) EXT - ECU on boy's eyes from above.

46. ECU on boy's eyes from above. Shot slowly widens to reveal him
lying in a window cleaning cradle as it moves down building away from
camera to reveal streets hundreds of feet below.

Shot slowly widens to reveal him
lying in a window cleaning cradle as it moves down building away from
(1a) camera to reveal streets hundreds of feet below.

London Records initially, and then from Rob
Stringer and Columbia. After London tried to
force us to work on a three-minute edit of the
track, we managed to wriggle out of that deal and
went straight to Jeff, who by then had a deal with
Columbia.

We were all incredibly keen to get back to
Heavenly – it seemed like a massive positive
going forward. Ahead of a deal being done with
Columbia, a bunch of head honchos from the
label came to our rehearsal studio to hear the
band play live, particularly to hear them perform
'Weekender'. Rob Stringer, their legal man Déj
Mahoney and Tim Bowen – apparently the
man responsible for signing The Clash – and
Jeff came down. When the small talk was over
and the band got ready to play, Liam refused
to perform. Stone cold he wouldn't have it and
fucked off. In his head, he didn't think it was
necessary to pander to music biz knobs. My
take was that his bottle actually went. He was
increasingly becoming more isolated from the
rest of us and obviously wasn't enjoying it much
any more. The rest of the band played through
four or five tracks without vocals, including
'Weekender'. Thankfully they were dynamite and
the Columbians were happy, but the whole thing
was tense and embarrassing. I'm still not sure
how I managed to manage that, but miraculously
I did, and we got an album deal done.

Jeff had the idea of doing a film – a kind of
mini-*Quadrophenia* – for the whole track. We'd
already worked with the director Wiz on the
video for 'Take It', and he came at it with a
load of energy. The idea was less that it was a
video for the track, more that the track became
a soundtrack to a film. The fact that Andrew
Weatherall remixed the track only added to the
excitement. We'd always wanted to get Andrew
to do something for us since writing those first
three songs; he was still our favourite DJ. *Boy's
Own* magazine was the first place to write about
us and we'd always wanted to play one of their
parties. Musically, this was the first Flowered Up
track he was up for having a go at, which added
a lot more clout.

When 'Weekender' came out, the reaction was a mix of pure excitement and quite a bit of shock. Not many people knew what Flowered Up were capable of as a band, but there were a few of our peers who were just made up that we'd hit a level that they'd always believed we were capable of. Then there was shock from people who'd heard the album and were now wondering where the hell this thing – this beast – had come from. So, for a short time, there was a renewed excitement that this was a new beginning.

Around the time that 'Weekender' was released, Barry [Mooncult, Flowered Up dancer], who was a glazier by trade, had been asked by the firm he worked for to fix a quarter window in a front-door panel of a three-million-pound mansion on a private road in south London. Literally the panels down the front door, a tiny thing. So the firm gave him the keys and the first thing he did was go and get another set of keys cut. This was before he'd even fixed the window. He knew the house was empty as there was a note on the gate saying that it had been repossessed by Midland Bank. He called and told me what he'd done, so I said, 'What's the address? I'm coming now.'

The house had been owned by a guy called Terry Ramsden. He'd made a fortune off betting on horse racing, had been arrested in California over Japanese bond fraud and was awaiting extradition back to the UK for trial. He'd tried to buy Walsall football club and was basically just a bit of a character.

About five of us moved in for a week. Once we were in there, we were going through wardrobes to see what was there. We found a load of Ascot day suits, complete with top hats that we'd wear in the jacuzzi. Straight away, we had the idea of having a party there. We knew the authorities would be notified that people were coming and going, so we had to do things quickly. There were different squatting laws back then – anyone would have had to go through the courts to get us out – so we did things by the books and put up signs saying it was being squatted legally.

Opposite: Original storyboard sketches for 'Weekender' by Adam Brockbank.

Above: 'Weekender' VHS cover.

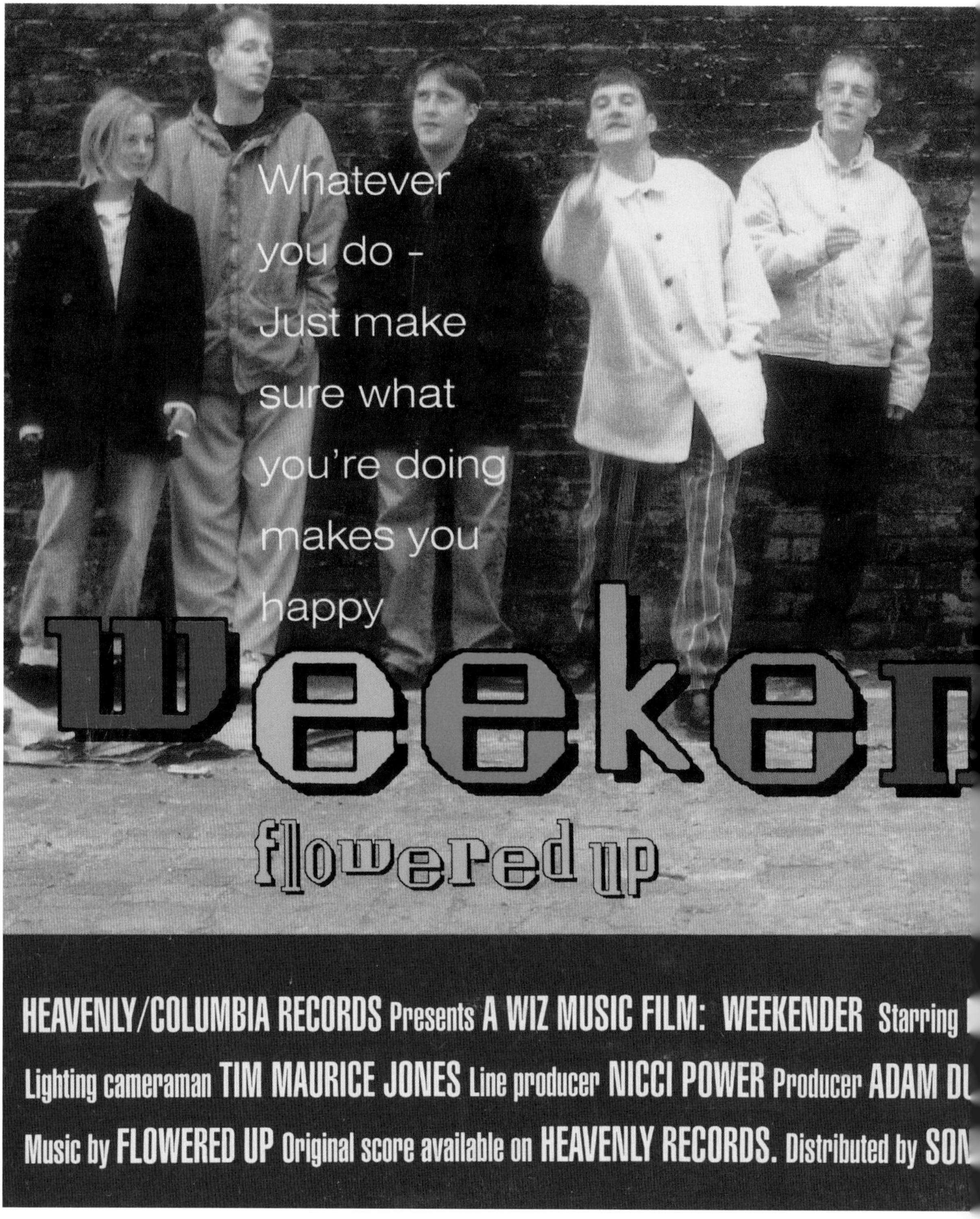

Whatever
you do –
Just make
sure what
you're doing
makes you
happy

weeke

flowered up

HEAVENLY/COLUMBIA RECORDS Presents A **WIZ MUSIC FILM: WEEKENDER** Starring

Lighting cameraman **TIM MAURICE JONES** Line producer **NICCI POWER** Producer **ADAM DU**

Music by **FLOWERED UP** Original score available on **HEAVENLY RECORDS**. Distributed by **SON**

ERED UP, LEE WHITLOCK, ANNA HAIGH

P Screenplay WIZ Directed by WIZ

HEAVENLY
... BELIEVE IN MAGIC

USIC ENTERTAINMENT (UK) LTD

COLUMBIA

Left: Flowered Up 'Weekender' flyer.

Next page (left): Flowered Up in Paris, March 1991; (right) The Heavenly shop, 50–52 Monmouth Street, WC2. Beneath the office during the Sony years (1992–93) was a proposed record shop. Unfortunately, it never had any stock in it, though it did host a Paul Cannell exhibition, Cannellism.

The party took about two weeks to organise. We booked DJs and a PA system and printed a thousand tickets that we sold at a tenner each. Paul Oakenfold and Terry Farley played, along with a couple of lads from the estate. We converted the bedrooms into bars and ran it like a club. The party itself was berserk. Gerry Conlon, one of the Guilford Four, turned up. They'd just made the film *In the Name of the Father* and he'd made a load of money. He turned up with about thirty hangers-on who all had cases of beer on their shoulders. Kylie was meant to be there; Hanif Kureishi went and based some of *The Black Album* on it afterwards. Every so often you'd hear 'Weekender' coming from somewhere – whether it was one of the DJs or in one of the bedrooms, people kept requesting it all the time. The police made several visits but were fully aware that if they stopped the party, they'd have a load of crazies flooding out onto a private road. They had to let it burn itself out.

Around six in the morning the PA shut down. The hire company had only been paid until 6 a.m. Whoever had booked the PA hadn't bothered to tell them it might run later. At this point there was a mansion full of hardcore veterans of acid house parties who weren't going to go home – they were on their fourth or fifth pill and raring to go. We paid the PA guys about four hundred quid to stay for another hour and a half, which is all they'd do. Through that period the house started to get deconstructed: sofas started going into swimming pools, twenty-foot curtains were torn down, all the banisters on the staircase got pulled up. The whole place was properly, properly wrecked.

By the end, it looked nothing like it had when we opened the doors. It was ruined. The last people to leave went on the Monday morning; they'd been roaming about dressed in their underpants and whatever was left of the curtains. Every penny we'd made on ticket sales and on the bar we'd spent. There was a massive drugs bill. In fact, we probably left there owing more money to someone somewhere. We walked away from there with nothing.

Below: Cannellism exhibition poster.

Opposite: Art of his head:
Paul Cannell in his studio, 1992.

Next page: Toasted Cheese Sandwich.

Sometime in 1990 Primal Scream's Bobby Gillespie visited Paul Cannell's house to look at artwork for potential use for future record sleeves. Before leaving, Gillespie absentmindedly discarded the brown paper bag that his takeaway lunch had been served in on the arm of the sofa. Paul viewed this not as a random act of littering but as the chance to create a piece of art commemorating the singer's work-related visit to his home. Some time afterwards, he presented the finished work, framed, to Jeff Barrett on the occasion of his birthday.

Toasted Cheese Sandwich is a few things. It is a multimedia piece, featuring paint, cut-up lettering from newspaper sources, a photograph torn out of *Rage* magazine (RIP), a standard brown paper bag, melted/hardened cheddar cheese and associated grease.

It is a comment on the throwaway nature of popular music, on food wastage and on consumerism.

It is a chance for some future civilisation to clone Bobby Gillespie from actual preserved DNA (actually, would this risk creating a kind of half-cheese/half-Gillespie hybrid?).

And it's a perfect example of how Paul Cannell thought and worked differently to everyone else. You can see it in the Scream logo, in the work he did with the Manics or Flowered Up and in the idiosyncratic, iconic Heavenly bird logo he created. Truly, a man once and forever art of his head. *Robin Turner*

Toasted Cheese Sandwich was a birthday present from Paul to me. He turned up with it one day after Bobby Gillespie had been round his house. Bob became aware of Paul's art through our usage of it on Flowered Up sleeves and Manics stuff, and he want to see if Paul had anything that might suit how he wanted the *Screamadelica* releases to look. From what I can gather, he took a toasted cheese sandwich with him and left the remnants on the sofa. So Paul thought, 'That would make a really good present for Jeff.' He was right. *Jeff Barrett*

DES PENNEY *Paul's manager*

Paul appeared in our lives soon after Flowered Up had recorded 'It's On'. I can't remember how we met him, he was just there, being introduced as this crazy artist who was a fan of the band. He wasn't someone we met through acid house. That in itself was bizarre, as pretty much everyone we met around that time was either through clubbing or through the drugs involved in clubbing – all of our dots had been joined there. Paul was definitely an outsider from that scene. From everywhere, really. He wasn't our natural type of fan, he was a hairy little guy who loved the Velvets and Dinosaur Jr.

We liked weird and wonderful characters and he really fitted the bill. He had a ferocious enthusiasm for all things music and art. He had a load of paintings he'd already done, one of which became the sleeve for 'Phobia'. It fitted the bill brilliantly. Next thing, he said, 'I do a bit of filming as well. I could do the video.' He reckoned he could bring it in for £500, which he did. He shot the band playing and did a load of animation over the top.

From the off, there was an element of darkness to everything he did. He had this idea that there was beauty in imperfection, but that also had something to do with the nature of the drugs we were all taking. I've always had a penchant for anything twisted, I love the look on people's faces when you suddenly go beyond their comfort zone. Paul was equally into that, and his artwork pushed whatever boundaries it could. It felt very much like the flip side of acid house: it was more narky, more angsty, as if to be saying that the honeymoon was over, this was reality. In many ways that wasn't a lie; it was representative of how things were turning.

When he did the original cover for 'Motown Junk' by the Manics, he delivered a collage that featured John and Yoko. John has a revolver right next to his head. Even at that point, for that track with those lyrics, it was considered a bit too on the money. It's also got what looks like a plane about to fly into a tower block, just to add to the uncomfortable nature of the image.

He was a very natural painter who was up for attempting new experiences within his art. He gave up painting with his right hand for a year, painted only with his left to see if he could master it. He always thought that to be a brilliant artist you had to be able to paint like a child. One time, we got him to do performance art at a Flowered Up gig at the Diorama. The whole thing was a mad party and there he was, in the corridor, nailing bits of wood together and chucking paint everywhere. People got really spun out by it but it was hilarious to see him surrounded by paint, drugged out of his mind listening to and reacting to great live music. That was him in his element.

I managed Paul for a few years, both for his artwork and his rock 'n' roll band Crawl. The saddest thing was that he was so impatient as a person, he just wanted to get on with things and he thought if he wasn't being paid he was getting ripped off. Which, in turn, led to him being ripped off for being impatient and taking money quickly. People would get him on his own and he'd end up swapping enormous paintings for a crap guitar.

He carved the Heavenly bird logo onto a rubber and did all the artwork for Primal Scream. The sun logo was a detail from a bigger painting that they focused in on. From there he went off and became resident artist at Creation Records. He didn't last long. A few months later, they signed Moe Tucker from the Velvets. They got him to do a single sleeve and he basically decided to retire straight after he did it – his career had peaked.

Opposite: Sleeve of a one-off single by Fabulous, released November 1991. Described as 'the least dour group you will ever see' (NME), the band drove around London in an Austin Maxi customised by Paul Cannell, modelled here by Malcolm McLaren.

Left: Flyer for label showcase at The Venue in New Cross on Bonfire Night (rescheduled for Camden Underworld the following month).

Below: East Village (Motherfuckers) – the High Wycombe four-piece whose demo tape blew Jeff away. The band made gorgeous, chiming Byrdsian guitar music. Their debut album Drop Out was released after the band had split up, but three members of East Village remain part of the Heavenly family. (L–R): Martin Kelly, Paul Kelly, Spencer Smith, Johnny Wood.

Jeff stopped promoting at the Falcon and fully immersed himself into acid house and clubbing. He disconnected himself from the Camden scene that he'd done so much to nurture. I still had roots there; East Village had been a part of the scene so I continued to hang out with people I knew like Andy Hackett and Sean Read. Through them, I was aware of their band, The Rockingbirds, from the get-go. I loved country music and thought their idea of putting a country band together was well timed. The first couple of gigs I saw were promising, but very quickly they became very good. Alan Tyler had written a fantastic set of songs and the band were all great players. Suddenly I thought, 'This band are amazing!!'

I remember telling Jeff about them on numerous occasions as we shared a mutual love of Gram Parsons and all of the things that The Rockingbirds were influenced by. The idea of signing a country band in 1991 was pretty far out there, even though we knew most of the people involved. They were not an easy sell.

After having tried to get Jeff to see them live a few times, I was with him one day when he was splitting up with his then girlfriend Val. He was pretty down and asked what I was up to. I happened to know the band were rehearsing so I said I was going to head up to see them, even though I wasn't. We grabbed a carrier bag full of cans of Red Stripe and headed up to where they rehearsed in the basement of a squat on Camden Road.

It was quite a magical moment. We got there just as they were about to begin. We passed a few cans out and two songs in, Jeff turns to me and says, 'Why haven't you told me about this band before?' That evening they played perfectly; the songs had been honed, they'd completely locked together and the harmonies were just beautiful. If we'd gone two months before it wouldn't have been the same. It was a real moment and I was so pleased he loved it.

Like the Manics, they seemed like the kind of band we couldn't or shouldn't sign, but really they were too good not to. Prior to those

signings, to the outside world, we could easily have been perceived as a dance label, even down to records like the Moonflowers single. The Manics and The Rockingbirds were the chance to say that Heavenly was whatever we wanted it to be. We knew those bands would polarise opinions. I think they shaped the future of the label. Accepting that a Heavenly recording could be anything was the first step towards the label becoming something brilliant. *Martin Kelly*

I was slow on the uptake with The Rockingbirds. Martin and my friend Val were going to see them often and really enjoying their gigs. They'd come back and tell me that there was this country band in Camden singing songs about Jonathan Richman that sounded like The Flying Burrito Brothers. It seems odd now that I didn't pick up on it and rush to a show. Especially when I think about what happened next, because we had a lot of fun together.

There have been times in the past when I've said The Rockingbirds album is my favourite Heavenly release, and it's still a record I listen to often. Everything about it was wrapped up in good times and it was a real pleasure making it. They made it with Clive Langer and Alan Winstanley and it was a hoot. It was recorded in Clive's studio, Westside, which was right in the heart of Frestonia (if you don't know it, look it up). Westside was quite a short walk from where I lived in Shepherd's Bush, close enough that I could manage to carry a crate of Red Stripe there every time I went without it being too painful. Every time I went, I'd leave my house, go to the office then walk to Frestonia. We'd then collectively drink the Red Stripe and then we'd go to the pub and somewhere in between the copious drinking the band managed to make a really, really beautiful record.

Alan Tyler's a great songwriter. His songs stand the test of time. The band were a bunch of characters, they liked a laugh and they could all play. I had known Dave Morgan and Dave Goulding from when they were in The Weather Prophets, who were signed to Creation. Andy Hackett I knew from out and about. He was with a bit of face . . . a funny

Previous page: The original Rockingbirds line-up.
(L–R): Dave Goulding, Dave Morgan, Andy Hackett,
Patrick Arbuthnot, Sean Read and Alan Tyler.

Right: The Rockingbirds' Alan Tyler
recording at Westside Studio, 1992.

face. He worked in a cheese shop and he used to try to give me cheese instead of money to come into gigs at the Falcon.

So they were a bunch of misfits and oddballs, pure Heavenly, really. When we did the deal with Columbia, we signed the band into that. It meant we had a really good budget to make the album – a Clive Langer/Alan Winstanley-size budget. A plenty-of-time-to-get-drunk-in-the-studio-and-still-make-a-record kind of budget.

When we started recording, Clive had just come back from doing a record in Austin, Texas. He's a classic old-school producer, he'd sit there and go, 'Do you know, I think what this track's missing is a fiddle. And a banjo.' And we go, 'Clive you're a genius!' Then we'd be thinking, 'Who's good at fiddle and banjo?' Probably thinking about some Camden-type person. Clive had just come back from producing the Bad Livers out in Austin. They were a punk rock bluegrass outfit. So he said, 'Let's get them. Let's go there and record the Bad Livers.' We had the budget and off we went – Clive, Alan Tyler and me. A guy called Texas Mike set up the session. I can still just about remember the flight. God, we were drunk. We got properly shitfaced on the plane. I probably got through forty fags. Texas Mike was a hospitable man, he looked after us properly, and the Bad Livers were really cool guys. The three of us felt a little bit privileged. When we came back we were full of praise for the city: 'Austin is amazing, so much fun. Margaritas by the pool.' That felt a little bit mean so we decided that we had to go to go shoot a video so that everyone else in the band could come and drink margaritas around the pool and meet Texas Mike and see this beautiful city.

After we made the album, the band went to Austin to make the 'Gradually Learning' video. It was July, which in Texas is pretty bloody hot. Like really, really hot. We had to get up to start shooting at 6 a.m. every day before the traffic and the heat started, which meant that days were mainly spent drinking heavily and mornings were incredibly badly hung-over. There wasn't really much of a plot. Andy Hackett is on a horse, I'm on

stilts, Dave Goulding is wearing full cricket whites for some reason. We shot around 6th Street, which was quite famous for its panhandlers and its transients, its hobos and people passing through. We met one chap passing through who went by the name of Armageddon. He became a good drinking buddy of ours for a while. I remember Dave Goulding getting so drunk and ending up with heatstroke and we had to carry him home. Armageddon didn't notice, he was carrying on the conversation with Dave not noticing he was comatose.

I don't really remember much about the Reading Festival show against Nirvana other than thinking it was a great idea. Well, I remember thinking it was a great idea six months before the time. Everyone around that time was just so pissed. We just drank all the time, all of us, and everybody loved booze. And somehow we still ended up getting on *Top of the Pops*, doing a Right Said Fred cover. *Jeff Barrett*

ANDY HACKETT
The Rockingbirds pretty much formed in the Falcon, where Jeff had promoted gigs. Dave Morgan, who'd been the drummer in The Weather Prophets, introduced me to Alan Tyler, a singer who wanted to get a country band together. I'd long wanted to play country music but I'd never met anyone else who was remotely interested in playing it, let alone writing it. Although it might sound odd from the outside, it wasn't that weird to be forming a country band in Camden in the 1990s. After *C86* lots of people were into The Byrds; their mid-1960s records were the roots of the sound of that scene. People had started digging deeper and listening to records like *Sweetheart of the Rodeo* and the Flying Burrito Brothers albums. Myself, Patrick [Arbuthnot, pedal-steel player] and Sean [Read, vocals and tambourine] were from Norwich and there was always a big country scene in Norfolk. You couldn't really get away from it. You'd go to a gig in a pub somewhere like North Walsham and the band might do a couple of Quo numbers for the rockers in the house, but generally it was country. You know, a great night out.

'Deeply Dippy' ... U.K. TOUR

The ROCKINGBIRDS
JONATHAN
JONATHAN

THE ROCKINGBIRDS
Man In The Moon
(Tyler)
Produced by Sean Read
Published by Bucks Music
HVN19B A
Heavenly

THE
ROCKINGBIRDS

THE
ROCKINGBIRD

COLLECTORS
CORNER
SELECT
-O-HIT

MOWTOWN JAZZ
SOUL BLUES

deliver a note-perfect performance - and in
apartment they confirm their uncanny knack
d lows of life to marvellous effect" NME 14

AY 24 NOVEMBER,
KETS £5 (£4 Concessions)

The ROCKINGBIRDS
JONATHAN
JONATHAN

Harcopak

JERICHO
SEPTEMBER . . :
th 5 L-kage +VICARS NEW MISTRESS
FR 6 THE JENNIFERS +revelation
SAT 7 THE ROCKINGBIRDS + The anyways
wed 11 REVOLVER + the daisies
th 12 urban tortoises + cellar rhythm
FR 13   t b a   THE
                                         ULTIMATE
                                         COOL
SAT 14 DEAD BUT DREAMING + FRUIT
TU 17 PURPLE RHINOS + beatnik
WED 18 the venus beads + filmstars
TH 19 silhouette
fr 20 HEAVENLY + guests
SA 21 THERAPY + the human torches
WED 25 TOP + SIX MILE CROSS
TH 26 T·B·A·
FRI 27 b·m·x· bandits + the saturn 5
SAT 28 formerly the virgin prunes
       the PRUNES + the bigger the

and in OCTOBER · · · FRI 4th - The Marionettes
                     FRI 12th · 1000 YARD STARE
                     Oct 5th CHAMULAND   Oct 17 - Goes Little Monkeys

Alan wanted the band to be as country(ish) as possible. I got Sean in, saying he could play anything and would be able to learn the bass in a week. He managed one song off the demo, so we got him in on tambourine, which is a bit mad considering he could brilliantly play more instruments than anyone in the band: there wasn't a lot of call for a saxophone back then. What really made it feel genuine was Patrick's pedal-steel playing. Half the bands in the country have got a pedal steel now, but back then people were like, 'What the fuck is that thing?' People thought it was a knitting machine.

We had a lot of friends going to a lot of gigs, so from the first time we played as a proper band the shows were packed to the rafters. Martin Kelly was one of them. He was really trying to convince Heavenly to sign us. Jeff was quite resistant but Martin convinced him to come and see us in rehearsal. We all lived in this short-term housing let in Camden, it was the art department of Camden School for Girls. We'd rehearse in the bathroom. Jeff came down one time with Martin and from the first note we played, he loved it.

Before we'd released a single, Andrew Weatherall wrote a piece about us in *The Face*. For some reason it was accompanied by a picture of us in Smithfield Meat Market in butcher's aprons covered in blood. I've got no idea why they did that, whether it was some nod to The Beatles cover. Maybe it was Jeff's idea, I can't remember. It just seemed very bleak when we were doing it.

We were the first band signed to the Heavenly/Columbia deal, the first Heavenly band to go through a major label. It meant there was a bit of money to spend. We recorded the album with Clive Langer and an engineer called Chris Potter who'd just worked with The Rolling Stones. Alan didn't like the mixes, possibly because they came back a bit Stonesy, so we got Clive's old production partner Alan Winstanley to mix it. I think he made it a bit less rocky, put in a bit more space.

One of the real highlights of that period was going to Austin to make the video for 'Gradually Learning'. Sony thought that track was the only thing on the album that had any chance of being a hit so they sent us out there to make a video. The premise was basically that anyone who could get the entire band to Austin for a week and bring something in on budget got to direct the video. We really didn't care how it looked or what went on screen, which is probably why Jeff ended up in it wandering about on a pair of stilts. We loved the idea of heading out to the heart of the action. This was before Austin became world famous for South by Southwest. We ended up staying in the same hotel where Don Letts had shot the video for The Clash's 'Rock the Casbah'. We flew in on 4 July, and as we descended into Austin all the firework celebrations went on. It was a hell of a way to arrive.

At that point we had cash, having just been signed. We were out every fucking night. The first night we got there, me and Dave Morgan ended up in a pick-up truck out in the desert at night with a flat tyre. The guy who was driving was called Bobby. He had a cell phone, which was pretty unusual back then, and he was going on about trying to get someone to come out and help. Me and Dave said, 'Fuck that, we'll lift the truck up and change the tyre.' We'd only been in the States for four hours and already we were stuck in the desert with this guy Bobby – someone we'd never met before and haven't ever seen since – doing amateur motor mechanics.

One of the problems back then was that The Rockingbirds never really had management. We never really wanted it. We all wanted to work with Heavenly. And it was all great until the money ran out. We used to love gigging – we played hundreds of gigs during the time we were on Heavenly – we were constantly on the road. During that time we really should have taken some time off to write some new songs. After a year and a half Sony finally decided they didn't want to carry on with us. They'd extended the contract and umm-ed and aah-ed for ages and we didn't have a load of new songs they could bank on.

Promotional jigsaw for the single release of 'Gradually Learning', featuring Andy Hackett on a horse.

Before that happened, we headlined the second stage at Reading Festival in 1992 under the banner of 'The Rockingbirds' Rolling Revue'. We were playing on the Sunday night while Nirvana played the main stage. We'd done a few of them before where we'd play our own stuff and we'd get guest singers from indie bands who were knocking around Camden at that point, like Silverfish and Th' Faith Healers, to do covers. Jeff always thinks big when it comes to things like that and he knew that through the band we'd got to know people like Edwyn Collins, Suggs and Vic Godard. We knew we were going up against the most popular band in the world at that time, but thankfully there's always going to be some people who don't want to see the most popular band in the world, and possibly even want to see a country band from Camden with a bunch of old faces guesting on various songs. The tent was packed and we had Suggs as compère; it was slightly shambolic but pretty good. A few years after that show, I found a bootleg tape of it on Camden Market. Rough and ready but good. A pretty good document of the band at that time, really.

Kevin Pearce is somebody that taught me a lot about music. I remember when I was up in London from Plymouth I bought a fanzine from Rough Trade called *Fun N' Frenzy*, simply because it was named after a Josef K song. Reading it on the train back home, I realised I'd just read one of the best music writers that I'd come across. I still think that to this day, actually. If you read Kevin's blog, *Your Heart Out*, I'd still say he's one of the best writers on music anywhere.

Kevin was the first person to ever tell me about the Manics. He dropped me a line to say that he'd been receiving letters from a kid called Richey Edwards which were like mini-manifestos, full of slogans and very passionate about his group and groups that he liked and where he wanted his group to fit in. I'd see Kevin around at gigs and I'd buy anything that he wrote. That recommendation was enough of a prompt for me to want to listen to Manic Street Preachers.

One of the things I loved about that period where people wrote and sold their own fanzines at gigs was that they weren't really there to sell you anything. They were just passionately expressing their love of a record or of a group or an artist, whereas the music press, whether you like it or not, are following a promo campaign for the marketing purposes of a record. In a fanzine Kevin could talk about Laura Nyro because he wanted to . . . because he had to, really. When you get a pure voice, somebody that hasn't been edited and is just communicating in pure thoughts and passions . . . sometimes those voices are ridiculously overenthusiastic. But I like that.

It may have been that Kevin came to me and said, 'I've got this idea for a book' – his own manifesto. I don't think he would have expected me to say, 'We'll publish it!' Me and Martin had never said we wanted to publish books. The only reason we wanted to publish it was because it was Kevin and because it was so fucking good. I've always liked the idea of Heavenly as being a conduit of communication. *Something Beginning with O* deserved to come out. We had a bit of spare cash so we put it out. I wanted people to read Kevin's writing. Still do. And, really, it wasn't that different to putting a record out. *Jeff Barrett*

KEVIN PEARCE
Something Beginning with O was written around 1989 and 1990. Initially it was a much larger project, but I was very into the idea of stripping everything right down to the bare minimum, using five words instead of a hundred, and creating something very instant, very visual, and very pop. It was pitched as being about obsessives and outsiders, but it was really all to do with my own obsessions, what I saw as important in the story of pop, and how by understanding the past we can move on to something better. It was, I confess, very much inspired by reading too much Nik Cohn, but also it was a protest against the way music was being written about, in the music press and particularly the sort of Johnny Rogan school of biography tomes.

And, yeah, mods and punk, and Paul Weller, Kevin Rowland, Vic Godard: these were my shaping forces. Nobody was writing about them back then, at least not in a linked sense, or in a way that tried to shed new light on these things. I could see all these connections, like the strangeness of The Jam's success, the early mods' attention to detail and Dexys' fixation with getting everything right, and that all seemed part of the same thing. But it wasn't just the contents, it was the approach, playing games with ideas and so on, creating patterns with the text and the rhythm of the words, and using lots of great literary quotes strategically placed alongside pop ephemera and song words, which was meant to be a bit like DJs and producers were doing with sampling. If that sounds pretentious, it was meant to be.

I tried to get publishers interested, but they really couldn't grasp the concept. 'It's not a real book.' 'Well, no, that's the idea.' I gave a copy of the manuscript to Bob Stanley, who was a mate, and he loved it. He passed it to Lawrence, and he loved it, and asked me to do a book on Felt, which never happened, but by then I knew I was on the right track. Then Bob passed a copy to Jeff at Heavenly, and he got it straight away, the idea of using lots of rare photos alongside the text, and said he really wanted to publish it. I knew Jeff through my fanzine *Hungry Beat*, and we were part of the extended early Creation community, then later when he moved up to London I went to a lot of the gigs he put on at the Black Horse, and so on. I had lost touch with him a bit, but I knew what he was doing at Heavenly, and had even pointed him in the direction of the Manics, which seemed to work out pretty well.

To decide to do the book as part of the label was brilliant. Factory were good at that, giving catalogue numbers to a club or a poster, but I don't think even they did a book in this way. And other labels had set up separate publishing ventures, but we knew it should be part of what was going on with Saint Etienne, Rockingbirds, and so on. It just felt right to do it with Jeff, and oddly he got quite close to doing records with Kevin Rowland and Vic Godard around that time, which was pretty weird, for when I wrote the book they had more or less disappeared, and even Paul Weller was without a record contract after the Style Council dissolved.

Because it was all new to us the gestation period was quite long. An old friend, Andy Beevers, helped enormously with many of the practicalities, and it was his idea to use the Mark Perry photo that we ended up putting on the cover, which was a brilliant move and a sort of statement of intent. Andy also put us in touch with Carol Briggs who did a fantastic job on the design and layout, she really got the context the words needed, and people like Jon Savage were very kind in helping out with photos they dug out from their archives.

When the book was finally published, in April 1993, the response was incredible, and a complete vindication of the risk Jeff was taking. There were all sorts of people who really got it, from Bikini Kill to Weatherall to Michael Bracewell to Simon Reynolds to Paolo Hewitt to Alan Horne, to young mods who got their mums to ring up to order a copy, and there are people around the world, somehow, who still quote lines back to me, and it's even been translated into Spanish.

It was the right time, back then, almost coincidentally, for the book, because a lot of the

music being put out – stuff like Massive Attack, DJ Shadow, Sabres of Paradise, Tortoise, the early drum and bass stuff, all of which I loved – seemed to fit in with what may be the best remembered quote from the book about how 'the best mods had the best record collections, the best wardrobes, the best bookshelves, the best minds.' Of course, none of these people would think of themselves as mods, but they were a lot closer to the true modernist spirit than idiots dressing up in Adidas trainers and target t-shirts and listening to Blur and Oasis, or whatever.

My one regret is not keeping more than a couple of copies, as they are worth a fair bit now. But, despite demand, it's not been republished, and never will be, because it very much belongs to a specific time, one when it was radical to consider meaningfully mods or Kevin Rowland, The Pop Group or The Action, and when in the pre-internet age information was less instantly accessible.

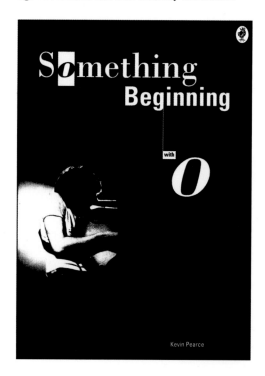

Something Beginning with O

Kevin Pearce

p3 line2 -
p3 para2
possibly
extensio
else. J
rejecti
indiffe

In
Ange
and
and
is

f

Club Forcing Approach
…are obsessed by clothes, music,
…ctional accessories or
…ted in little

visual of life
Rock Dreams

BACKGROUND INFORMATION

O is a short book about obsessives, outsiders and inter-connecting events. It is a unique journey through British pop history, with carefully chosen stops along the way. O gives a brand new perspective on the great cultural events.

The story starts with the '60s mod uprising, the lifestyle, mythology and ramifications, and continues through to the closely connected '70s Punk Rock explosion. Definite themes recur in the text: strangeness, obsessiveness, plunder and constant change.

These themes and trends are developed in the last part of the book, which examines three major characters who emerged from the '70s Punk Rock explosion and who embody "the o thing". These characters are Vic Godard (Subway Sect), Paul Weller (The Jam/ Style Council) and Kevin Rowland (Dexys Midnight Runners); three characters naturally linked.

O is approximately 15,500 words long. It is deliberately short and to the point, stripped-down for maximum impact. A more comprehensive, less immediate text would not suit the subject matter. O is deep without being in-depth. It is persuasive and provocative. O should be very visual, with plenty of photos. It would look very striking in stark black and white.

O is carefully structured. There is a definite sense of how the story is shaped, what counts and where it fits. Scale plays a very important part. Things of equal importance are covered in equal depth. There is a natural symmetry to the chapters on the '60s mod uprising and the '70s Punk Rock explosion. There are many vital connections back and forth in the text, reflecting pop's natural nerve-like tangle of linkages and lineages.

The Heavenly Sunday Social took place in the most unassuming of London venues – the basement room of a pre-furbished pub somewhere between the West End and the rest of the world. The resident DJs, Ed Simons and Tom Rowlands, are now world famous as The Chemical Brothers. Back then they were The Dust Brothers. Three singles into their career and living on borrowed time name-wise after the original owners asked for it back, Tom and Ed were recording their debut *Exit Planet Dust* at the time the club began its thirteen-week run.

During those weeks, The Dust Brothers exploded. They were the main attraction. Their supporting cast included many of their peers, people like Andrew Weatherall, Justin Robertson, Tim Burgess and David Holmes, all of whom were happy to play second fiddle to the crazed block party the headliners would throw down until the lights went up.

The idea for the Sunday Social came after hearing The Dust Brothers DJ week after week in the back rooms of clubs and at house parties. They played like their lives depended on it and the music was wildly exciting. Sets would hammer hip-hop instrumentals into tweaking acid house, gleaming techno and psychedelic rock 'n' roll. We weren't club runners, we were a record company and a press office that had a pretty good idea about what a party should feel like.

The summer of 1994 was pretty much fever pitch for rock music: Oasis were still pure, untapped potential, with *Definitely Maybe* just around the corner; Blur's 'Girls and Boys' was ubiquitous; Manic Street Preachers were somewhere between rock 'n' roll and a hard place – *The Holy Bible* was just out to universal praise but Richey was already on a self-destructive path out of the band; the long-awaited second Stone Roses album was due in the autumn; Primal Scream were headlining Reading Festival on the back of an unashamed rock album and a handful of very savvy dancefloor remixes (the best of which was, naturally, the work of The Dust Brothers).

Club land was a lot less interesting. Wherever you went, you brushed up against tribes. Clubs would expect you to dress accordingly and to act accordingly to get past the person on the door. Randomness was out and things were just a bit boring – which was exactly why we decided to start a night up, knowing next to nothing about club promotion but a thing or two about how to throw a party and who should play it. *Robin Turner*

VOICES

Jeff Barrett *Heavenly Recordings*
Robin Turner *Heavenly Recordings*
Martin Kelly *Heavenly Recordings*
Ed Simons *resident DJ, one half of The Dust Brothers (then)/The Chemical Brothers (now)*
Wendy Barrett *Jeff's wife, door person at the Heavenly Sunday Social*
Pete Wiggs *regular and guest DJ, Saint Etienne*
James Dean Bradfield *regular, Manic Street Preachers*
Beth Orton *regular, solo artist*
Nick Dewey *regular, now co-manager, The Chemical Brothers*
Stuart Bailie *deputy editor, NME, broadcaster*
Sarah Cracknell *regular, Saint Etienne*
Chloe Walsh *regular, press officer at Heavenly*
Alexis Petridis *writer Mixmag (then)/Guardian (now)*
Des Penney *regular, manager of Flowered Up/ Paul Cannell*
Sean Rowley *regular, TV producer (then)/DJ, broadcaster and club runner (now)*

JEFF BARRETT: I remember Robin coming into the office shortly after he started working there raving about hearing The Dust Brothers DJing somewhere. Possibly in Manchester. I knew who they were because Robert Linney [former Heavenly accountant] had just started managing them out of the office.

ROBIN TURNER: It was actually hearing Tom and Ed playing the Job Club at Gossip's on Dean Street around the end of '93/start of '94 that made me start thinking about starting a club night. They'd left Manchester by then. I used to go down there a lot when they were playing. They'd be doing a little alcove there, the equivalent of the third room. I was twenty-three and up for it – doing press for Underworld opened a few doors at clubs that had always been banged shut in my face before. I'd go to the Ministry when Darren Emerson was playing, and you'd get Richie Hawtin playing a four-hour Plastikman set and it was all a bit boring. Tom and Ed were the same age as me and they had loads of the same musical references. We got on and they had a really great set of mad mates who used to go to all of their DJ gigs. In the spring of 1994 they did the back room of a venue on Kensington High Street called the Park: Boy George and Danny Rampling in the main room, Tom and Ed making a racket in the back. There was a sofa on the edge of the dancefloor and I remember Tom's girlfriend (now wife) Vanessa and his brother Huw diving off the speaker stack face-first onto the sofa to some mad acid record. It felt like a vibe, and a really funny one too. And it felt like something we should try to do as our own club.

MARTIN KELLY: Heavenly was always on the periphery of the dance scene. We came from a rock 'n' roll background but we were releasing dance music, getting incredible remixes done of tracks. But clubs were pretty rotten around then. I remember going to a club called Merry England at the Café de Paris and just thinking it was full of wankers.

JEFF: I thought we were clubbed out. Robin is a bit younger than me and Martin and arrived in London after acid house had exploded. We'd been through that intense period, from Shoom onwards, and felt like that was it for us.

MARTIN: At the end of March, Saint Etienne played the first ever show at Shepherd's Bush Empire. We'd all been expecting a late-night bar, but we got kicked out, so we all piled back to Jeff's old flat round the corner in Cromwell Grove. Tom and Ed were part of the gang that came with us. Back there, Jeff was playing a load of records like 'Across 110th Street' by Bobby Womack and 'Under the Influence of Love' by Love Unlimited.

JEFF: We were all smashed, lying on the floor with our heads between the speakers. I'd be putting on records and Tom and Ed were going, 'What the hell is that?' It was those records Martin mentioned and then things like 'Time's Up' by O.C., hip-hop records I'd picked up in Soho. And from there, the idea of

repeating that kind of night but as a club seemed to make a bit more sense.

ED SIMONS: We were really excited to have people to hang out with in London. One of the things that really inspired us all to do the club was that impromptu party back at Jeff's after a Saint Etienne gig. We all bonded over a load of brilliant records he was playing and the relationship kind of grew from there.

MARTIN: Robin and I decided to go and have a look at some venues. Jeff and I had been to the Albany on Great Portland Street years before to see some Canadian comedians. Possibly Penn and Teller, if they're Canadian [editor's note: they aren't].

ROBIN: We saw this place and it had a broken clock on the wall and sticky carpets and an Aussie landlord who thought we were taking the piss when we said we thought we'd get fifty people in on a Sunday night.

MARTIN: We booked the place and I'm pretty sure Jeff still wasn't feeling the idea. Then he came up with the name for it and it all clicked into place for everyone.

ROBIN: I'd been trying to come up with a name that had a kind of 'pop' feel to it. Clubs were called things like Gosh! and Déjà Vu and Strut. The Heavenly Sunday Social felt utilitarian, it was functional; it was odd and felt like something that might go on in a miners' institute in the Valleys. It was the perfect name for what it was, a projection of what you wanted a club to be. The flyers were strips cut from an A4 sheet photocopied; they were as basic as you could get away with without scrawling 'NEW CLUB PLS COME THREE QUID IN' on a piece of bog roll.

WENDY BARRETT: I thought the idea of a weekly get-together where you could hear great music was perfect. We all thought that it would be pretty low-key. We had no idea it would go so crazy.

MARTIN: The first week I couldn't be there the whole night as Tash from the office was promoting a gig up the road with Dan Penn and Spooner Oldham. I got there later on and it had kicked off.

ED: The first one was pretty quiet. There were maybe fifty people, mostly people that we knew. The second week, Bob and Pete played, and it was roadblocked. The third week I remember I had a big night and I had to pull myself together to get down there. I ended up arriving pretty late and there was a queue right around the pub, people desperate to get in. It was a pretty easy club to pack. It wasn't that big but seeing that felt pretty amazing. The first few weeks we were playing this mad party that happened every Sunday afternoon – at a hairdresser's in Kentish Town. We used to play on a roof terrace before slugging down to the Albany. We put together a set of records that we stuck quite closely to every week – the kind of hodgepodge of instrumental hip-hop and rare-groove bits that we picked up in Eastern Bloc in Manchester off Richard Moonboots. We were playing pretty mad records, stuff like 'Dead Homiez' by Supersuckers, heavy acid stuff like 'Lobotomie' by Emmanuelle Top, Sly & Robbie's 'Boops', The Beatles' 'Tomorrow Never Knows', as well as loads of our own stuff. We were pretty proud of the music we were playing, it was completely different to everything else out there. We started pretty much every week with 'Strange Games and Things' by Love Unlimited Orchestra, a really strange slow-burn instrumental disco track that never quite peaks. It ended up being like a weekly call to arms.

PETE WIGGS: The first week, someone dragged one of the chairs from the upstairs into the middle of the floor as a makeshift podium. It became a thing that had to be done every week. There was this weird determination to place the chair in the middle of the floor. Then people would get up and on it and dance. We'd head down there early every week. We'd all meet upstairs before the doors opened. I remember we used to drink flaming Drambuies before it started, which is really naff. But it seemed to start the night off pretty well. It took a while to get to the right level of drunkenness needed to get up on a chair in the middle of a packed dancefloor in a grotty pub. The Drambuies probably helped.

MARTIN: Once Tom and Ed started, you'd look around the room and the look on people's faces was pure elation. I guess it's like what people say

the really early days of acid house were like – a communal spirit. You definitely had that feeling that you were doing something that other people didn't know about yet, something special, something illicit. I remember having that feeling at Shoom – you knew the outside world was unaware that you had a secret that you wanted everyone else to know, but at the same time you weren't going to be the one to tell anybody, cos then it would be out. The actual club ended up being very close to the ideas we'd had initially. None of us could have predicted how it was going to pan out, but in terms of the way it was envisaged, as a place where like-minded people could hang out and drink and hear great music, that's pretty much how it was.

ROBIN: One of our first ideas was to produce a weekly newsletter called the *Broadsheet* that we could hand out to everyone when they walked in. It had lists of people's favourite records, charts from DJs, gossip from the previous week, even a weekly soap opera written by an old college friend of Tom and Ed's called C.J. Magnet. This was before the internet and before mobile phones, back when you actually had to talk to people to find things out. It was an attempt to try to create a community. It told people what they missed and what they had to look forward to. I'd put it together on a shitty old word processor on a Friday, cut and paste mad pictures onto it and photocopy a load of them, hoping that we'd make enough money on the night to pay me the twenty-quid copy charge back.

JAMES DEAN BRADFIELD: We'd just finished mixing *The Holy Bible*. And I'd just moved up to London out from my parents' house for the first time. I was feeling burnt and a bit lonely. I was drinking in a pub on Westbourne Grove on my own one night when I bumped into a drunk Pete Wiggs and Robin Turner. They would be crapping on about some guys called The Dust Brothers playing down this club they were involved in. Meeting them was kind of like reconnecting with my past with Heavenly. I remember being there and thinking that 'Chemical Beats' was the best thing I'd heard since *AmeriKKKa's Most Wanted* or *Fear of a Black Planet*. Also 'Under the Influence of Love' by Love Unlimited. I'd never heard a record like that played

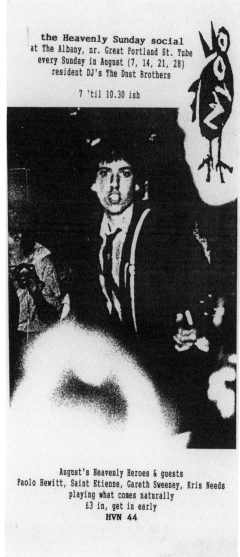

Under the influence: The Heavenly Sunday Social at the Albany, autumn 1994.

the Heavenly Sunday social
at The Albany, nr. Great Portland St. Tube
every Sunday in August (7, 14, 21, 28)
resident DJ's The Dust Brothers

7 'til 10.30 ish

August's Heavenly Heroes & guests
Paolo Hewitt, Saint Etienne, Gareth Sweeney, Kris Needs
playing what comes naturally
£3 in, get in early
HVN 44

at that volume. It made me think that they were trying to rock 'n' roll-ise everything, which I thought was brilliant. Also, it was on a Sunday. Sunday is always a good piss-up day.

BETH ORTON: I definitely got caught dancing on the bar at the Albany a few times. Nobody really cared though; no one was going to kick you out. For any reason.

PETE: When the Social started, we weren't busy as a band. I seem to remember having fun and not too much work for the whole time it was on. I was living in Cleveland Street in a studio flat, one street away from the Albany. Myself and my then girlfriend just moved into the flat when the Social started. I'd been to the pub before in the daytime, but I didn't know there was a room downstairs, some kind of mental sweatbox.

WENDY: I did the door with Tash and our mates Lou and Claire. It was three quid to get in and we had a rubber stamp with the Heavenly bird on it. We had a little table at the bottom of the stairs right behind where the DJs were. There was a big neon star right by us, and another stairway that was the fire exit out onto the street. When it got really busy the queue went up the stairs and into the pub. If we had any mates who wanted to get in, we'd sneak them in through the fire exit; people seemed to come from everywhere. Tash eventually got sacked from the door for letting everyone in for free. We cashed up in the little room behind the bar and somebody worked out how much we could pay the DJ. The warm-ups usually got fifty quid. We had a great spot on the door because it overlooked the dancefloor and there was this never-ending supply of beer. By the end of the night, we'd be up on the little table, dancing.

NICK DEWEY: At the Albany there was a clock on the wall downstairs, permanently stuck at five to twelve. It was on the wall behind where the decks were, and there wasn't anything else to look at in terms of visuals. So that was the focal point. It seemed to be symbolic of something really important even though no one had a damn clue what that might be.

PETE: One of many reasons why the Social was great was because there wasn't any of the usual crap you got at clubs. There was no guest list, there wasn't any door policy; it was egalitarian. It did mean it was horribly packed . . . no one really cared as long as they were inside. I remember when I played records down there with Bob, I'd only just started DJing around that time. It was a fairly wayward set, but people were asking what things were, there was no heckling. We were made to feel very welcome – it was great to be playing stuff that wasn't house music and not get some idiot having a go at you.

STUART BAILIE: The *NME* student kids were all wittering on about Megatripolis and Club Dog like it was the start of a new era. I didn't get it. The Social was exciting in a different way. It was happening on a night where people don't normally go out, and it had a lot of emphasis on people becoming mates. There was an interesting mix of cool faces and music fanatics. I imagine the sixties clubs like the Bag O'Nails and the Speakeasy were like that.

ROBIN: I remember one week finding myself at the bar stood next to Paul Weller. There was a polo-shirted, modish looking guy stood next to him clearly in awe. He blurted out, 'Mate, *All Mod Cons* made me the man I am today!' Without missing a beat Weller looked him up and down and said with disdain, 'And that's supposed to make me proud?' I pissed myself and immediately asked him what he was drinking. The answer, obviously, was Löwenbräu.

SARAH CRACKNELL: I remember having my arse pinched by Paul Weller as I was walking up the stairs at the Albany. It was very funny to turn round and see who'd done it, a massive cheeky grin on his face.

MARTIN: I really remember records like 'Live Forever' and 'Weekender' standing out. Tom and Ed played them alongside their own records and those were the points where you'd really stop and go, 'Fuck.' I remember someone coming up to me and going, 'What the fuck is this?' It was 'Tomorrow Never Knows'. They were convinced it was some remix. It was the original, played off the original vinyl, just out of its normal context.

Tom and Ed had the ability to make all those records meld together. That was their secret.

ROBIN: The idea initially was that the club would run for four weeks, every Sunday in August. After three weeks we knew we had to keep going. We were having too much fun. We hit the phones hard the next week to try to corral everyone we could into playing. I don't think anyone we rang turned us down, no matter how far they had to come. Word must have spread pretty fast.

CHLOE WALSH: I'd grown up in Glasgow where I'd gone to a lot of clubs. I hadn't really been to many since I'd lived in London. The few that I'd been to didn't really have the same energy as places like the Sub Club and the Arches, or the Haçienda in Manchester. There wasn't the same sense of shared euphoria, maybe because you didn't get such loyal, regular crowds. So that lightning bolt of excitement when a long-standing club favourite was played was missing for me. The London clubs I went to seemed soulless in comparison. The atmosphere in the Albany was the closest thing to the Slam DJs at the peak of the Sub Club, which was my favourite club up to that point. Did it change the way that I thought about clubs? Well, I've never seen poppers on the dancefloor before. So it changed the way I thought about poppers.

ED: Playing down there was always very intense. There was no booth and the decks were on a table. You knew that if it had been a sunny day, it would get a bit rowdy. The decks would jump all over the place. It was a total pain in the arse.

NICK: Every week, Tom and Ed would come straight from the studio clutching some new classic to try out alongside all those great remixes they were making at the time. They'd play all of these mad hip-hop instrumentals, psychedelic rock tracks and stuff like the Leftfield remix of Renegade Soundwave. It got heavier and more intense as the set went on. It was more like a rock 'n' roll show in the way it exploded from one track to the next, but totally unlike any band you'd ever seen. I just remember thinking that was the best music. That it was the music I'd been waiting to hear all my life.

ALEXIS PETRIDIS: I remember the first time I went. I'd moved to London about two weeks before, I was at journalism school. I spent ages trying to get in, got in, Jeff was DJing and he was playing 'Friday Night, August 14th' by Funkadelic, which I'd never heard played in a club before. I'd only been to either indie nights or hardcore raves or techno clubs before that. It was a Sunday evening, everyone was off their faces and there were pop stars everywhere. I was like, 'Fuck me, this is what living in London's like.'

DES PENNEY: Entering the Albany was like being unleashed back into a world I thought had died. Summer '92 through to when the Sunday Social started was the worst time of my life. Nothing going on, I was an out-and-out junkie. For whatever reason, I got back in touch with Jeff and he got me to come down. It was a revelation. It put me back in a positive place, somewhere where there was still this great music and a people surrendering to it. It really gave me a sense of purpose.

SEAN ROWLEY: Things did take a turn for the worse for me after a few weeks going to the Sunday Social. I was working on *The Big Breakfast* at the time so I needed to be up and about very early on a Monday. The nights themselves were getting more and more sprawling and pretty soon I was missing from work on Mondays. I went through a succession of lies such as, 'I went out this weekend and I got spiked. It's put me off acid for life.' After a few weeks, Tuesdays started to disappear, then Wednesdays. After a while of not turning up, I got confronted by the head of the production company Planet 24 on a Thursday morning. Without thinking it through, I said, 'I was out on Sunday, jogging, when I got run over and I've been in a coma for forty-eight hours. I've had a scan and I'm all right now.' I was pretty sure I wasn't going to last too much longer at *The Big Breakfast*.

NICK: I threw myself in with both feet. You had to, really, it was all or nothing. It wasn't the sort of place you could stand at the bar trying to look cool. Once you were in, you were in, and there was no escape. You went to the toilet at the start of the night as there was no way you'd get all the way over the other side of the room when it was in full swing. I've been back to the Albany since and it's only about two feet from one side of the basement to the other, so they must have really packed them in. There wasn't really a dancefloor – it was more like a pile-on. It was a bit like when you play football at primary school and you form a big swarm that moves around the pitch with no proper passing, or tackling, just everyone hacking away at the ball. It wasn't really dancing by the end of the night; it was more like the sleeve of The Pogues album *Rum, Sodomy & the Lash*. Everyone clinging on for dear life. And the heat was unbelievable. You'd be soaked to the skin by the time you stepped outside at the end. I can't imagine anything worse now but, at the time, I loved every single second of it.

CHLOE: I went to almost all of them, but I can only remember about ten minutes of any of them – ten minutes total, not ten consecutive minutes. My memory is murky, as was the club. It was rowdy and sweaty and frenzied. I first laid eyes on a lot of people who would soon become some of the very best friends I've ever had. All of them red-faced, covered in sweat, splashing beer all over themselves as they pogoed on top of tables.

MARTIN: When we booked Tricky, I don't think anybody realised just how crazy his music would be. He'd been coming down for weeks as a punter. He turned up one week and the doorman refused to let him in saying he was clearly trouble. Robin didn't know him but snuck him in anyway. Every week he'd come down saying he was going to bring us music he was making – this was six months before *Maxinquaye*. He never did, so we offered him a slot on the final night, partly to try to hear these tracks he was on about. David Holmes played on the same night and refused to go on after Tricky, assuming he was going to play some kind of godlike set that couldn't possibly be followed. What happened was Tricky played one very bizarre, very brilliant hour of music that sounded like the inside of an acid-addled mind. I remember leaning over to tell him that the record he was playing – 'Been Caught Stealing' by Jane's Addiction – was on at the wrong speed. He just looked at me and said, 'I know.'

ROBIN: The basement was packed from when the doors opened, so most people heard the entire warm-up set. It meant that atmosphere started ramping up very early on. I played a few records for the first hour or so, and then the warm-up went on from 8 til 9.30 (or 10 once the landlord had applied for a late licence, a few weeks in). For some people, playing the warm-up was intensely nerve-racking – Tim Burgess got so nervous he crouched behind the decks and got Chloe – his then-girlfriend – to put a series of killer 7-inches on for him. There was something about how the terrible lighting, the cigarette smoke and the anticipation of what was to come all elevated hitherto ignored records. I have such a vivid memory of Sean Rowley playing 'Sail on, Sailor' when he warmed up. It's a relatively unknown 1973 single recorded by an unrecognisable version of The Beach Boys, but at that point, in that shitty pub, it sounded like a platinum disc spinning on a celestial jukebox.

SEAN: The club always got tagged as eclectic, which missed the point. It was far more focused than that word implies. I'm obviously not a snob, but I did get very protective of it. Very much, 'If you don't get it just fuck off.' The anything-goes philosophy got very misinterpreted. Not within that night, more with the kind of clubs that came after and what the Social got lumped in with. There were great, life-affirming moments in the warm-ups that really did have that magical 'all back to mine' feel. You could play a northern record next to an acid record next to God knows what. What was really special was that each warm-up DJ had a different take on things. Even if it didn't quite work, you didn't really mind that you'd got there early because you knew you were about to be delivered the goods by Tom and Ed. The guests really were like support bands. Some were fantastic, some weren't quite right. No one cared. You got there early and hung in there.

NICK: Some people from 'dance world' were quite snobby about it at the time. I remember someone describing it as 'like a student disco'.

BOYS OWN

SPRING

The charge to the bar and the ensuing crush, proved to much for the weak hearted and many left to the strains "Road to Nowhere" (via Mr Dean Thatcher). Leaving the people who really wanted to be there and not just to be Mr "Next-big-thing-nosey-parker!"
Catch Flowered Up at the Boy's Own "All day affair" and up at the Hacienda in the Spring, with bands popping up from Bromley, and all points sarf of the river, It looks like being a singer will be this years alternative to "serving up" and why not it's alot less harmful to your health.

Flowered Up 1 - The Rest 0

The Heavenly S
HVN 44, No.
Disco Evange
More Injokes

Socials come and Socials go, and, by G
bring you top Heavenly Hero and rouge
witnessed a worse for wear J.C. attemp
record, a drunken fool and a soundsyst
the landlord had started to kick people
totally reliable Dust Brothers do the
gets. Dirty gits. What's coming up? Jus
on the 25th, into October and the 2nd w
debut of Red Snapper with Mr Dean Thatc
single and their L.P. - both are amazin
- Big Bobby G, Nick Warren and Daddy G,
Holmes, loads of other bods, honest. Any
cool, if a bit pricey...hence why we're
two. Mr Teeny, Principal Skinner, Ralph Wiggum...collect
we're trying to find someone to pay for the thing. Liqui
several other nitrate manufacturers are being approached

The Damage (The Sunday Social)
So, Mondays are out of the question from now on then...
The 11th, what a night - Ashley Beedle playing a select
described as "eclectic", followed by a Dust Brothers se
On", "Weekender", "Across 110th Street"... music doesn'
playing "Rise" by PIL has got to be one of the best So
and one of the finest selectors we've had so far, than
had to be Ali, the doorman, who saved us lot from havi
total chap. If anyone was thinking that we're getting
that - we just want to enjoy it as well
right off it

The Heavenly Sunday Social Bro
HVN 44, No. 5, 4th September
Top Propaganda And Bullshit
NO LIGHTWEIGHT BEHAVIOUR. EVER.

Five weeks in and we bring you the Social debut of Andrew Weatherall (unless you count his very
appearance the first week). Top boy, last minute confirmation and such anticipated. As always,
at the end, 'fresh' from recording their first l.p. which is (without trying to sound too smug)
men will weep openly. The Social will be carrying on for the next couple of months, for as long a
Our guests will be: Ashley Beedle, Johnny Chandler, Red Snapper (live) with Dean Thatcher, Tim
Holmes and Nick Warren and Daddy G (Massive Attack). Please fill in the mailing list/post your det
Sunday Socialism, 72 Wardour Street, London, W1V 3HP)
on coming 'cos it's firing off on a weekly basis...
P.S. What's all this shite about not being able to play a "rock" record in a "dance" club? We'll han
anyone and stand on the stairs and watch the reactions. It's a fucking blast

e Heavenly Sunday Social Broadsheet
HVN 44, No.4, 28th August
Total Cack With A Firm Helping Of Propaganda
"It wasn't us who penned..."
DOES ANYONE READ THIS SHITE?

Mr Needs has just rocked the house at the Reading Fest to the pre Primals crowd and should by now be
crowd 100th the size of last night. The Dust Brothers didn't play Reading but were probably down the front
opid as ever. The Primals, at the time of writing, were due to be playing The Brothers mix of 'Jailbird'
man Mick Jones
ple keep on com
ohnny Chandler
ber 2nd will
of these bods,
ng the most st
ool - much the
Adverts over.
ld keep on r
tened in the
features th
on t'other,
for coming d

SOCIALISM

The Heavenly Sunday Social is over - 'til the season of goodwill at least. Now The Dust Brothers can finish their first album
(featuring the semi-legendary "Let Me In Mate, I'm The Inmate"), the Heavenly office can function on a Monday, all our guests can
go back to playing proper gigs for proper money, you lot can get on wqith your lives. Last week's "Damage" - how weird was
Tricky?? How good were the Dusts??? Many a tear in many an eye, especially when big Mark Jones got up on the speakers and ai
guitared his way through "Weekender" for the last time. Well done to the ten people who blah'd in by putting lipstic
the backs of their hands. Us lot had it back in a flat in Goldhawk Road, got egg raided by the neighbou
the police. Martin, Sean Rowley, Neil and Claire, Nick and Robin deserve respect for carryi
watching "Rude Boy" completely wasted, finally collapsing at 11.30 pm after no sle
fellas. Amazingly, no one died. We'll keep you posted about any seasonal Socials an
top live entertainment which should happen early next year. Until then, you'll be ab
miserable that it's all over. Thanks for writing back to us, your name has been ente
in a draw in our filing cabinet...)
Blatant advert time...the rumours are true - Socialism is spreading across the nation.
movement by donning a limited edition t-shirt bearing said slogan in either blue or re
"P&P"), from Heavenly Sunday Socialism, 72 Wardour Street, London, W1V 3HP. First come,
delivery. Top fucking shirt it is too...

Until we meet again, love from Jeff, Martin, Tash, R

The Heavenly Sunday Social
HVN 44, No. 1, 7th August 1
A load of Propaganda

Heavenly Sunday Social - it's not about trip hop, it's not about phat bea
things used to be. It's about drinking, dancin
record collections to the public, it's about m

'Beer, beer, that's the reason we're all here..

Pure Dust Brothers charts

& The Ladyetts -
izards

n, oh dea
h Sweeney
id the job,
h this pla
od as it u
a loud as
The Week...
Brothers had finished playing. 1000
the fact that he's (A) a top bod, (B) a top funk master, and (C) a tobacc
yhem due...)...No.2, Nick (Deek) for walking into a lamp, having the bulb explode against his head
ywhere. Nick then walks away, unscarred, but totally phazed (e.g. monged out of his tiny mind). On this
has not been booked to play a Social, he is a danger to himself and to others and he badly needs
3, Wendy (she who takes your money on the door) for telling Mr. Chandler to do the dirty deed on the
showing, we should definitely book Wendy on the decks when we get our extra hour.....No.4, Tash (2nd week)
a visiting Heavenly hero in the gents, and for going completely unheard...sob...no star spotting this wee
was down here, they were all cool as fuck, loving it, dancing, drinking, chatting, the whole lot. That's
is all about...Top weirdness award goes to the two yell-Krisna'd up girls who arrived late and s

EVERYBODY'S LOOM
FOR THE LAST GAM
IN TOWN

This is probably a point for raging debate, but what the
debate. I put it to you that there hasn't been a band which s
'LONDON' loudly in everything it records, says and wears since
of "Sten Guns in Knightsbridge" ...... Come on lets hear it th
you say, do me a lemon, Lois, Filas, Gabbiccis and pimples, i
and besides sounded like Big Country. "BIG AUDIO"
I suppose. Their long players are like
at the look

That was so off the mark. It was serious about music, and was totally in the hands of people who knew what they were doing. I discovered some of my all-time favourite records down there and the club shaped everything musical and beyond for lots of us in a way.

ED: At that point, it was amazing for us to be playing with the likes of Andrew Weatherall, Ashley Beedle and Justin Robertson, people whose names we'd read in magazines. Suddenly they're warming up for us. Andrew played an incredible set that was put together so brilliantly, completely differently to how he would have done it his own clubs. Jeff's set was inspirational too. He played some fantastic records - mad Italian disco house records you'd forgotten about, and then things like Sister Sledge, 'Thinking of You'.

NICK: Andrew Weatherall's set was amazing. The next day, we all went out and tried to find the records he'd played, things like 'Kung Fu Man' by Ultrafunk, lots of early electro, his remix of 'Weekender' and the odd totally brilliant Clash b-side. It took ages to track them down – it was much harder to find music when there weren't any blogs crapping on about it the next day. Shazam was still a comic book character.

PETE: There were times when I'd pray for a night off, but I was petrified that someone would come and knock on the door and drag me down. So I'd usually just head down there before that happened. It was pretty addictive once you started going.

ROBIN: Every week you kept hearing these mad stories of things people had done down there. Some guy leching over girls was set on fire with a bottle of amyl and a lit cigarette. Someone chucked a pint over him to put him out. Then there was a guy getting a blowjob on a pile of coats behind the decks. I'm not sure if it was the smell of the place or the fact that it was so packed to the bloody rafters, but the one thing that place wasn't was sexy. Call me old fashioned, but I'm not really sure how that one happened.

WENDY: Sunday night back then was early closing, but no one was ready to go home at half-ten. Sometimes we carried on at home, pissing the neighbours off.

ED: Looking back at it the whole thing sounds very hedonistic, but for me it was never druggy. It was just one endless bottle of Budweiser.

MARTIN: The Social couldn't really have gone on much longer at the Albany. I think we – Heavenly and Tom and Ed – were all very aware that it needed to stop. It was getting out of hand, numbers-wise. On the last night, Brian, the landlord, estimated there was 1600 people either inside the building or outside trying to get in. The capacity of the basement was about 160, comfortably. We usually got 300 in somehow. That last night, Brian was stood on the bar taking a panoramic photo of all the people locked out, probably to tell the brewery this was just another average Sunday night for him down the pub.

SEAN: By the end of the run, I was questioning so much of what was going on in my life. I'd walked out of my job thinking there was much more fun to be had out there; that there was much more than just taking Keith Chegwin round people's houses at 7 a.m. Pretty soon I was pursuing the *All Back to Mine* idea that I began to formulate in those weeks that the club was running. It eventually became a TV series and an album and eventually evolved into *Guilty Pleasures*.

CHLOE: These days I can't make it through a bottle of wine on a Sunday night – never mind a bottle of amyl. Nowadays, something like that would kill me. But I'm glad it was there, even if it's the reason my memory is shot to bits.

JAMES: If the Sunday Social were happening now, it would definitely kill me, and I wasn't even taking drugs.

SEAN: One of the great gifts that life can bestow on you is to actually have, for a brief moment, a place where you can go and literally lose yourself. I was lucky enough to have that for that period of time at the Social. I'd never in a million years dream of going back, but I wouldn't swap the experience for anything.

ED: 1994 was one of those great summers – an amazing time for us. It was the first time we'd had our own club. We were making *Exit Planet Dust* on the weekdays and DJing every weekend. And it was one of those rare, really hot summers – well, rare back then. The best thing about it all, at the end of the day, was that the people I met at the Social are people I've been friends with now for twenty-five years.

MARTIN: I remember going back to the Albany a year or two after the Sunday Social finished. It was exactly the same downstairs except for some reason they'd put a Northern Uproar poster on the wall.

ROBIN: While it was going, we knew the Heavenly Sunday Social was vital and important and different, but we also knew that it had to stop when it did. None of us really wanted to be club runners, and charging three quid on the door wasn't ever going to make us rich. The one money-spinning idea we did have was selling a t-shirt with SOCIALISM printed in bold on the front at the last Albany party. We obviously left the box outside the pub on the last night. Those fifty-odd shirts either ended up as landfill or as fashionable undergarments for local rough sleepers. Over the next few years, the idea of what the Social could be warped a little. We met two DJs – Richard Fearless and Jon Carter – who went on to become residents at our nights at the much-missed London venue Turnmills (first as the Social, then as the Heavenly Jukebox). Richard was just starting to make records under the name Dead Elvis, latterly Death in Vegas, while Jon was initially inspired to start a band – Monkey Mafia – at the Albany, as an attempt to channel the spirit of that place in full swing into a live group. Tom and Ed carried on playing Social nights as they became bigger and bigger. Their first compilation album, *Live at the Social, Volume 1*, captured the sound of their mind-bending DJ sets in the years following the Albany.

In the summer of 1999, we opened the Social on Little Portland Street. It can't claim to channel the spirit of the Albany seven nights a week. That would be impossible, if not totally irresponsible. That said, it's been a pretty incredible clubhouse for a bunch of all-day drinkers and late-night thinkers ever since it opened, a kind of acid house Cheers bar. We've been lucky over the years to play host to everyone from Aphex Twin to Adele via Beck's smallest London show and Bon Iver's first. That said, the most perfect night was possibly a musical time tunnel when Tom and Ed dusted off the original Sunday Social set for a one-off fundraiser twenty-five years after we all first fell in love with those records. It was, for some of us, akin to witnessing The Beatles reforming to play *Revolver* in full. Now I'm just keen to hear how that music sounds in another twenty-five years.

Below: Ticket for the one-off Heavenly Sunday Social boat party on 22 June 1997. The trip up the Thames featured music from The Chemical Brothers, Armand Van Helden and the Heavenly Jukebox. Special guests on the day were Primal Scream, playing the first live show in support of their yet-to-be-released album Vanishing Point.

Above: 'Shoot the Boss *captures the spirit of contemporary British multiculturalism in a way that really hasn't been accomplished since the end of the '70s' (Spin) Jon Carter aka Monkey Mafia.*

Opposite: *Paris-born singer and producer Vanessa Quinones (Espiritu) was signed to Heavenly in the early '90s and again in 1996 when she released the pioneering drum 'n' bass album* Another Life.

Espiritu
CONQUISTADOR
MIXES BY
ANDREW WEATHERALL/
SABRES OF PARADISE
A Very Heavenly Limited Edition
007
Of 400
HVN 24P

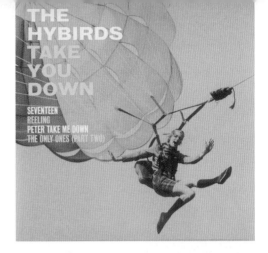

THE
HYBIRDS
TAKE
YOU
DOWN

SEVENTEEN
REELING
PETER TAKE ME DOWN
THE ONLY ONES (PART TWO)

Below: The Hybirds' Richard Warren and Tash Lee McCluney in Abbey Road Studio, 1996.

Opposite (left): Dot Allison – formerly of One Dove – released her first solo album, a collection of spectral pop songs called Afterglow, *for the label in 1999; (right) 'Second nature to us, the girls in the hood/my friend took your guy, I told ya she could'. Q-Tee was the voice on Saint Etienne's early track 'Filthy'. In 1996, she released one killer slice of UK hip-hop for the label called 'Gimme That Body'.*

We loved working with Annie Nightingale. All of us at Heavenly were obviously very aware of her, she'd been ever-present in our lives, really, whether it was on the radio, *Top of the Pops* or on *The Old Grey Whistle Test*. But she wasn't just someone who'd been there and done it, she was someone still at the cutting edge. Her shows on Radio 1 were fantastic, her enthusiasm and passion for the music she was playing was totally genuine. It was mad that Annie was on the radio every week playing the most genius, upfront music. This sounds a bit patronising, but ladies of a certain age weren't given platforms to share their enthusiasms. That show was an anomaly.

She is such an enthusiastic person; she was so into every aspect of making the record. I remember we'd sit in the Eagle on Farringdon Road and we'd be going through the tracklisting and she'd be eulogising each and every track she wanted on there. She knocked my socks off, she really jumped in fully. The album was never about using Annie as a brand and just putting something out; she was working out what went where and how it would all sound and how it flowed. And all the decisions she made were spot on.

So, doing the record was quite a simple decision, and a lot of fun. Plus we just couldn't resist that title. *Jeff Barrett*

ANNIE NIGHTINGALE

I'd been doing a Sunday evening request show on Radio 1 for twelve years, broadcasting weekly all the way through the 1980s up to 1992. Each week, people would ring in for their favourite Smiths record or a Prefab Sprout track. Lots of the same indie bands would get requested week in, week out. Around the end of the eighties, I began hearing all this fabulous new music. It was dance music, really, and it kept arriving on 12-inch singles with wonderful long remixes and extended tracks that people like Andrew Weatherall were making. Most of the tracks would be bought in specialist shops on recommendations as I wasn't getting sent them by record companies because, if they had

them, they didn't know how to promote them. It was a real shift from what had come before and musically it was much more up my street. Those tracks began creeping into my shows from 1988 onwards and it became a much bigger part of it after Primal Scream's 'Loaded' came out.

Eventually, with a change of scheduling person at the BBC, I got moved to a slot later into the night. I didn't mind because it meant I could play more of this new music that I loved, rather than three-minute edits of things that had been out for years. I had completely fallen in love with this incredibly exciting scene and had started going out clubbing with Bobby and Innes from Primal Scream, having met them in Brighton where we all lived.

I was playing dance music before Pete Tong arrived on Radio 1 at the start of 1991. John Peel was the only other DJ playing similar records; it was seen by the powers that be as a weird niche. The station was very out of touch with what was going on around the country – with the real underground. After they brought in Pete Tong, and his show really worked, a lot more dance DJs arrived at the station and they tried to catch up with rivals like KISS and pirate stations all over.

That love and obsession went on for years. Still does, really. I'd be doing the show and each week I'd get calls from people saying, 'Where can I get that track?' In those days some of those records were only pressed on 500 12-inches. Fewer, maybe. Once they'd sold out, you couldn't get them. Someone might have something taped onto a cassette off someone who had a copy. Otherwise they ceased to exist. No one was making compilations of that stuff. There was no iTunes or Spotify or YouTube. Those white labels were precious items and people were desperate to get hold of them. I knew that because I was getting calls every week to the show where you'd have people going, 'I've been out in Bristol and I can't find this record. I have to have it, can you play it? Can anyone help?' I knew what that feeling was like. Music wasn't there at your fingertips like it is now.

More and more, my Radio 1 show was becoming a meeting point for people all over the country who'd been out clubbing and who were maybe all back at somebody's house after a club. They'd started calling the show *The Chill Out Zone*. It really wasn't very chilled out. From about two till five on a Sunday morning you'd be playing these amazing records then you'd have people ringing in trying to piece the night together. They might be trying to find a rave somewhere; they'd be out driving, in a field somewhere, trying to find the location: 'I'm near Luton, I can see lights but I can't find it. Where is it? Help!' Or you'd get people calling in with simple requests like, 'Can you tell our mate to hurry up because we've run out of Rizla?'

We were totally getting away with it – it was like a huge interconnected party on the air. So I thought, 'Let's do a compilation.' And, at that point, compilations were desperately unfashionable. They were things like *Now That's What I Call Music* and the Hits albums that provided a great service for pop kids, but there wasn't a point where dance music was being collected and lovingly pored over. That whole culture was so exciting and I wanted to make it more available and to reflect the scene which was clearly out there, happening every weekend. I'd met Jeff through the Scream. He seemed to know everyone involved in the scene, all the DJs and bands who were making this fantastic music. I went to meet Jeff with the idea of compiling a bunch of those tracks and he said, 'Let's do it.'

Jeff was a real guiding force. I didn't know anything about rights or how we got permission to use things, especially if they were unreleased. Or if they'd been limited editions. He just said, 'Give me a list' and he got on with tracking them down. He made it happen. I don't think any other label could or would have done it. Heavenly, and Jeff in particular, are so free. It's why they've stayed ahead of the game for so long, doing their own thing.

Annie on One became a bit of a soundtrack for a certain type of 'up all night' person – people who wanted to keep the vibe going and didn't want to let go of the weekend. People have been staying up all night since rock 'n' roll started – you might as well give them a good soundtrack. That compilation completely changed the perception of me in the media. Until then, there was an older Radio 1 audience who'd known me through the eighties, playing those indie records on a Sunday, but they maybe hadn't known that I'd fallen very hard for acid house.

It's not an exaggeration to say that album completely changed my life. It got people to see me in a completely different way; I was part of a completely different scene, connected to a different audience who thought and acted in a different way to the old rock crowd. I can't stress enough that it gave me a new lease of life. I even ended up with a residency at Gatecrasher in Leeds! Years later, I met Danny Boyle – this was a year or two after the Olympics. He told me he had a copy and that he loved the *Annie on One* compilation. That really blew me away. I love his films and his taste in music. I have to say, I was terribly proud of that.

Previous spread: Inside the Chill Out Zone: Annie Nightingale recording her show at BBC's Yalding House, Clipstone Street, W1, in 1995.

We'd been told that we had to hear Beth's songs by some very persistent people, some of whom I didn't really like. When we eventually got Beth's original demos it was obvious there was something there, even if they didn't live up to the hype we'd been hearing. They weren't brilliantly recorded, but there was the start of something. At that point she was in a band with her brother, and it wasn't right for her voice: they were a rock band and her voice wasn't suited.

When we spent some time together, she played me the music she'd made with William Orbit, and I started to get a feel for places we could go. When we met up, we'd sit and listen to Goffin and King records and girl groups and Dusty Springfield, and then we might go dancing to Andrew Weatherall together. That's how *Trailer Park* came together, because that's how we were living.

Beth was a part of our deal with Deconstruction, but they really let us just get on with making the record with no interference and no pressure to do anything in a particular way. Andrew wasn't brought in as a nod to their dance world, he was brought in because he was the right person to mix those tracks.

I knew that putting out 'I Wish I Never Saw the Sunshine' as a limited edition 7-inch was the right thing to do. It was a really personal thing for Beth and me as we had listened to The Ronettes' original together a lot, it was one of the ways we really bonded. It was a song that created a relationship for us, and a working place. It was a touchstone.

We never called Beth a folk artist, or a dance act or the comedown queen. She was pretty original. We never labelled her in any way, really. There are shades of folk in her music, but at that point folk wasn't really part of the language. When we were making the record, there were no set reference points. I thought we were making an experimental singer-songwriter record like 'Any Way That You Want Me' by Evie Sands or *The Delta Sweete* by Bobbie Gentry. If you think about how those records sounded, they were built on

experimental elements and they weren't easily bracket-able. Beth wasn't easily bracket-able, which is a good thing.

And, man, it sounded good when you were coming down, which is never a bad thing.
Jeff Barrett

BETH ORTON
A tape of my songs was given to Jeff Barrett at Heavenly. They were recorded into my ghettoblaster at home and they went on to become the core of *Trailer Park*. I knew about Heavenly in a distant way through my old friends The Rockingbirds and through Saint Etienne. Their beautiful record *Foxbase Alpha* held something for me. They didn't make a 'type of music'. I would stare at their record sleeve searching for clues but they seemed to have an identity that was all their own. There was nothing typical about them. One of the reasons I loved it was their cover of 'Only Love Can Break Your Heart'. I've been a Neil Young fan since I was little. I loved their version and, more than anything, was inspired that they had a hip-hop beat underneath it. Looking back, I think it was one of the ways I made the unconscious connection that I could combine the different styles of music that I loved even when the sounds weren't the obvious choices.

Soon after Jeff got the tape, we met one afternoon at the Ship on Wardour Street for a drink. With the late-afternoon light streaming through the cigarette smoke, Jeff's kind words of encouragement felt like a lullaby. All the characters that would pop by – including Tom and Ed from The Chemical Brothers (although they were still the Dust Brothers then) – made it seem like part of a particularly lovely dream. Much like Tom and his unassuming sweetheartedness, there was no outward sign of what wildness lay beneath. I felt a sense of hope and curiosity, but had no idea of the adventure I was about to take with these people.

Before meeting Jeff I'd recorded a song with Red Snapper and asked them if they might be up for being my band. They were too busy, but their bass player Ali Friend was up for it. With Ali as my first musician on board I was already beside myself with auspicious good vibes. We arranged to meet up to see Bert Jansch, who was playing a gig in London upstairs at the Garage. I was surprised Ali even knew who Bert was. All too typically I got to the gig late and missed the whole thing. As I arrived I bumped into Ali as he was leaving. He was there with his friend Ted Barnes. I was devastated to miss the gig and they both said that Ted 'can play like Bert, he knows all those tunings'. It was quite some claim but they made me laugh and I decided to give it a go.

In the midst of this period, Tom Rowlands asked me if I'd like to sing on a track of theirs. 'Alive Alone' ended up being the last track on the first Chemical Brothers album *Exit Planet Dust*. Like so many of the best songs, it made the listener feel it had been written just for them. I sang those words as though it was, with all the sorrow and longing and loss that my heart was feeling at the time. When we recorded 'Alive Alone' I only heard that one section of the song that my vocals were on, and I didn't know what came next – I hadn't ever heard the full finished track.

A few weeks later I was at the Heavenly Sunday Social at the Albany. It was maybe the first or second night of the club being open. It was like an early squatters' rave – it felt like we shouldn't be there. Right at the end of the night the whole place went quiet and a track started with a voice I knew vaguely but it took me a minute to realise it was me singing. It sounded so beautiful but so shocking too: to hear something I'd sung, so internal in nature, blasted across the club. Before I could get used to hearing myself that huge beat kicked in and the whole place booted off. The room went completely mental. I stood amid the chaos in disbelief, until someone dragged me onto the dancefloor. Probably Jeff!

After playing Ted and Ali my songs they helped with the arrangements and brought in some beautiful chords and changes. I loved Ted's playing. He wasn't actually anything like Bert,

he had his own identity and feel and sound. Between Ted and Ali the songs were elevated and expanded, and I heard my two-chord songs come to life in ways that made me want to constantly get up from my playing and hug them, or lay on the floor in a heap overwhelmed and just listen to the beautiful music they were creating. I asked 'Wildcat' Will Blanchard to be my drummer. He was in The Sandals, they were a groovy acid jazz, hip-hop cool-as-anything bunch of handsome dudes band. I knew Wildcat from club nights he put on, like Tongue Kung Fu. Sean Read, my old mucker from The Rockingbirds, stepped in to play some piano. Sean easily channelled my love of classic West Coast music.

I was slightly in awe of all my bandmates; each one of them brought a sound and a feel that marked important musical ley lines. It was a time of lad culture and club culture; I was writing folk songs alongside it all and suddenly I had these like-minded souls treating the songs like they were worth their time to dig into. There were so many moments like when Ted added his guitar to 'She Cries Your Name' or Ali his bass to 'Touch Me With Your Love' where I was brought to tears or just simply left speechless and floored by the beauty of it all.

I'd never felt part of a gang before, but with Heavenly and the band, it definitely felt like one. For a while our clubhouse was a pub on Dean Street – the Crown and Two Chairmen – where Tash (who worked there) and I started doing nights. Those Acoustically Heavenly nights were really where I learnt how to perform live, sat on a bar stool in front of a bunch of mates in the upstairs room of a pub. We were playing covers as well as our own stuff and we'd play one after the other, like DJs going one-on one-off. So many of the faces from the Sunday Social showed up there, week in, week out. Even though the sound was as different as could be, the spirit was the same.

When it came to making my first record, I saw making music like putting together a collage. I didn't read music (still don't) and was

inexperienced, so I would see music visually.
I'd been writing since I was eight years old; I
recorded my first song aged eleven with Dougie
MacLean, the beloved Scottish folk singer, as
my guitarist. We played into a tape recorder in
the office of the arts centre my mum helped run
in Norwich. My love of folk music was ridiculed
mercilessly in my house, but I grew up with
my mum working all day and into the night at
the arts centre. The likes of Bert Jansch or
Dougie, and countless other incredible bands
and musicians, would come through town and
perform, often trying out their new material
in the place where I spent the majority of my
childhood. From the ages of eight to thirteen,
that was my schooling.

A few years before meeting Jeff I'd worked as a
runner on various pop videos to earn cash, one
of which was Primal Scream's 'Higher Than the
Sun'. Douglas Hart was directing the video. My
main job was to hold a spotlight on Bobby
Gillespie for hours on end. I don't know how
many times I listened to the song during the day
but, over and over, I was under the spell of its

gorgeousness. I learnt about Andrew Weatherall
through this experience and became a convert to
Primal Scream and Andrew's work.

I met Andrew Weatherall through Jeff. I don't
know where I got the balls to ask but at some
point – with the collage in mind, and with all the
enthusiasm and innocence inherent in my bringing
together of dream collaborators and the support
of everyone at Heavenly to back me up – I had the
courage to ask if Andrew might be up for producing
the record I was hoping to make. I think it was
hard for any of the label or my new bandmates
to see how he would fit the picture, but Andrew's
take on dub and his love of the best bass sounds
ever, the way he created an ambience and space,
made him my dream producer. I thought this
would be the only record I'd ever get to make. I
wanted to include all the formative elements of
the music I'd grown up with. I was intimidated but
I was cheeky as hell, and all of this gave me the
confidence to ask. Andrew's warmth and kindness
came through; I think he must have liked my gall.
He wasn't up for recording and producing a whole
record but he said to come back to him when that

part was done and he'd see about mixing. I was over the moon.

As the recording process went along it became ever more clear that no one in the band, except for me, wanted what we were making to be remixed. Such care was put into those recordings. I wasn't oblivious to what we had recorded already – I could see we had made something beautiful in its own right – but I was torn as I so wanted to see through the vision with Andrew. Victor Van Vugt, who had come on board as producer and was brilliant at bringing the band together, mixed the album. In the end Andrew went on to mix three songs: 'Touch Me with Your Love', 'Galaxy of Emptiness' and 'Tangent'. There I was in the thick of one of the most male-dominated universes you could imagine, but in terms of no one putting on airs and graces, I was certainly an equal – I was pretty feral back then! Andrew being into remixing what was basically an out-and-out folk record will forever make me smile. Andrew – like so many of the

fellas I got to spend a significant amount of my music-making with back in the nineties – was an absolute fucking gentleman. Working with Andrew on those songs allowed me to expand and experience my voice with a different kind of power; it was liberating. He drew out of me in sound what I was feeling my way towards using words and melodies.

By the end of all the many explorations that made *Trailer Park* what it came to be, we had created something unheard in music at that time. A blend of sounds that had not existed until then, even if I say so myself! It was a big old group effort and the most beautiful trip. So many incredible people I met and worked with, nothing forced or considered, it all kept unfolding in its own unusual way. It was Heavenly who were up for supporting the curiosity, never questioning, always a 'yeah!' and never a 'nah'. Heavenly was the only home that could have allowed for this all to come to life. I will hold these experiences and memories dear, always.

Previous page: Beth Orton and Terry Callier rehearsing prior to recording together for the Best Bit *EP, 1997.*

Next page: 'So fast like a rollercoaster, in and out you seem/Like a dream, so fast you're gonna side-stream'. Four-piece Mancunian teenage rock 'n' roll band Northern Uproar released two albums for Heavenly.

got LIVE if you want it!

Espiritu
Tuesday, 6th June

THE HYBIRDS

HEAVENLY
BODIES

ickot No. 299

presents

Dot Allison Live
March 2nd: London, Improv Theatre
...nham Court Road, W1
...(DJ...Jeff Barrett)
Do...
Do...

NEW BUFFALO
ABOUT LAST NIGHT

The debut EP featuring 16 Beats and Just A Little Time.
Available now on CD from all good Independent stores.

"Once in a blue moon, a record stops you in your tracks with it's spine-kissing beauty. 'About Last Night'
is one of these exquisite blooms. Stunningly simple, effortlessly original." - NME

"Delightful... the dreamy vocals and lo-fi tone poems are pretty near perfect." - Uncut

Heavenly
recording
www.heavenly100.com

Famous Times
& Hybirds

...LY PRESENTS

LIVE AT THE SOCIAL
VOLUME 3
...IXED BY ANDREW WEATHERALL
RICHARD FEARLESS

HEAVENLY PRESENTS
got LIVE if you want it!

...et No. 014

Tuesday, 13th
northe...

HEAVENLY
got LIVE if
north

HEAVENLY RECORDINGS
HEAVENLY PRESSOFFICE
NEW TELEPHONE NUMBER 0171
OUR ADDRESS AND FAX NUMBER REM...

Bluebird

BETH...

HEAVENLY & DECONSTRUCTION

INVITE YOU TO THE FLAMIN...
9 HANOVER STREET
LONDON W1

ON WEDNESDAY 3RD MAY
7PM TIL LATE

FOR A DRINK
A LARGE DRINK
A VERY LARGE DRINK

FEELIN...
HEAVE...

TUNES PROVIDED BY

MONKEY MAFIA
PAOLO HEWITT
PLUS SPECIAL GUES...

...ton Trailer Park

"Q-TEE"

SJM and HEAVENLY present A MONTH OF
NORTHERN UPROAR
15th, 22nd and 29th of September at THE ROADHOUSE
NORTHERN UPROAR plus guests
AFUNKYPUNKROCKPSYCHEDELICSOULFULBEATHAPPENINGSOUNDTRACK

debut single ROLLERCOASTER available 2/10/95 on the Hea...

Dot Allison Mo'Pop
Her new single released on
Heavenly Recordings
March 15th. CD/MC/Ltd 7"

northern uproar:

HEAVENLY PRESENTS
got LIVE if you want it!

THE HYBIRDS
Tuesday, 20th May

...et No. 293

Bitten

What does it mean to be high in a basement? How does one get there?

I always thought that name was such a beautifully ambiguous statement. To Heavenly and the world beyond, it was a killer compilation album that captured the sounds of an underground dance music scene. To the artists involved in the record, it was a wayward way of life, a rallying call for heads-down hedonism and an invitation to join an eyes-closed, lost-in-music moment.

Dance music has been a key part of Heavenly's output since day one. The label grew out of acid house and subsequently never lost sight of the dancefloor. Rock 'n' roll records were regularly remixed and reshaped (and still are). Tribal lines were blurred wherever possible because, really, that's how we all consume music, isn't it?

Pieced together by artist/producer/DJ Sally Rodgers, *High in a Basement* was a vivid snapshot of London's house music underground in the mid-1990s. That scene was producing transcendent music specifically to be played in small rooms kitted out with killer soundsystems. Although that scene has long since mutated and evolved, the spirit is still there as new generations still strive to catch the feeling in basements, lofts, fields or house parties whenever they can.

Robin Turner

SALLY RODGERS

A Man Called Adam started out making records for Acid Jazz, one of which – 'Techno Powers' – had been a big record for Harvey and Choci from the Tonka Sound System. Then we did the whole Ibiza '90 thing, releasing 'Barefoot in the Head' and recording an audacious, bonkers and self-indulgent record for Big Life, who at the time had Coldcut and The Orb as well as Yazz and Lisa Stansfield. It was an odd mix. I think they wanted me to be one of those pop birds, but we were always closer to the other side of it, we were far more interested in making underground dance records. So when we got dropped, Steve

[Jones, one half of A Man Called Adam] started a label, Other Records.

Dance music was shifting then. On the one hand, there was the rise of the superstar DJ and mega clubs like Cream and Renaissance. It was called progressive house back then but really it's the equivalent of what you'd call EDM now. On the other, you had clubs like Kenny Hawkes' and Luke Solomon's night Space at Bar Rumba on Wednesday nights. They were bringing over DJs like Derrick Carter, Chez Damier. It was a much cooler sound. They were playing records released by Latino labels in New York and Miami, a lot of French records too . . . records that had an American garage sound to them; records that were jacking and swinging and not just following a Teutonic thump. We were jazz kids when we were younger, so these records made a lot of sense for us. Much like the original Chicago records, this was more black, more gay, more swingy. We'd found a house music to fall in love with.

Alongside Space, there were parties happening in places like Plastic People and at clubs in east London. This was the very early days of Shoreditch, back when places like the Blue Note were up and running. Those parties catered to something of a stoner scene, it wasn't like people were clattered on ecstasy in a massive space waiting for Sasha to come on.

Before long, Other Records was part of a scene with UK labels like UStar, Nuphonic and Luxury Service, and producers like Rob Mello and Zaki Dee, the Idjut Boys and Ray Mang (aka Laj). We were all trying to collaborate and work together on tracks. It was an intensely creative time, with a healthy amount of friendly competition between artists. We were a gang who all knew each other, we were always listening to each other's tracks and going away going, 'That's brilliant, we'd better make our next one better.' It's how real creative scenes have always functioned.

We came up with the idea of doing a compilation of this new UK house sound, so I took the idea to Jeff, who was up for it immediately. He'd been our press officer back in the early days and I'd always kept in touch with him. Although there have always been rock 'n' roll bands or acoustic artists on the label, Heavenly has always known, respected and released dance music. Back then I was one of the only women in the very masculine world of house music production – Jeff dealt with that in the opposite way a label like Big Life would have. He was always respectful of me as a person of taste. He has the same integrity towards gender issues as he does towards everything else, and that was massively important.

The album came together under the name *High in a Basement*. It always felt evocative of a blues party or a rent party. It felt warm, like it was something put on by and for friends, something intimate. It could almost have been a Coltrane album title. When I look at the picture of our old studio in Gospel Oak that's on the sleeve of the album, it almost has a sixties feel to it. A load of us sat around and decided on what would go on the record, pitching in favourite tracks or mixes. I had the final say, though.

In the years since the album came out, lots of the labels associated with that sound stopped releasing records and the whole nature of the industry has changed massively in the digital era. High in a Basement is really just a snapshot of a scene being lived in by a load of people in their twenties. And even if that specific scene has gone, there's always going to be people in their twenties getting together to sort their own scenes with their own music. Sometimes I find myself DJing in clubs that are put on by young people who are all making their own tracks and doing their own thing – it feels good to know that people are still striving for that same experience.

Right: Sally Rodgers and Steve Jones, of pioneering house duo A Man Called Adam.

Right: Sean Read and Alan Tyler, of Famous Times, made two records for Heavenly, including a song that could easily sit alongside Neil Diamond at his very best ('The Blue Man'). Pictured here in Camden, 1997.

Opposite: Richard Sen was Bronx Dogs, whose grimy electro music reflected a pre-gentrified east London at the end of the '90s. Richard was resident DJ at the short-lived Social spin-off night Metal Box. Picture shot in Falconberg Court, W1, 1998.

THE BLUE MAN EP

Sarah Cracknell introduced me to Jez Williams in the mid-1990s when he was in Sub Sub. She'd known him since the eighties when he played in a band called Metro Trinity with her friend Johnny Male. They made a really lovely jangly New Order(y) EP called 'Die Young'. When Sarah was working up songs for her first solo album, the band she put together was made up of Johnny Male and Guy Batson, who were now Soul Family Sensation, Jez on guitar and Robin Goodridge from Bush on drums.

I got to know Jez quite well after that, and thought he was an incredible guitar player. We asked him to play guitar on the forthcoming Saint Etienne album, which became *Good Humor*, and he made a real difference to the sound of that record. While recording in Malmö he told me that Sub Sub were no more, and that the same people were morphing into a new band called Doves. He reluctantly agreed to send me their music, but it took forever to prise anything out of him. In the meantime I heard they had played the Falcon in Camden and were supposedly mind-blowing. I rang Jez and said, 'Why the fuck didn't you tell me you were playing down the road?' He pretty much said he hadn't wanted to bother me.

That was just as the 10-inch of 'The Cedar Room' came out on Casino [an offshoot of Rob's Records] and was the best thing Jeff and I had heard in ages. I remember some conversations about whether or not we could get involved, but then the news arrived that their label boss Rob Gretton had died. It was a bolt out of the blue, especially for Jeff, who'd worked closely with Rob when doing PR for New Order and Factory. We wanted to be respectful but following a tip-off from Chris York [SJM Concerts] we contacted the band and their manager Dave Rofe to see what their plans might be. A couple of days later a CD of the first album arrived and Jeff and I jumped on the train to Manchester.

I vividly remember listing to *Lost Souls* for the first time on a Discman on the way up and thinking it was the best debut I'd heard since the first

Stone Roses album. Fully formed and ready to go, it's still one of my favourite records. We sat in the beer garden of the Briton's Protection on Great Bridgewater Street. They asked how many we thought we might sell. Sticking my neck out I said, '100,000.' They were all pretty gobsmacked. 'Really? We thought we might do ten thousand if we were lucky?' I couldn't have been more wrong. It went platinum [awarded for 300,000 UK sales] within its first year.

The timing for hooking up with Doves was perfect. Our deal with BMG had soured and it was time to move on. EMI were keen on working with us and Doves were the perfect way to kick things off.

Doves rarely turned in singles under five minutes long. It usually fell to me to do radio edits. The challenge of getting the band playlisted earned me nicknames from Jimi like 'Razor's Kelly' and 'the Butcher', but getting 'There Goes the Fear' down from seven minutes to under four and A-listed on Radio 1 made it all worth it. *Martin Kelly*

JIMI GOODWIN

Truth be told, even when Rob [Gretton] was still alive, we were collectively wondering whether his label could properly push the music we'd been working on. There was a question about whether Rob's Records had the juice to really make it fly. There's always been a quiet ambition in our band; you might not always see it, but it's there.

That said, we counted ourselves as very, very lucky. We'd previously made an album as Sub Sub that we were really proud of, but now we'd been given a second chance to make a debut album. Rob facilitated that and paid for it. We were staying with Rob out of love and respect, but with *Lost Souls* we'd finally made this record that we knew we should have made years before. So, with Rob's blessing, we had started looking around to see if anyone might be able to offer something that we all felt was lacking from the set-up we had.

With *Lost Souls* pretty much finished we met a few labels, but when we met Martin and Jeff

Title spread: Doves live at the Royal Festival Hall as part of Forever Heavenly, the label's eighteenth birthday celebrations, September 2008.

Below: Doves ride a Manchester Metrolink tram, 2000.

Next page (L–R): Andy Williams, Jez Williams, Jimi Goodwin.

in the Briton's Protection we immediately loved their vibe. It helped that Jeff had done Factory's press and he'd partied in the Haçienda like we had. It felt like they weren't bullshitters up from London. I'm not saying anyone else was a bullshitter – we just immediately assumed they were, our detectors were on high alert. And with Heavenly it just clicked. Jeff didn't trot out the Mondays or anything to impress us, they just said, 'We really, really love this fucking record.' And we believed them and thought, 'You know what? These guys aren't so different to us or Rob.' There was no spiel, just passion. We knew the label, we knew the pedigree. I'd been obsessed with 'Weekender', I'd bought it on video back when it came out. I knew they were people who didn't just do easy things. We knew

about the Social and we had massive respect for what they'd done with The Chemical Brothers. So we decided that we should pitch in with them. When we signed we wanted to do the right thing so we gave all of our advance over to Lesley, Rob's widow.

After *Lost Souls* came out we got a bit freaked out by the success. It went Top 20, but all along we'd thought we were going to get a pasting for having the audacity to pick up guitars after being a dance band. But we did know we'd made a great record. There was a lovely honeymoon period after the release. You've dreamt of going to New York and playing your music live over there to a crowd of people who want to see you. Now we were actually doing it, it was everything we'd dreamt of, it was just great. We toured America with The Strokes just as they were first getting known, it was ace.

The smoke was clearing from touring when we went in to start recording *The Last Broadcast*. We'd spent nine months on the bus with thirteen guys. You're still young enough to find some romance in that, but it was a massive wake-up call when the bus pulled back into town. It's a massive cliché, but we had twenty years to write *Lost Souls*; we had a fucking year to write *The Last Broadcast*. I was pretty daunted, getting my head back off the road and into the studio.

We'd done most of *Lost Souls* in New Order's place at Cheetham Hill with Jez recording us. When we started recording *The Last Broadcast* we didn't have a base but we recorded in places that made us feel comfortable. We were working out of Jez's spare bedroom, out of my spare bedroom, Andy's front room and rehearsal rooms in Stockport. Although it might sound ballsy as a finished thing, the confidence in the band during the making of *The Last Broadcast* all came from Andy and Jez. Honestly, I was still finding my feet after coming off tour.

We were so proud of making *Lost Souls* for about thirty grand that we wanted to continue working that way. You don't need to pointlessly

throw fucking dough at this. We were going into Revolution Studios in Cheadle Hulme, which is where loads of seventies bands had recorded. We wrote and finished a lot of songs in the studio. We'd also go to cottages in the middle of nowhere and set up Pro Tools. That's how we got round not having a studio of our own. Technology was happening that way: we had two big racks of hardware, and anywhere that could go, we could record. We'd rock up in places like Ramsbottom with car boots full of instruments; we'd go down to Kendal near the Lakes and record stuff like 'New York'. Making the record, we mainly worked on our own, though we recorded in the Dairy in Brixton with Max Heyes, who'd done a lot of work with Brendan Lynch and Paul Weller, and we did some bits with Steve Osborne. Steve was very much the go-to guy for when we were having trouble with tracks. He helped us massively with 'Caught by the River' and with 'Satellites'. I love Steve to death, and apart from Ben Hillier who we worked with on *Some Cities*, he was the only person who could do things that we couldn't do in the studio.

'There Goes the Fear' was one of the first songs written for the album. The nucleus of it was pretty much all Jez's. He had done a demo at home very early on. I remember first hearing it in a minibus on the way back from a gig before we'd signed with Heavenly. Somehow we'd been booked to play a gig in Bristol, mid-afternoon at some free festival in a park. Apparently it's where Geoff Travis and Jeanette Lee from Rough Trade saw us and hated it. I remember I was feeling a bit dark, voicing a bit of arrogance, and that came across on stage. 'Well this is a load of fucking tripe.' We got word back that they thought we were awful. Anyway, on the way home, Jez had this tape and played it. All the crew were in the van so everyone was hearing it the same time as me and Andy, so we were a bit freaked – that wasn't how we did things – but there was no denying that he had something brilliant. Jez is a very, very focused writer. He's amazing; me and Andy can't wax lyrical enough about his energy and his vision. He really did pick up the baton and he showed us that we hadn't done everything with *Lost Souls*.

We had a great first album, we'd made the record we actually wanted to, but there was so much more to do.

We'd been very lucky that everything up to that point had been done without any real pressure to deliver or to perform in a certain way. Before the album was finished, we were suddenly being really pushed to do a tour with Travis. We'd been lucky, we'd never had to do support gigs before. Travis were out on their first arena tour. We didn't feel ready, but people were saying, 'You've got to be ready.' It meant we had to finish the record to a deadline. We went to Real World – Unreal World, really – and we committed to a tour in February, which meant the record needed to be finished by Christmas. And we did it, and the whole circus started again.

We knew 'There Goes the Fear' was a strong opening gambit, but Jeff was totally convinced from day one that it should be the first single. He was on the blower going, 'I really think "Fear" should be the first single.' We were sat there thinking, 'Really? It's dead long, and we've already got away with that once with "The Cedar Room".' 'No, listen, it'll be amazing.' 'OK, we'll trust you here . . .' After all, we were all very much in unison that it was a stone-cold fucking killer.

I don't know anything about marketing – and I shouldn't do – but I do know that there was a stroke of genius with the single release when it was decided that it was only going to be available for one day. It proved we had a fanbase and it pushed it to No. 3. I don't know where it would have got to without that happening. And another genius move was getting that video made by Julian House. Without a doubt, it was the best video we ever had done.

The following year was crazy. The album went straight in at No. 1. It all rolled on and the gigs got bigger and bigger. At the start of 2003 we won Single of the Year at the *NME* Awards, which were being held at Hammersmith Palais. Vernon Kaye off the telly had to pick up the award on our behalf as Andy, Dave Rofe, Robin and me

Opposite: The artwork for each of Doves records was designed by long-time collaborator Rick Myers.

HEAVENLY RECORDINGS
&
EMI:CHRYSALIS
invite you
to celebrate the release of

doves
lost souls

the debut long player
at
The Scala, Kings Cross
on
Wednesday 29th March 2000
from
11:00pm till 3:00am

Heavenly
recording

were all on our way back from the toilets when it got announced. We were walking back down the steps, there was a spotlight searching around the tables. We'd already had a bit of party at the hotel the night before, I'd seen Jez at breakfast and he told me he was going to do one back to Manchester: 'Fuck this for a game of soldiers, I'm going home.' The rest of us met in a pub in Shepherd's Bush. I remember seeing Topper Headon and he was like, 'Nice one, spirit of punk and that!' When I got back to our seats, I saw Chris Martin from Coldplay and he said, 'Fucking amazing. I've got to go up in a minute. Do you want to come up with me and get your award?' He genuinely meant it. He wasn't trying to get in our heads or anything. He didn't need to. He thought we could have more fun, but I'd gone and retreated into a shy phase.

You don't often get time to think when you're in the middle of it but we all knew it was everything we'd ever dreamt of. We knew that things weren't handed to you on a plate; we worked really hard. We got better and better as a live band, as you should do – I mean, if you're not getting better after relentless touring, you should get off the fucking road. But really, I think we even knew at the time that that whole period was the ride of our lives, man.

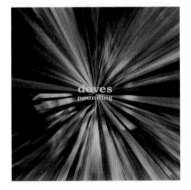

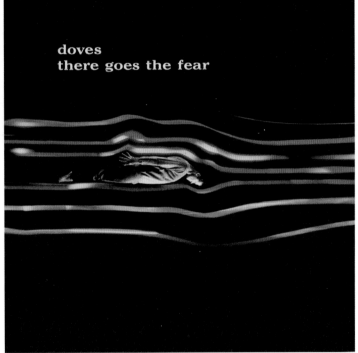

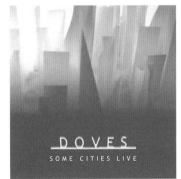

'I want my days and stolen nights, I want my life back...' Mancunian bliss-pop duo Snowblind (Jane Murphy and Paul Williams).

Dick O'Dell pitched Ed Harcourt to Jeff and myself just after we'd done our deal with EMI. We knew Dick through house music, he'd run Guerrilla Records and before that Y Records in Bristol with The Slits and The Pop Group via Rough Trade. Dick was certain that Ed was perfect for Heavenly, but he'd brought in a bit of a sleeper. We weren't immediately bowled over but I used to find myself playing the demos over and over while working late in the office. The songs really got their hooks into me and when I mentioned it to Jeff he felt exactly the same way. Over a period of time Ed's music really crept up on us, the songs were getting under our skin.

We went to see him play at the Cashmere Club, below a pizzeria in Marylebone – not the kind of venue you'd ever see a new band in. The first show we saw there was a bit bonkers and we weren't entirely convinced he was capturing what we liked about the demos. After another show I went back to Jeff saying, 'Come and see him again, I think he might be getting it right.' At the third show he'd nailed it and we were in. We really hit it off with Ed. He was young – twenty-two at the time – larger than life and bloody funny.

When it came to releasing Ed's music, we tried re-recording some of the tracks from the original demos and it just wasn't happening, they just weren't as good. So why not just put out the demos, then? We'd played them so much and had a severe case of demo-itis. They were great, so why change them? Releasing them as *Maplewood* bought us some time while Ed recorded the first album, but the EP took off and had a life all of its own. People felt the same way as we did, and it was the perfect way to launch Ed onto an unsuspecting public.

For me, Ed is like Heavenly's Randy Newman – an unbelievable talent who doesn't need to have hit singles. Newman was signed at Warners for years without having a hit, but made scores of great albums that sold really well and influenced a ton of other writers in the process. Ed is a similarly classic singer-songwriter. It's rare you hear people who can effortlessly craft a song so well, who can move you along with lyrics that act like stories.

I remember a year or two after we signed Ed I heard Tony Wadsworth, then the chairman of EMI, on the radio talking about what artists he liked at that time. He said, 'I love Ed Harcourt. One of the great things about having bands like Coldplay and Radiohead is that they allow us to have artists like Ed.' In a perfect world you would have certain, talented, artists who can do what they like, develop at their own speed, carried by bigger-selling acts. It's how the majors should work and it's how society should work, really. *Martin Kelly*

ED HARCOURT

In the time I spent with Heavenly, I went from being a fresh-faced boy to a completely grey-haired, haggard old husk of a man, covered in tattoos. No regrets – those seven years were some of the very best of my life.

When we met, I was living in Sussex in my invalid grandmother's old farmhouse. I had the run of the entire house, where there was a baby grand piano that belonged to her that I began writing songs on. I'd amassed a load of instruments and musical things and I had a 4-track recorder, so for two years all I did was compose and record in this idyll in the heart of the countryside. Everything I recorded was incredibly lo-fi. I was obsessed with Tom Waits and also listening to Beck and Sparklehorse and Eels, those kinds of American alternative acts. Also Nick Drake and The Beatles were a constant in my life. Those influences really affected the early demos, you can really hear it in the recordings.

Eventually I got convinced by friends to send music out as it was just living in my head and on those cassettes. I knew nothing about how things worked or what you were supposed to do to get a record deal. I used to make copies of the demos and send them in the post to myself so they'd be copyrighted. After sending out demos to four managers, I went with Dick

O'Dell, who really got it and understood it even if I didn't at that point. Dick thought we should send them to Heavenly as it would be a good home. Fine by me.

Around the same time, it seemed like a good idea to make myself publicly visible. I moved to London and started doing gigs at these open-mic nights in a little dive bar called the Cashmere Club. The first time I ever played my songs was at my brother's birthday in there. After that I asked the girl who ran it if I could come back and play again. Dick managed to get Jeff and Martin down as they loved the demo. That night, I didn't play one song off the tape we'd sent them, I just played this weird, junkyard, backwards-flowing music that they hadn't heard. That no one had ever heard. I don't think I really cared about what anyone's response to my music might be. I was so young and it didn't really register what I was doing.

The second time they came down, I'd hired in a vibraphone player with me and, again, we did completely different songs. I even ended up playing a saw. Dick was getting really frustrated, thinking I was deliberately shooting myself in the foot. I was incredulous: 'Maybe I don't want to play those songs? They're too poppy.' The third time, thank God, I gave in and conceded. I had a full band and actually did what I should have done all along. They went into a frenzy about it and we started working together.

Heavenly decided they were going to release the demos untouched. They wanted the first thing people heard to be these raw recordings. The thing is, they were genuinely raw. When it came to mastering I had no idea that they might need decent audio files to work from. I turned up at Metropolis with my 4-track and all the cassette tapes and I didn't have any mixes of the songs. I was trying to mix live on the 4-track while Miles Showell, who was doing the mastering, was looking on perplexed, going, 'What the fuck are you doing?' I didn't know any better. When it came to mixing 'I've Become Misguided' the tape would give off this horrible electronic distortion every time I tried to play it. So Miles took it out, got out a hammer and bashed the tape with it. Not sure how that worked but it seemed to sort the problem out.

It was amazing that I was being allowed to do this kind of stuff. It was such a pivotal start to my career. People still come back to that record, and it was one of Jeff and Martin's great ideas – keep it simple, keep it as close to its pure form as possible. There's a charm to naive recordings – like the early Beck record *One Foot in the Grave*; there's something odd and otherworldly about it. When I re-recorded a couple of the songs for *Here Be Monsters* I never managed to recapture the magic of those original demos.

If putting the demos out wasn't enough, Heavenly then let me make a film to go with them. *Raccoon Boy* was some weird trip I'd dreamt up; I don't know how the fuck it got made. I had a song I'd written called 'Raccoon on My Shoulder' that I played to my ex-girlfriend, who was a video director. She thought it was properly out there and suggested making a film to go with it. So she pitched it, and I told Jeff, who had quite a twisted sense of humour and was totally into the idea. We shot a load of footage in my flat and in Highgate Park. We had two raccoons made for it – an animatronic one that sat on my shoulder and was fitted through a leather jacket and had a hook so I could move his head about. Then we had another one that was operated by three puppeteers. Somehow we managed to convince EMI to spend thousands of pounds on this absolutely deranged film. That kind of behaviour on a major label seems like such a distant idea now – the idea that someone in accounts is going to give the thumbs-up to a debut record made up of demos and an accompanying film where a new artist has sex with someone while a raccoon taunts him from his shoulder.

The years after *Maplewood* were incredible, a torrent of ideas, many of which made it onto records, and a huge amount of love as part of a wonderfully dysfunctional family. I fulfilled my

entire five-album deal with Heavenly, which is a pretty amazing feat for an artist like me in the twenty-first century. Towards the end of my time at Heavenly I'm not sure any of us knew what to do, though. When it came to delivering records, I was coming to them with thirty songs, two double-albums' worth of new recordings. Maybe things petered out towards the end, but I feel incredibly lucky to have been given that chance. There was a bit of pressure from EMI for me to continually write singles, which was fair enough – they weren't going to let me make an industrial noisecore record, even if I did give it a go. I don't know why things didn't connect with the public, and really it doesn't matter – you have to keep on doing what you do, making music and trying to turn heads.

One of the most significant things I took away from those seven years of beautiful excess (and occasional downright madness) was what I learnt about life and music. Jeff was a very important mentor to me. I really feel that when you're working in music with people of a younger generation, you have a duty to pass on knowledge and passion. I grew up listening to music passed on to me from my older brothers; Jeff was like an older brother in that respect – he turned me on to records by people like Big Star, Nina Simone, Carole King, Spooner Oldham and Dan Penn that properly influenced how I wrote and thought about songs. I feel like Jeff's like the Bill Murray of the music world. Lots of hits, some misses but, Christ, you don't want to think about a world that he's not around in.

new single
out 28th june

22-20s

shoot your gun

Devil in them: 22-20s brilliantly rewired the blues with heavy punk-rock energy for their 2004 debut album.

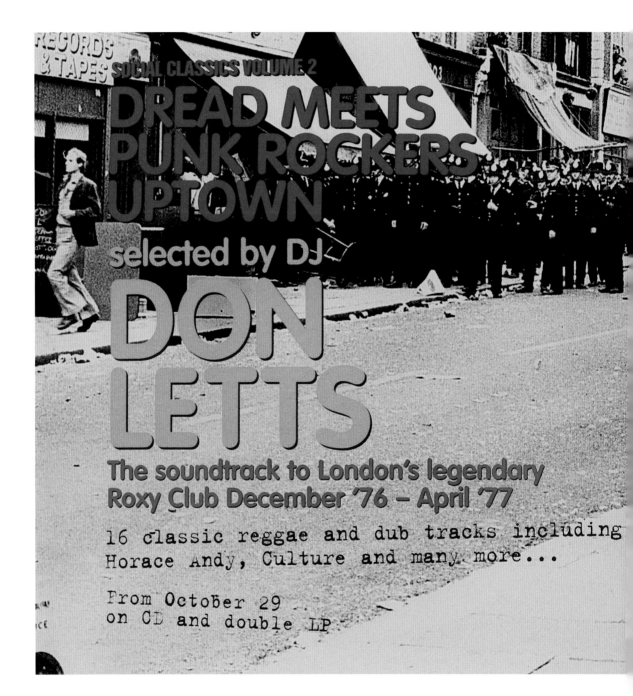

SOCIAL CLASSICS VOLUME 2

DREAD MEETS PUNK ROCKERS UPTOWN

selected by DJ

DON LETTS

The soundtrack to London's legendary
Roxy Club December '76 – April '77

16 classic reggae and dub tracks including
Horace Andy, Culture and many more...

From October 29
on CD and double LP

ng Tubby, Junior Murvin,

Don Letts is musical royalty. He's someone who's been there as history has been made and whose actions in the past have influenced the way we think in the present. Whether he's arrived armed with a Super 8 camera, a burning-hot sampler or a bag of super-heavy 7-inches, he's helped change the direction of travel. Without a doubt, he is the don.

Dread Meets Punk Rockers Uptown came about in the period when Heavenly started working with EMI. Coincidently, the Social had just opened in Little Portland Street. Every night featured a different soundtrack, whether it was greatest hits firing off from a rebellious jukebox or friends and family playing their favourite records. The Social Classics off-shoot connected everything up – they were a way of taking the sound of the Social back home, wherever you were.

When we were approached about putting out Don's first ever compilation album it wasn't a tough decision to make. The proposed tracklisting was a flawless primer in dub and reggae. Many of the records he'd played at the Roxy had become cornerstones for us in the years since punk rock broke. The ones that weren't – those deeper, heftier cuts – were Social classics we just didn't know yet. Like all perfect playlists, it sounds timeless and otherworldly. And a lot of people thought the same. *Dread Meets Punk Rockers Uptown* met with universal praise on release and went on to win *NME*'s compilation of the year. A second compilation album – *Dread Meets B-Boys Downtown* – headed west to the Roxy in New York at the birth of hip-hop. A different scene, a different sound, a different story. The Don remains the same though. *Robin Turner*

DON LETTS
So how did the Dread meet the Punk Rockers Uptown? By DJing at the Roxy, playing dub reggae to disaffected white kids back in '77. Let me set the scene.

By the mid-seventies the establishment had managed to alienate its own white youth. It didn't have to try hard to alienate me since I was a first-generation, British-born black of Jamaican descent and already well pissed off . . .

In 2000 Sam Bully and the late Nils Stevenson approached me with the idea of doing a soundtrack of the tunes I played as DJ at the UK's first punk rock venue the Roxy back in 1977. I knew Sam as a notable character on the punk scene and Nils from his time working with the Banshees. The Roxy was so early in the day that there were no punk records to play – UK ones anyway. So I played what I liked – bass-heavy dub reggae. Lucky for me, the punks liked it too. They could relate to the musical reportage quality of the lyrics, the heavy basslines, and they didn't mind the weed either. This unlikely combination would give rise to the 'punky reggae party', which would ultimately get the nod from Bob Marley. That was the background to Sam and Nils's concept. Ultimately it was a niche idea that needed someone with vision, someone that understood the dynamics of music and its possibilities. So they went to Jeff Barrett.

Now, Jeff was a musical maverick that had that served his apprenticeship from the ground up. We're talking record shop manager and live music promoter, not to mention running his own clubs and setting up records labels before launching Heavenly in 1990. Oh yeah, his time as a musical grasshopper also included a stint at Creation Records working for another musical Svengali, Alan McGee – so this brother knew his shit. Consequently his only advice for the proposed project was to ignore the commercial aspect and keep it real. I soon came to realise that music wasn't a hobby for Jeff, or even a job – it is his fucking life. His passion for music is at the core of who he is and, as such, he's a dying breed in a world of non-musical accountants. Personally I owe the brother big time cos it was his decision to release *Dread Meets Punk Rockers Uptown* on Heavenly in 2001 that re-launched my life as a DJ, because truth be told I hadn't played out since those halcyon days of the late seventies. So when you're out there grooving to my bass-heavenly selections, spare a thought for the likes of Jeff – there ain't many of 'em left!

Dread meets B-Boys downtown

Social Classics Vol 3

The Hip Hop sound of New York '81-'82 as selected by Don Letts

The new movement came with its own style, language, dance moves and attitude. From where I was standing it was similar to punk in that it appeared to be a reaction against the over-produced black music coming out of the U.S at that time, which seemed removed from the harsh realities of life in the Bronx. Again in time honored tradition the youth set about creating their own soundtrack in a very punk DIY kind of way. - Don Letts

Exclusive album launch party on August 10th (see over)

Three six-stringed Heavenly singer-songwriters
(L–R): Muswell Hill guitar genius James Walbourne,
New York anti-folk musician Jaymay and
Mercury-Prize-nominated Irish artist Fionn Regan.

NME

FIFTY YEARS OF SEX, DRUGS & ROCK 'N' ROLL!

NEW MUSICAL EXPRESS

WORLD EXCLUSIVE! NIC & NAT ON LIVING WITH THE LIAMS

BRITAIN ROCKS
Down the front at T In The Park, Move and Lost Weekend

Where *did* he get that coat?!?

Celebrity fans, awesome gigs and a brilliant album

The Vines

20 JULY 2002
£1.50 (US $4.50)

PHOTOGRAPHY: ANDY WILLSHER

NME.COM
MUSIC NEWS UPDATED EVERY HOUR!

NO WONDER EVERYONE WANTS TO SHAG CRAIG NICHOLLS!

9 770028 636147

29>

The Vines demo arrived in the Heavenly office one Friday afternoon in the early autumn of 2001. Within an hour, we'd mobilised to sign them. Seventeen tracks long, their CD was one of the most complete and fully realised sets of songs that had ever dropped on the label's welcome mat. While some tracks howled with the kind of teenage rage that had fuelled pop music since sixties drugs went bad, others chimed with the kind of celestial melody that made the first Stone Roses album or *Waterpistol* by Shack so gloriously addictive, echoing the times when sixties drugs were very, very good. When the songs from those demos were eventually recorded, over the space of four years and two albums, you realised every transcendent harmony, every yowl, every cymbal smash had been worked out meticulously on that original CD. They were pretty much perfect.

In 2001 there had been a global resurgence in guitar-heavy rock 'n' roll thanks to disparate American outliers The Strokes and The White Stripes. The Vines hailed from Sydney. In the eyes of the music press at that point, New South Wales was as much a cultural backwater as old south Wales had been when Heavenly signed the Manics. The fact that frontman Craig Nicholls would consistently cite Suede (then on the verge of splitting due to ever-decreasing interest from the public) and a pre-stadium Muse as influences only served to lower expectations further. It meant the records and live shows would hugely confound preconceptions.

The Australian three-piece (soon-to-be four piece, though not all the same pieces) signed to Heavenly affiliate label Capitol in the States (with a proviso that Heavenly released in the UK). The UK chose the first single and had two tours before work began in the rest of the world; there was an *NME* cover that declared them 'The Must-See Band of 2002' before anyone else had started working the record. Two years later, the press turned on the band, with a viciousness that went far beyond 'substandard second album'.

Right from the start, Craig's behavior had been erratic. Those around the band put that down to a prodigious bong habit and an unhealthy appetite for junk food, though neither of those proclivities could explain a temper that regularly saw band members or crew 'sacked', or people in the immediate line of fire physically lashed out at. Over the years, cracks appeared and quickly got wider and wider until eventually Craig was diagnosed with Asperger's syndrome. Life in a touring rock 'n' roll band was pretty much the worst career choice for anyone living with that condition.

By the time of the diagnosis, founding member and perpetual wise counsel Patrick Matthews had left the band on stage during a gig for Triple M radio at Sydney's Annandale Hotel and headed for an easy life. A new line-up of the band made one more album for Heavenly (the brilliant and sadly overlooked *Vision Valley*).

This is a conversation between Patrick, permanently sunny former-Vines guitarist Ryan Griffiths, and the band's long-suffering former manager Andy Kelly. *Robin Turner*

ANDY KELLY: The Heavenly experience in the UK was so much fun. I'm glossing over the bits that weren't fun but none of that stuff was due to Heavenly. I remember the very first time I met them. I arrived on the morning of a Doves listening party at the Social [the first playback of *The Last Broadcast*, February 2002]. Robin met me at the door. I'd only ever emailed him at that point, probably one phone call. It was twelve, or eleven in the morning, and Robin said, 'Here you are, I love you. Now let's have a Cocksucking Cowboy.'[1] That was my introduction to Heavenly and I thought, 'This is going to be all right.'

RYAN GRIFFINS: They had a few catchphrases. My five-year-old, Isla, says, ''Ello mate.'

ANDY: The first show you played at the Brighton Freebutt, no one had seen you. Martin Kelly was down the front shouting, 'She flies!' because you were actually good. We've signed this band and they are good. That became a catchphrase. I think it's even on the back cover of *Highly Evolved*.[2]

PATRICK MATTHEWS: Someone suggested that maybe we could talk about the 'serenity in the maelstrom' rather than, I guess, the maelstrom itself.

ANDY: I don't remember how much serenity there was. There weren't too many moments of serenity in that Heavenly office.

PATRICK: I went to the Social a lot but not to the Heavenly office. James Oldham talked about how they'd have parties at the office that started at 10 a.m. on a Monday. But I missed that. Well, not missed it but . . .

ANDY: You were asleep.

RYAN: You were wrapping it up.

ANDY: Trying to get a replacement key sorted at the K West Hotel cos you couldn't find your old one.

PATRICK: I first met Robin in LA. He came to the Viper Room gig, then came back to LA when Heavenly realised they were going to work with us via Capitol.

ANDY: That gig at the Viper Room. I wasn't there but [co-manager] Pete Lusty and Andy Cassell's story was that it was not good and at the end, Andy Slater[3] came up and famously said, 'Start looking at real estate guys.' And then, 'You guys got girlfriends or wives? Ho, ho, man, your lives are about to get REAL interesting.'

ANDY: I wish I could remember how the structure of the deal worked. You were signed to [Australian label] Engine Room and they played a big role in how that got divided up. Heavenly had the UK and released before anyone else.

PATRICK: Only because you guys, the managers, said, 'We want to go with Heavenly.'

ANDY: That would've been the thing about Heavenly. The people were so awesome, so enthusiastic and loved music. They loved you guys so much.

PATRICK: Although it didn't occur to me at the time, Heavenly immediately responded to the side of The Vines that wasn't the hard rock. I think Capitol saw 'Active Rock'.

ANDY: 'Active Rock' and 'Modern Rock'. You can see why they got Andy Wallace [*Nevermind*] to mix 'Get Free'. Heavenly understood the other influences . . .

PATRICK: And the uniqueness of it.

ANDY: And the uniqueness of Craig. They love a frontman in the UK.

PATRICK: What if Heavenly had signed us for the world and Capitol weren't involved?

ANDY: It would've been different without the Capitol machine. Going into the president's office would've been different . . . for starters, it wouldn't have been Andy Slater sitting there playing Neil Young on his guitar, getting down.

PATRICK: 'Oh sorry, guys, didn't see you there.'

ANDY: 'Hey, guys, come in.' 'Er, we've just been waiting out at reception for twenty-five minutes, you knew we were here.' Arguably you wouldn't have sold as many records.

PATRICK: We wouldn't have. And we wouldn't have had a Coppola[4] directing a music video. Or David LaChappelle.[5]

PATRICK: The flipside of that is we could say, 'What if Heavenly weren't involved?' If it hadn't have been for Heavenly in general, and Robin in particular, none of the things I remember most fondly about London would have happened. We'd have these big nights, and although they were chaotic the conversation was so much better and more organised than if we'd just got pissed with Carl from The Libertines.

ANDY: It was great having the Social as a headquarters. Maybe it wasn't serenity in the maelstrom but it was just a tiny bit of sanity. Even though it was total insanity in there.

PATRICK: In the UK, the distances we had to travel for shows didn't send Craig mad.

ANDY: The crowds were really exciting.

PATRICK: The UK was ahead of the US at the start. March/April 2002, we were still doing every interview that Capitol could drum up for us in the US, whereas in England we were way ahead, doing our first *NME* cover to coincide with the first single. When the US got ahead, we got Letterman.[6]

RYAN: In London, we really racked up that bill. Robin had something to do with that.

ANDY: At the Edgware Road Hilton. It was so much money! Twenty or thirty thousand Australian dollars. There were a few nights where we became the party. First you did a show somewhere with The Libertines and Carl and Pete came back and were up in your room ordering bottles of wine on room service. And the next night there was the huge party in the lobby. You were exceptionally lucky not to be kicked out. Someone who will remain nameless but may have had ties to Heavenly was in the toilet snorting something off the ground when the security guard came in. I was pulled aside by that security guard and he said, 'You are going to have to leave.' My legal defence, your honour, was, 'We have spent SO much money at this hotel I'd really appreciate it if you could overlook it and we'll get our act together.' And they agreed. That was a good night, though.

PATRICK: That event was preserved for posterity in my *NME* diary. 'People who shall remain nameless.'

ANDY: Yeah, but while we're talking about it, it was Robin. And we love you for that. I'm not sure of your mental state at that time, Ryan, but when you were playing *CD:UK*[7] you came up after a rehearsal and said, 'There's all these, like, machines coming down. I don't know what they are?' And I said, 'Cameras?' You said, 'I don't know.' And I thought to myself, 'Very good thing they're miming.'

RYAN: I blame Heavenly.

ANDY: My memory of London is totally shaped by being in Soho and going to the Heavenly office. I guess as managers we went to the office more than you guys.

RYAN: I reckon it would've been very nice, rocking up there without us.

ANDY: There was a great bunch of people there. Spence, he was fantastic. Robin worked basically under a stairwell from what I remember. Martin and Jeff shared an office. There were a lot of people packed in. But it was a lot of fun . . . It was so different coming from Australia. The Heavenly experience makes you want to retain the fun, the fandom. And that gets harder the longer you do it. Also, all those things that could've been intimidating, like *Top of the Pops*, they just made it more fun. So there was huge pressure but you got insulated from it.

PATRICK: That pressure ended up being felt elsewhere too. For example, *NME* drove the hype, put us on the cover, 10-out-of-10 reviews. Then James Oldham interviews us at Coachella, and Craig locks himself in the toilet for hours.[8] We –

the band – didn't think Craig was going to hurt himself, but I'm sure James thought Craig seemed like someone cracking under a lot of pressure, and I think James was definitely having a moment thinking, 'What have I done?'

ANDY: He was just in the dressing room at the wrong time. No one could control any of it. Plans are hard enough to make work in rock 'n' roll anyway.

PATRICK: A few years later, I said to James, 'We must've been the very last band that you guys anointed the saviours of rock.' And he said, 'Well, there was The Arctic Monkeys.'

ANDY: He left before that, though, before The Vines' second album, and it was never the same for The Vines after that at the *NME*.[9]

PATRICK: Maybe we should all try to remember the first time Craig threatened to fire us?

ANDY: Management wise, he didn't threaten me directly but he did threaten to fire Andy Cassell in LA when you were recording the first album. Andy had refused to carry his guitar case. That was early on. I don't think I ever got threatened with firing...

PATRICK: 'I like you, Andy. I wouldn't do that to you, Andy.'

ANDY: I thought that too until he buzzed on the office door in 2008 saying he had a knife collection and he was going to come up and kill us. So that wasn't bad – seven years of not being threatened. I considered the knives to be notice of termination of contract. Were you ever threatened with sacking, Ryan?

RYAN: I never got a sacking.

PATRICK: I don't think Craig knew how to press your buttons. Unlike Hamish [Rosser, The Vines' drummer]. He was always on about sacking him.

RYAN: Whenever there was an issue where he was isolated – self-imposed, invariably – I'd be sent in. I wasn't happy about it. I didn't get threatened in the early days. I actually don't think in Craig's eyes Hamish was ever really in the band.

ANDY: He saw him as a contractor. One gig at a time.

PATRICK: With me it wasn't that I would be sacked, more he'd tell me that I didn't write the songs. So I didn't get the sack. Until I actually did.

ANDY: Well, you left the band in one of the best band-leavings of all time.[10] Just walking off the stage in the middle of a show. And then watching a bit of that show. And I remember you saying, 'That sounds pretty good.'

PATRICK: All Hamish. Hamish sounded great.

ANDY: For a while, you'd just be watching it hurtle all the way to its ultimate conclusion.

RYAN: I remember touring with The Living End[11] and Scott [Owen] saying to me, 'You're lucky it's so unpredictable.'

ANDY: It's so funny the view on the other side of the fence. You're just thinking it would be so good to play a tight set every night.

PATRICK: Yeah. I remember one time about seven years ago Chris played the wrong chord. It was crazy.

ANDY: Thinking about Jeff with regards to you guys, and I remember the first time you played *Later... with Jools Holland*. Craig was wearing a Vines t-shirt with the sleeves cut off and Jeff was like 'He can't wear his own t-shirt! You've got to tell him to change it.' And I was like, 'Ooo... aaa... I can't tell him ...'

PATRICK: Got to save those moments.

ANDY: Got to save myself.

Opposite and next page: Vines photos taken from Hamish Rosser's personal archive and shot before and around the release of Highly Evolved.

RYAN: Self-preservation.

ANDY: If I tell him, he'll wear two Vines t-shirts. One around his head. I don't think Craig wearing his own merch was Jeff's preference. I can't remember if that was the same *Later*... – because you played it twice – as when between songs Craig was crawling around under the stage. One time Lou Reed was on. And he liked it.[12] There was definitely one where Craig was crawling around under the stage.

PATRICK: The second one Jools had Nick Hornby sitting at a little table where he would sit down and interview him, and so he's quite close to the action and he was looking worried.

ANDY: Rightfully so. That's that thing I was talking about, people would be watching you and be genuinely scared.

PATRICK: Well, he [Nick Hornby] was in harm's way.

ANDY: He was.

PATRICK: And I don't think Craig had read *High Fidelity* at that point.

ANDY: Not at that point. He later went on to read it and say it was one of his favourite books in the music genre.

ANDY: What was Craig's relationship with Heavenly?

PATRICK: Robin calmed Craig down a lot because he was so entertaining.

ANDY: Yep, loved Robin.

PATRICK: Quick fire.

ANDY: Robin and Stu from EMI.

PATRICK: From Robin's perspective, he probably didn't realise that, because Craig would still be acting crazy. Same thing with Rob Sheffield, who interviewed us for the *Rolling Stone* cover.

Rob definitely kept Craig calm. He was happy to just talk, but Rob thought he was making him demented because all Craig would do in the interview was smoke bongs and talk about The Strokes and The White Stripes.

ANDY: But that was Craig on a good day – that was his good place. He's talking about his interests, he's performing his favourite leisure activity.

PATRICK: No food was thrown.

ANDY: There weren't too many writers who could do that. So Rob did pretty well there. And Robin.

PATRICK: But the converse... Andy Slater thought he was probably really helping Craig out by talking to him, really helping Craig reach a creative plateau.

ANDY: Probably until that time he came on the tour bus in Milan that night and Craig called him 'a devil man'.[13]

RYAN: I had a friend on the bus – he still talks about it. He couldn't believe that Craig would talk to the president of the record company that way.

ANDY: So, Robin, good influence on Craig. I suppose now is the right time to ask if you wouldn't mind coming out to Australia and helping Craig out with the rest of his life.

PATRICK: Talk shit with Craig for half an hour every morning.

ANDY: Listen to Suede and Muse, two of Robin's favourite bands.

RYAN: Robin would've been the closest to Craig across any label. Band members, management [laughs].

PATRICK: He was rock 'n' roll.

ANDY: Well, just the good parts.

1 A shot made up of Baileys poured over butterscotch schnapps. Not a sex act.

2 The Vines' debut show in the UK was on 5 March 2002, in Brighton. James Oldham, reviewing for *NME* on 16 March 2002: 'This is one of the most sensational debut gigs that your correspondent has ever seen. Without question, The Vines are going to be this year's Strokes. A few more gigs like tonight and they might even turn out to be a whole lot more.' It wasn't only *NME*. The *Guardian* gave **** for the London show: 'It's like listening to all your favourite bands at once' (Betty Clarke). When the album arrived four months later, *NME* wrote: '*Highly Evolved* is the sort of shiver-down-the spine debut that gets you thinking that if The Strokes were the John the Baptists of rock then just maybe . . . No pressure, mind.'

3 Andy Slater was president of Capitol Records from 2001 to 2007. Slater previously managed artists like Macy Gray, Fiona Apple and The Wallflowers. One of Slater's first signings to Capitol were Chicago band OK Go, who were in the studio next door to The Vines at Sunset Sound Factory in mid-2001. *The Face*, cover feature, January 2003: 'About three weeks into the [Vines'] sessions at Sunset Sounds Factory, Andy Slater, president of Capitol Records, bumped into Craig in a narrow corridor. He was so intrigued, he made it is his duty that day to listen in on The Vines recording. 'I was at the studio, this kid walked in and he had this immediate presence,' he told the *Los Angeles Times*. 'He wasn't looking at anything in particular, just wandering around the studio kinda looking at the air. Sometimes artists are tapped into some other dimension that enables them to articulate things we want to say but sometimes can't. He felt like someone who was tapped in.'

4 Roman Coppola directed the video for 'Get Free'.

5 Directed the video for 'Outtathaway' and shot cover and feature for *The Face*, January 2003.

6 The Vines played the *Late Show with David Letterman* on 19 August 2002. Reading from his teleprompter David Letterman introduced them matter-of-factly: 'Our next guests are an acclaimed rock 'n' roll band from Australia. Their debut CD is entitled *Highly Evolved*. Here they are, kids, The Vines.' At the end of a frankly deranged performance that ended with Craig in the drum kit, Letterman smiled his gap-toothed grin broadly and shouted (over guitar feedback) to his sidekick, Shaffer: 'How 'bout that? Is he all right, Paul?' 'Can't say,' said Paul Shaffer. 'Can't say for sure.' 'The Vines,' said Dave. 'We'll be right back, everybody.' The CBS Orchestra broke into the Australian sixties band The Easybeats' 'Friday on My Mind' and The Vines left the stage. When the show came back from the break Paul said, 'I hope they're not neglecting their studies.'

7 The Vines played *CD:UK* on Saturday, 6 April 2002. Patrick in the NME.com diary: '[*CD:UK*] was mental. When we left, all these kids were screaming and rushing up to our limo with tinted windows. When they peered in and discovered we weren't the Sugababes, I think they were disappointed.'

8 *NME*, 'Why The Vines Are The Must-See Band of 2002': '[Craig] starts to say that when he was seventeen he seriously thought about

killing himself. "I thought it might make things easier . . ." Craig starts hyperventilating: "Look, I can't do this . . ." He heads to the toilet and locks the door. We tell the band about his panic attack, they barely look up. Ryan just says, "Don't worry about it. He does this sort of thing all the time."'

9 Paul Moody praised *Winning Days* in a profile for the *NME* saying it was better than The Strokes: '. . . it is *NME*'s solemn duty to report that the results are truly startling. Forget any notions of a *Room on Fire* holding pattern or, as Patrick claimed to *NME*, a 'part-metal album', it's the perfect reflection of their schizophrenic live shows.' Sadly, the album review in *NME* wasn't written by Paul Moody. They panned the album, giving it 5/10, saying the band were actually much worse than The Strokes. '. . . In following up their classic debuts Oasis went supersonic with *(What's the Story) Morning Glory?* while, in contrast, The Strokes refined their sound for *Room on Fire*, *Winning Days* does neither. It retreads the same terrain as its predecessor without getting anywhere near its heights. *Highly Evolved*? *Winning Days* is anything but.'

10 *Rolling Stone* (Australian edition), June 2004: 'The drama started during the opener, "Outtathaway", when Nicholls kicked out and connected with a photographer from a local paper. Nicholls then leapt into the crowd and reportedly had an altercation with some fans. When he returned to the stage, Patrick Matthews put down his bass and walked off, leaving the band to play as a trio. Nicholls then squealed through songs, making little effort to sing. At one point he mocked the crowd, calling them sheep.'

11 The Vines toured the US in 2004 with fellow Australian bands Jet and The Living End as support. The tour was called 'The Aussie Invasion Tour'. Reviews of The Vines' live show were scathing. *New York Post*: 'Jet outstripped The Vines on every count, from performance to production to personality . . . It was sad that Jet, which had the encore-demanding cheers, wasn't given the time to return to the stage, while The Vines, who did do an encore, did it because of ceremony.' *New York Times* (Kelefa Sanneh): 'Last year (was it only last year?), when The Vines first arrived in the United States, they were celebrated as retro-rock saviours, but they're really alternative-rock scavengers, borrowing bits and pieces from Nirvana, Oasis, Blur and others. Next week The Vines will release their second album, *Winning Days* (Capitol), a rather tired-sounding collection of rehashed rave-ups and risible pseudo-psychedelia. The album achieves nothing more than hard-rock competence. Their concert often achieved less.'

12 The Vines played *Later . . . with Jools Holland* on 19 April 2002 with Del Amitri, Susana Baca, Stereophonics and Badly Drawn Boy. Then again on 16 April 2003 with Lou Reed, Goldfrapp, Kings of Leon, Ladysmith Black Mambazo, Stephanie McKay (and Nick Hornby). In Jools's interview with Lou Reed on the 2003 show Lou points to Craig and says: 'Boy, if he lives long enough it'll be great.' Jools says, 'That fighting with the drum kit, that really is a thing, isn't it?' and Lou says: 'Hey, I want him to do it ten times in a row . . . It made me feel good to see that. The spirit lives.'

The Social, 5 Little Portland Street, W1. Envisaged as the Cheers bar for the acid-house generation, it opened in June 1999.

Two further Socials were opened in Arlington Square, N1 (below), and Pelham Street, Nottingham.

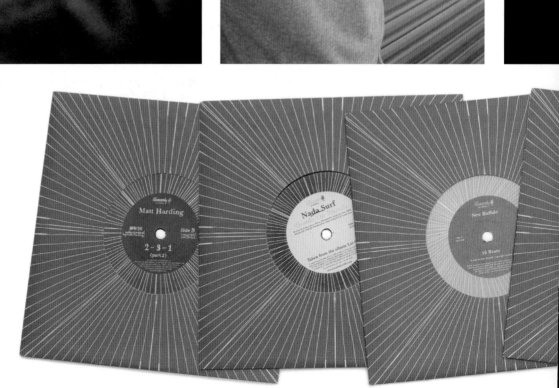

The faces behind a fistful of Heavenly 7-inches released in 2001.

Above: Electric Moccasins of Doom (Wildcat Will Blanchard and Matty Skylab).

Opposite: Omega Amoeba and Matt Harding.

The Magic Numbers were the last band we signed from the pre-digital era. The internet was there, and although we were using iTunes and emails, they were very much a pre-MySpace band who we heard about and tracked down in a very analogue way with a bit of old-school detective work. Wildcat Will called to tell me he'd seen a band playing at the Colony Club, just round the corner from the office: 'They're called The Magic Numbers, they're like The Mamas and the Papas crossed with Fleetwood Mac. Amazing harmonies, I just know you're going to love them.' It was one of those recommendations you don't get very often. I loved the name and it just stuck in my mind immediately. I remember looking in gig listings in the *NME* and typing the band's name into a search engines, probably Yahoo or Ask Jeeves at that time, and finding nothing. The only information Will had was that the lead singer was called Romeo. Nothing else.

Not long after, another friend – Jon Chandler – told me he was playing drums in a band called Absentee who had this amazing guitarist called Romeo. Turns out it's the same Romeo from The Magic Numbers and Jon had his number. I called the number and a really lovely sounding, softly spoken guy answered. We chatted and I told him I'd heard great things about his band and I asked if he could send us any music. He said he'd drop a CD in. But he didn't, so I rang again a few days later saying, 'I'd really, really like to hear your band.'

The next day, this CD in a crumpled maroon slipcase turned up, hand-delivered to the office with four quite random songs on it. I told Jeff that this was the band we'd been told about and put it on but . . . it was a bit disappointing, to be honest. The songs were all very mellow ('Try', 'This Love', 'The Mule', 'Which Way to Happy'), and it didn't have the vibrancy that Will had enthused about. By the time I heard about their next show at Water Rats, there wasn't much of an appetite to go. I'm not sure why but I forced Jeff out of the door to come with me: something was pushing me towards them even when it seemed so against the odds that we'd like them.

That night, when they played – BAMM – it was there from the first song; from the moment they walked on stage, really. They didn't look like any other band at the time but they looked cool and they blew our minds. I remember looking round at Jeff after a couple of songs, both of us slack-jawed at this fully formed, phenomenal band. Those are the moments you live for.

After the show we talked our way backstage and Jeff immediately hit them with, 'I want to put your records out.' He's the best person in the world to deliver that message – I know that because he once delivered it to me. There were beaming smiles and a lot of excitement. The next time they played, Geoff Travis from Rough Trade was there and, although he was clearly blown away, he kept back because he could see that we were already on it. He was just one gig behind us, and if we hadn't have gone to the Water Rats things may have turned out very differently.

Those early shows were amazing: every gig became an event. Being pre-social media and pre-file sharing, if you wanted to hear their songs you had to see them live, and if you'd seen them live you wanted to hear the songs again. It meant you saw so many of the same faces every time they played. You just went time and again, and they grew and grew and grew. It blew up so quickly that they'd sold out the Forum in Kentish Town before their first 7-inch was available, before anyone had heard a note of recorded music. It also gave us a weird kind of confidence where we felt we could invite anyone along knowing that they would love them. When the album arrived it became the biggest-selling record on the label. It spent a year on the charts before being certified double platinum in the UK. A lot of people agreed with us about those songs. Like the Heavenly Sunday Social, The Magic Numbers grew on word of mouth. Their gigs felt like a secret club you were invited into. Anyone was welcome as long as they knew about it. In a digital age, that might not have happened. There would be crappy camera phone footage of songs, people would form opinions based on little snatches of music on an Instagram post, and the

whole thing would have felt far more public. I'm glad it happened like it did, it felt natural and it was fun. The Magic Numbers was such a great moment for the label as the band encapsulated so much of what we all truly love about music.
Martin Kelly

ROMEO STODART
The Magic Numbers were two families. The Stodarts and the Gannons.

We wanted to create music that was timeless.

We wanted to create a band that you could believe in.

We wanted to break your heart whilst lifting your spirit.

We wanted to make a classic debut album.

In 2004 The Magic Numbers were playing live almost every other night around London, making friends that soon grew into a following that spread the word the old-school way, by word of mouth. People told people about this new group comprising of two sets of brothers and sisters, who were singing a kind of country-soul-pop music with three-part harmonies. From the outside things seemed to be happening very quickly, but I'd been writing songs and playing empty venues with our drummer Sean for ten years before this momentum started building, and for us it really was always just a matter of time . . . but it sure took its sweet time. Honestly, though, it was only when our sisters Michele and Angela brought their magic to the band that anyone start taking notice, as then we discovered a sound. There was an energy between us that was somewhat frenetic, it was powerful; we knew we had something special and unique and, because of that, it also made us very cautious and protective.

Fifteen years ago it felt like we were on top of the world, capable of anything, full of promise, full of innocence – but also full of anxiety, still recovering from loss and having nothing.

We literally had nothing but each other and this music. So many dreams of ours started coming true, from selling out shows and hearing people sing along to our songs in the crowd, to being given the opportunity to go into the studio by Heavenly. The biggest dream was to make a record. Jeff and Martin's belief in the band and myself as a songwriter at that time really gave us that extra confidence and boost that I think every artist needs, whether they'd like to admit it or not. So there we were, about to make this record. Going into the studio can be a very daunting experience for a band, especially when the only real experience you've ever had is some home recording with a 4-track. We chose to work with Craig Silvey because we loved him straight away as a person and felt like he understood what we wanted to achieve. He was amazing at putting us at ease and not having us react to that red-light fever that sometimes creeps up on you. He wanted to stay true to what he'd seen us do live and just try to enhance that sonically as best as he could.

We had a shared vision of not wanting there to be too many overdubs on the record, as the core elements between the four of us when we played live was already telling the story in the way we had arranged the songs. It's funny now to think that we ended up playing these huge

festivals with literally a guitar tuner between us as we didn't want anything else to colour the sound of our guitars being plugged straight into our amplifiers.

It's always the songs for me that make a great record and we had the songs.

My sister Michele and I sat at our mum and dad's and said, 'Right, let's write a song in D major.' And I started pulsing on that opening chord, and Michele's bassline took us on a journey like always: that melodic, hooky, driving thing that she does is key to what makes this music. We had so much fun writing 'Mornings Eleven' that I feel the spirit of that moment was captured in the song. We never really said it out loud to each other at the time but we both knew we were trying to write our very own 'Good Vibrations'. We'd have never thought that it would be the opening song on our debut album.

Some of the songs on this album just appeared fully formed. 'This Love' in particular was written pretty soon after I had learnt of our grandmother's death in New York, where Michele and I had grown up. I was heartbroken that I wasn't there for her in those last days, especially as she had raised me as a little boy. I can clearly remember playing that opening triplet guitar figure, and the words and melody just came pouring out like they were

The Magic Numbers would love you to celebrate with them on Thursday 9th June to mark the forthcoming release of their debut album. They will also be playing live on the night

The Tardis
52-56 Turnmill Street
Clerkenwell
London EC1M 5SH

Nearest tube Farringdon

Party starts at 8pm and continues till late
This invite admits one

Heavenly Sagatiba Heineken

always there. The same thing with 'Which Way to Happy', I remember the feeling of playing catch-up to what was coming out. Over the years I've learnt that it's a very rare thing, songs appearing fully formed like that. It still surprises me when they do arrive like a memory of some kind. 'Love's a Game' felt like it had always existed – in fact for a very long time I would ask people, 'But does it remind you of anything?' I remember playing 'Forever Lost' to the band, us rehearsing it and having fun with the arrangement, but I have no recollection of writing it.

So many songs came from such sad places – the end of a long-term relationship, death in the family, feeling so lost and vulnerable, this yearning for something else, to be someone else – but I guess unknowingly we disguised it with harmonies and hooks. 'Love Me Like You' was definitely one of those. No one spoke of the meaning of the song when I first played it, we all just dived straight in and started having fun with hooks and skips in the rhythm. It was the baby of the bunch, as it was only written a few months before we began recording, whereas 'Try' was probably the eldest of almost two years. Then there's the duet between Angie and myself 'I See You, You See Me'. My mum and dad were arguing downstairs and I knew it would only be a matter of time before they would make up and

laugh about how ridiculous they were both being. I based the song on that kind of love, one that sees through everything. Angela's voice on that still melts my heart.

I'd bought a set of these glockenspiel tone bars from a charity shop in Hanwell one afternoon, walking home from signing on at the job centre and, all the way back, I was thinking about this much more tender arrangement of a song I'd written called 'Hymn for Her'. The climax of the song on the third chorus was originally how it was all throughout. I remember that day working on it with Michele and Angela, and as we were so excited about how it turned out we decided to play it live that night to a small few.

There's so much love and hope and joy and honesty in that first album. So much fun in the arrangements, so much youth and innocence in our voices. It encapsulates a very precious time within the four of our lives. I'm still our biggest fan.

Fifteen years later we still want to create music that is timeless. We still want to be a band that you can believe in. We still want to break your heart whilst lifting your spirit. But we can't ever make that first album again. We captured that moment in time. Upon reflection, it surpassed all of our wildest expectations.

Below: Greetings from Republica Evescarra: lo-fi instrumental electronic duo Ellis Island Sound (Pete Astor and David Sheppard), 2002.

Opposite: 'I've got blonde on blonde, on my portable stereo/It's a lullaby, from a giant golden radio'. New York power-pop trio Nada Surf released their third album, Let Go, *through Heavenly in 2002. Their second album,* The Proximity Effect, *was subsequently reissued through the label.*

Jon Savage has been part of the Heavenly extended family since the start. Whether dementedly heckling the Manics with shouts of 'punk rock!' at the Heavenly gig at the Camden Underworld in December 1990, or providing a piece of evocative proto-psychogeography for the sleeve notes of Saint Etienne's *Foxbase Alpha*, Jon was a welcome presence, always bringing his razor-sharp wit and a wonderfully deep and wide musical knowledge with him.

One of Jon's most positive qualities (there are many) is his willingness to share that knowledge. It's one thing to possess a record collection that effortlessly spans every interesting cultural shift since the birth of rock 'n' roll, it's quite another to feel duty bound to enthusiastically pass that knowledge on. Jon's books do that and so do his lovingly compiled CDs, whether released commercially or burnt from iTunes and handed over.

Having left the capital for Wales in the mid-1990s, Jon's visits to the Heavenly office became rare events. When he did arrive, it was invariably with a fistful of those homemade CD comps. They each contained unearthed gems and oddities from that monumental record collection. Filthy electro, post-punk oddness, the unearthed roots of gay music and the alternate greatest hits of baggy were all cleverly pieced together. As was a transcendent collection of 'hobo rock' songs hand-picked from mainly forgotten records of the late 1960s and early '70s. *Meridian 1970* is as close to Jon's original iTunes compilation as the licensing department at EMI could get. It is a record that allows the listener to step out of time and place as it brings the sounds of a Midwest dustbowl right into your headphones. *Robin Turner*

JON SAVAGE *author, cultural commentator, record selector*

Meridian 1970 came about at my fiftieth birthday party in 2003. I had a few friends of my age up to stay and we started playing a pile of old records that we'd actually liked in the late 1960s and early '70s, as opposed to the ones you were told that you had to like. Records like *An Old Raincoat*

Won't Ever Let You Down by Rod Stewart, the first couple of James Gang albums, the first Neil Young album. It was fantastic and a little liberating and it prompted me to make up an iTunes playlist of tracks I'd loved from that period.

Pretty much anyone who'd been in a big 1960s group ended up making a solo record, whatever their position in the band. And coming out of the hippie era, there was so much wastage on albums around that time. A lot of albums were released with only one or two good tracks on them, sat between a lot of filler. After digging through the same records a few days later, I made a playlist of a load of the tracks and burnt a few CDs. I like to share great music, so I often carry a handful of compilations around with me just in case I bump into a friend. One day, walking down Kensington High Street, I bumped into Jeff and handed him a copy of this particular playlist. A few days later he called to say, 'Let's do it on Heavenly.'

The album was an attempt to rediscover this forgotten musical hinterland. A lot of work has been done re-evaluating it since, but then it was still something of a forbidden zone. These were records made after the height of hippiedom. It was a reflective, downer period which meant that a lot of the albums were, on the whole, quite turgid, so there was a question of digging out the nuggets. There were a few tracks we wanted that we couldn't clear – 'Tangerine' by Led Zeppelin, 'Available Space' by Ry Cooder, 'Can't Find My Way Home' by Blind Faith – but on the whole, it's very reflective of the playlist I made in 2003.

The cover of the original CD I made was the front cover photo off *The Ballad of Easy Rider* by The Byrds. The sleeve we eventually made had a very evocative photo of a row of US mailboxes. The impression from both pictures was one of open space. I was a big fan of West Coast music at that point; lots of the music of that period was very much to do with mental space becoming physical space. If you take LSD and you go to parts uncharted then you probably aren't going to want to live in the city any more. Although I loathed it at the time, Woodstock

was a large-scale presentation of that idea. And living in England back then, that kind of space didn't really exist.

As ever with compilations I've done, I wasn't trying to make a major point – I just liked those songs. They were records I'd really liked when I was sixteen or seventeen, and that's an important, formative period of one's life. There's no point me saying I was only into The Stooges in 1969, as I didn't really know their music until *Raw Power* came out. This was my soundtrack until Bowie. If there is a thread that runs through the songs then it's one of freedom. That's what I craved the most as a sixteen- or seventeen-year-old.

When *Meridian 1970* was released it stopped me being a critic and made me an enthusiast. You put together these kinds of compilations because you like the music. There's a bit of compromise in what goes on them but that's part of the process. The idea is simple: I like these records and I think you'll like them too.

Pop-culture historian, expert record selector and long-standing friend of the label, Jon Savage.

I was working from home one day and a fella from Manchester called Graham Thomas got in touch. Graham was a promoter up there. He used to do nights at the Bierkeller, putting on bands like Working for a Nuclear Free City, Polytechnic and Nine Black Alps. I was living in Batson Street by Greenside School, working in my boy's bedroom on my old iMac. My wife Wendy was working at the school and she came home for lunch. As she left, she asked if I was in tonight. 'Yeah, not going anywhere.' Just after she walked out of the door, I was contacted by Graham who said, 'I've got something that I think you should hear.' And he sent me a demo of 'People Help the People' by Cherry Ghost. Emailing tracks as MP3s really wasn't a big thing at this point.

When I played it, I thought, 'Jesus Christ almighty, that's a hit song.' An amazing voice, it was absolutely an instant hit. I called him up and asked who it was. He told me it was a guy called Simon who used to have this group, blah blah blah. I'd never heard of the group. He told me they were good, a bit Americana and that Si was a maths teacher. And he's got a song called 'Mathematics'. And he sent that, and it was really good, real serious quality. I asked if he was doing any gigs. 'I know he's playing tonight in Glasgow, but I'm not sure about anything else. I'll try to find out.'

So I quickly grabbed my toothbrush, headed to Heathrow and went to see him play in Glasgow. It was good timing because just as I got to the venue, I saw someone in the queue that I knew: Ellie Giles, who now manages Bill Ryder-Jones. Ellie was a scout in Manchester working for Polydor. As I got to the door, I saw her and her boss, Simon Gavin, getting out of a taxi. So I snuck behind them in the queue and tapped them on the shoulder, to groans of, 'You bastard.' They really thought nobody knew about Cherry Ghost.

I saw the gig and I loved it. I really loved it. It pushed all my southern soul buttons but it was coming via Bolton. He was singing blue-collar love songs, really, in a similar way to how someone like Dan Penn sang them about the south. He was just singing about the north of England and painting these great pictures of northern working-class life and delivering them with this brilliant voice. After the show I hogged him, I didn't want to let him out of my sight and let Ellie and Simon anywhere near him. I really wasn't messing about. And that spontaneity and that hogging worked because he chose us.
Jeff Barrett

SIMON ALDRED
I was almost thirty by the time I met Jeff. I'd done a lot of things wrong by then, so I was ready to get it right. I'd worked out how to write a song, who was talking bullshit and who was authentic, who could play the drums. When I met Heavenly, they felt familiar. They were – to quote Michael Barrymore – my kind of people.

Cherry Ghost wasn't a band when I met Jeff. It became one out of necessity as the songs I'd written needed to transform, from just being strummed by me in Mexican-themed bars (literally where Jeff 'discovered' me) to a more fully realised 'band' sound. It was always my intention to have more than me on the stage, and to have an expansive sound. Getting signed provided the impetus.

When I was writing the songs that became *Thirst for Romance*, I was very introspective, and finding Manchester claustrophobic. The light, the slate-grey skies . . . it felt like there was a lid on it. And on me. The scope of the music I was writing made it easier for me to breathe. It allowed me to stretch my imagination and reach for something more. Nowadays, Manchester doesn't feel as small to me; I'm happier.

Making the first record, I had a quiet drive and an ambition. I felt ready for the exposure and I wanted people to hear the songs. The peripheral stuff that quickly came when the record was released, though – the radio sessions, the photographs, all that – I wasn't really prepared for. I enjoy being anonymous and I never really got that kick from the audience and their

applause that I think great performers feed off. Really, the writing and recording aspect was as far as I'd thought things through. It was nice to not be skint for once, and it pushed me out into the world on a personal level, so I'm forever thankful of the experience.

There were so many memories of good times with Heavenly: Jeff jumping up and down on the bed to 'Do I Love You (Indeed I Do)' at in a room at the Malmaison by Manchester Piccadilly as security were hammering on the door; drinking games with The Little Ones in the Social; Martin singing

'We Got to Have Peace' to my mum, pissed up at my first gig in Salford. Very happy times. Heavenly were always hugely supportive of everything I ever wanted to do musically. Honestly, they were the best cheerleaders I could have asked for, I love them dearly and I gained so much confidence from them.

When I was bored of my writing and needed something that didn't revolve around a guitar, Heavenly encouraged me to make the Out Cold record. It was an important process. Then, when Birdy covered 'People Help the People',

HEAVENLY RECORDINGS
present
an acoustic performance by
CHERRY GHOST
plus guests
TREVOR MOSS & HANNAH-LOU
ON
13th December 2011
AT
Bush Hall
310 Uxbridge Road, London W12 7LJ

Advance tickets priced £17.50 from the venue or www.wegottickets.com

www.cherryghost.co.uk   www.heavenlyrecordings.com

Previous page: Simon Aldred of Cherry Ghost on stage at Hallé St Peters Church, Ancoats, Manchester, 22 December 2013.

a new door opened in terms of presenting opportunities to write for other people. It coincided with a time when I was enjoying the structure and consistency of being home a bit more. Houses, kids and all the grown-up shit kicked in, and it just made the world of co-writing a bit more appealing, so Cherry Ghost wound down. I miss singing and writing for myself but I also really enjoy meeting people from different musical backgrounds. Working like that has made me appreciate who Heavenly are more than ever. The mainstream monetises everything and there's so little integrity in most

of the music. I'm lucky – I've written with some brilliant people but, on the whole, it's a brutal fucking world. For Heavenly to still be fighting the good fight in amongst all that is nothing short of a minor miracle. It gives me hope.

When Jeff approached me to get back on stage to play at the Heavenly weekender at the Trades Club, it was a no-brainer. I'll always feel part of that family, and I can't think of a better reason to sing and play again. And it'll be great to watch the next generation of artists do their thing as well. The Heavenly roster, as always, is fantastic.

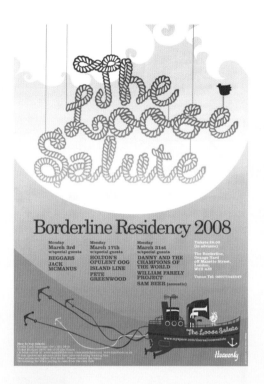

Below: Cornwall's finest country-surf quintet, The Loose Salute, dealt in rustic, folk-tinged sounds and in 2008 Heavenly Recordings released their debut album *Tuned to Love*.

Opposite: In summer 2008, Heavenly Recordings released *Morning Tide*, the debut album of The Little Ones, a Los Angeles-based sunshine pop band who updated the baroque 'n' roll sound of The Zombies and The Left Banke.

Opposite: Sacramento-based freak-folk artist Sea of Bees – aka Julie Baenziger. Heavenly Recordings would release the hushed, fragile folk of Songs for the Ravens and 2012's Orangefarben.

This page: Welsh artist Pete Fowler's live illustrations from Trevor Moss and Hannah-Lou's intimate tour of the UK's last remaining tin tabernacles.

Beggars, a rock 'n' roll quartet from Reading, only released one single on Heavenly – a cranked-up and furious version of Leonard Cohen's 'The Future'.

Edwyn Collins, Orange Juice, Postcard Records – they were all part of the reason that we do what we do. I don't know that we'd have formed East Village if it wasn't for Orange Juice. After punk, their aesthetic joined so many dots. No one was going to form a punk band then, it was dead. Edwyn and Postcard presented a different way of doing things, seeing things. Something fresh, something exciting and new.

Years later, I'd gotten to know Edwyn pretty well after Saint Etienne recorded some tracks with him at New River, his studio in Alexandra Palace. It was just as he'd recorded 'A Girl Like You' and I remember him and Seb playing us the rough mix. His last live performance before his stroke was at mine and Sarah [Cracknell]'s wedding. I asked him if he'd play 'A Girl Like You', which he kindly did. It was a special moment.

When Edwyn was in hospital I got a call from Grace. She sounded pretty determined, saying, 'You and Sarah have got to come and see Edwyn tomorrow.' We'd wanted to go and visit but were waiting for the right moment. This was definitely an order, so we got over there straight away. I was quite shocked at how badly it had affected him. He recognised Sarah and I, just about. We went back to the hospital a few times over the coming weeks and saw gradual signs of recovery. Grace told me that Edwyn had finished a new album prior to the stroke – recorded but not mixed. I asked if I could hear it, but she seemed certain that no one would want to release it. That was where the idea hatched.

Everything was part of Edwyn's rehabilitation: folks visiting him in hospital, finishing and releasing the record and, finally, the gig at Dingwalls. Grace was, and still is, a force of nature, and made everything happen for him. It was incredible to watch his progress at that time, especially his wildlife drawing, which he'd had to remaster using his left hand.

The gig at Dingwalls was incredibly special. A few had concerns that he might not be ready, but here was a guy who'd overcome unbelievable adversity and was up on the stage, singing songs – beautifully, I might add – that many of us thought we'd never hear again. It really was one of the great Heavenly moments. *Martin Kelly*

GRACE MAXWELL AND EDWYN COLLINS
in conversation in Helmsdale, Scotland

GRACE: It's hard to remember how we all met, it goes way, way back.

EDWYN: I produced the second Rockingbirds album [*Whatever Happened to The Rockingbirds*, 1995] up at our old studio, New River.

GRACE: And you've been working with Andy Hackett and Sean Read ever since. We must have met Martin and Jeff around then. We were struggling a lot financially at that point.

EDWYN: It was when I was making *Gorgeous George*.

GRACE: Edwyn's first studio was in Alexandra Palace. He shared it with this guy and they each did six weeks on, six weeks off. So we had six weeks to make The Rockingbirds album then the other guy was back in. And then he had six weeks to make *Gorgeous George*, the album with 'A Girl Like You' on it. And then he got booted out. It was a crazy time. We knew Andy from way, way back in the day because I used to call him 'Stage Door Johnny'. He was always this wee guy with rosy cheeks who'd be hanging around after gigs in Norwich. 'Edwyn, he wants to come back again!' Eventually he got onto the stage. You can accuse Hackett of many things but a lack of perseverance is not one of them.

EDWYN: Before my stroke [20 February 2005], I'd mixed four of the tracks for *Home Again*, which was fully recorded. And then I got sick.

GRACE: We hit the pause button.

EDWYN: I spent six months in hospital. After six months in hospital, I hated the place. I was so glad to be getting out. Sometimes I'd be bored, sometimes I'd be frustrated and sometimes scared.

GRACE: I remember Seb [Lewsley, Edwyn's long-time studio partner] said to you that he had the raw mixes of the album . . .

EDWYN: And I said, 'It's not good enough.'

GRACE: We were travelling backwards and forwards to Wimbledon in the car to therapy sessions and we'd been listening to the rough mixes, which sounded great. Seb said, 'Do you want me to finish them?'

EDYWN: The bass wasn't right. I wanted louder bass, I wanted it to sound different.

GRACE: Edwyn looked at me, terrified, and said, 'We have to wait!' He wanted to be better enough to get back in the studio. At that point, none of us had any idea how long that recovery process might be. In the early part of 2007, we'd made it back into the studio. He had just started singing again in the house. He couldn't write songs at that point.

EDWYN: One song, 'Searching for the Truth', came later.

GRACE: We got back into the studio, as Edwyn said he was ready to tackle the mixes. I remember looking through the glass at the control room and I could see Edwyn and Seb falling about laughing at something. I couldn't hear them but I could see everything and I had a real moment where I felt that was like normal life again after what had seemed like such a long time since the stroke.

EDWYN: When it came to mixing it, I wasn't right in the head. Apart from a song like 'Home Again', the simpler songs, I don't think I was doing the right job. And I was frightened. Six months in hospital had got me frightened. It took me a long time to reconnect with things. I'm still not really right in the head.

GRACE: Martin and Jeff got in touch with us about putting the record out when Heavenly was going through EMI. It was during the time that EMI was being bought by Guy Hands. We thought Heavenly's remit was to bring new, young, exciting, vibrant artists into the deal, not to sign an old lag like Edwyn! But they really wanted to do the record, it was just a question as to whether EMI would want to support them in that. If it had been just a couple of months later, I don't think they would have supported it. I remember going to EMI for an initial 'meet the team' meeting. Even before Edwyn's illness, I'd been out of the music industry for a while. I ended up in this big conference room with Jeff and Martin and all of the EMI people and they all introduced themselves and told me their jobs. I came home howling with laughter that they'd been taking me so seriously. It was like something off our mad old telly show, *West Heath Yard*. Every single meeting I've been to is the same old shit, it's hilarious, and there I was back in it. In retrospect, it's all turned out fine, but, really, it wasn't fine then. Nothing was set, nothing was clear, there was no view of what the future might look like. Edwyn and I were very good at putting a brave face on things.

EDWYN: Sometimes, I'd sit in our garden in Kilburn and the trees would move and shake and blur . . .

GRACE: Like his sense of reality wasn't working properly.

EDWYN: I'd be thinking, 'Where am I?' And I'm in my own garden. It was very weird.

GRACE: When we started working with Heavenly it was around about two years after the illness. Looking back, I'd say that was still very early days. It was a very intense period. Some people think that if you don't get functions back quickly then it's not working, but we were just at the start of getting back on top.

EDWYN: There were years of recovery in front of me.

GRACE: Every step of the way, I'd ask Edwyn, 'Do you want to do this? Are you sure?' And he'd say, 'Yes.' But really he was making a massive leap of faith with me. He was determined, but there was such a lot of vulnerability there.

EDWYN: Every day, Grace was with me. If I'd have gone walking in the park, I could have got lost and I'd have had no idea how to get home.

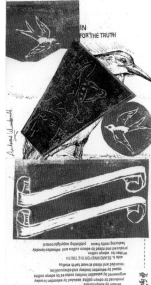

GRACE: So thank God that in the middle of all this stuff, we were with Heavenly. They didn't ask any questions, they didn't push us to do anything. They'd ask us what we wanted to do and they were unquestioning when we suggested things.

EDWYN: They trusted us.

GRACE: Coming out of that period in the hospital, we'd gone straight into full-time therapy. Putting the record out with Heavenly marked the time when Edwyn's speech and language therapist said that they were becoming more and more redundant as real life was becoming his therapy. We made ourselves so busy. It was great to move away from it being full-time therapy to day-to-day life and the experiences that would help reshape things. Obviously the record was a massive first big step; the next thing was to play live again.

EDWYN: I wanted *Home Again* to be heard in a live situation. The previous albums hadn't been so easy to play. A song like 'Liberteenage Rag' is all live, it's folk mixed with my sound . . .

GRACE: The two records before *Home Again* were real studio records and Edwyn hadn't been in the mood for much touring. This was before any illness. Edwyn never trusted technology on stage, which would have been needed to make those records work live. With *Home Again*, it felt like it was time to 'get the band back together again'. And then the pause button was hit. It was a very, very big deal to get back on stage. The first show back was a massive deal, it was being broadcast as part of the BBC's *Electric Proms*, which was taking over venues all over Camden. Although we had Jeff and Martin's confidence, there was some flurry of worry from the people who'd sorted out the gig – the lady who did the plugging at EMI and the lady from the *Electric Proms* – when they met Edwyn properly to discuss the show. The gig was announced. I was in this weird position of a) taking umbrage that people were questioning whether Edwyn could do it or not and b) thinking, 'Oh shit, can we actually do it?' I went all defensive, but I made myself ill in the run-up to the gig, thinking it would all be on me if the gig didn't work . . .

EDWYN: If it all went tits-up!

GRACE: I was worried it would be a massively awkward, humiliating let-down. Edwyn was struggling to get the flow . . .

EDWYN: To hit the right notes. My singing was quiet, it was weird.

GRACE: Heavenly poured oil on the troubled water by taking umbrage on our behalf, which was wonderful – but really my stance was just covering up my own insecurities and fears. Maybe it was my fault, and I was encouraging Edwyn to do something he wasn't ready for. But you had to be . . .

EDWYN: Bold.

GRACE: I'd talked myself into it, I was believing my own hype. I knew everything was getting better and better, but whether it was enough? I remember on the day of the gig we had a really brilliant soundcheck. And something told me right then that we were going to be all right. Ultimately though, what it comes down to is that Edwyn is a massive ham.

EDWYN: Cheers for that, Grace.

GRACE: Ultimately, when he got up on the stage and everyone in the room was rooting for him, the big ham in him emerged and he totally pulled it off. And then we all got completely smashed afterwards – apart from Edwyn.

EDWYN: People were rooting for me. Roddy [Frame] came along and played.

GRACE: Roddy, Carwyn Ellis, Andy Hackett, Sean Read and Paul Cook from the Pistols. The band on stage was like the bloody A-Team. That said, I don't think the audience went in assuming it would be a stroll in the park, but it didn't feel like a judgemental room in any way. It was the loveliest thing, people wanted Edwyn to pull it off . . . and him reacting to that. You don't get many nights like that which are landmarks. After that, Edwyn did loads of promo, press and radio stuff. The last thing we did for that album was a single release of *Home Again* where we did a golden ticket that meant you could win a piece of Edwyn's artwork that had been adapted by another artist. Each prize was one of the artworks by people like John Squire, Nicky Wire . . .

EDWYN: Billy Childish, Harry Hill . . .

GRACE: Someone won one of them – I can't remember which artist – and got in touch to ask if they could swap theirs for the Manic Street Preachers one. Get tae fuck! Get what you're given! What a bloody cheek.

Previous spread: When Edwyn Collins's 2008 single 'Home Again' was released, Heavenly invited twenty-five artists and musicians to customise a piece of artwork created by Edwyn during his rehabilitation. Seen here are pieces by Pete Fowler, Andrew Weatherall, Irvine Welsh, Paul Cook, Billy Childish and Nicky Wire.

Below: Edwyn Collins's London studio, West Heath Yard.

Formed in Brighton in 2010, TOY's motorik shoegaze would be key not only to Heavenly Recordings but to the British psychedelic landscape across the 2010s.

Between 2012 and 2016, Heavenly Recordings released the band's self-titled debut album, Join the Dots, *and* Clear Shot, *both produced by Dan Carey.*

Oscillating between weird folk and hallucinatory art-pop, often within the same record, Liverpool's Stealing Sheep released Into the Diamond Sun, Not Real *and* Big Wows *on Heavenly Recordings.*

Getting Beyond the Wizard's Sleeve to remix the Temples record just seemed like a no-brainer. We didn't really get involved. The way that Erol Alkan and Richard Norris worked, they might have sent us a little bit of something to give us a taste of the direction they wanted to go in, which was exactly the direction we wanted, and then it was like, 'Right, we're not going to play you anything else until it's done, and then you're going to come around to the studio, I'm going to dim the lights, someone can skin up and you can listen to it.' And it didn't disappoint. Temples are a psychedelic group. The Wizard's Sleeve version was Erol and Richard giving them a slightly more modern psychedelic sound than what was coming out of their studio.

Sun Structures was a really big record for us. A really significant one too. Remixing tracks by Temples seemed a bit pointless as a marketing idea, although we did try a couple. Remixes are often there to extend the lifespan of a track in an attempt to cater for wider and wider tastes in club world. Doing the whole record as one continuous piece of psychedelic music made total sense with this band. It ended up being a whole new home-listening experience by a couple of producers who we absolutely loved. *Jeff Barrett*

RICHARD NORRIS *producer, one half of Beyond the Wizard's Sleeve*
Psychedelia wasn't fashionable in the mid-1980s. Back then, I was helping run Bam-Caruso, a label that specialised in unearthing sixties psychedelia in the spirit of Lenny Kaye's *Nuggets* and Greg Shaw's *Pebbles* albums. We were releasing compilations that collected up a lot of the records that had been made in the rush to find the next Beatles, back when A&R people were quite happy to give pretty much anyone a one-single deal. There are hundreds of one-off singles on labels like Pye or Decca or Phillips, where you'd get bands having a decent go at it, creating the most mental backwards phased freakbeat monsters only to subsequently never be heard of again.

Bam-Caruso was out of step with everything around it. At that point psychedelia was, at best,

Julian Cope with a turtle's shell on his back. At worst, it was Neil the hippie off *The Young Ones*, a bit naff, like an Austin Powers pastiche rather than a load of extreme, mind-expanding music. It wasn't a big scene and, for years, you never saw the word psychedelic used positively in a review apart from in *Strange Things are Happening* - Bam-Caruso's in-house magazine. I first met Jeff through *Strange Things* . . . because we were really interested in Loop, who he was working with through his Head label. They were part of a nascent psych scene with Spacemen 3 towards the end of the decade.

In early September 1987 I'd gone to interview Genesis P. Orridge for *Strange Things* . . . at his house on Beck Road in Hackney. Alongside all the psychedelic stuff, I found myself getting into more and more electronic music. I knew house music through going out to gay clubs, places like the Pyramid, which Mark Moore did at Heaven, or the Mud Club or the Bell in King's Cross, where I used to DJ. For me, clubs were running in parallel to guitar music and the psychedelic stuff that the label was doing.

For a few months in London there had been rumours and whispers about something called 'acid house'. There hadn't been anything written about it at that point. When I went to interview Genesis, he pretty quickly said, 'Have you heard about this new music?' I said it sounded like what I'd been looking for – a form of true psychedelic dance music. So he said, 'Let's make an acid house record next weekend!' The next day, I started rallying a load of the Bam-Caruso people together and he brought some Psychic TV people, and the following weekend we went into this tiny studio in Chiswick to try to make acid house music under the name *Jack the Tab*. Without ever having actually heard any.

The *Jack the Tab* record was more about the idea of acid, the psychedelic-ness of acid itself. It still sounds completely mental because it was all done in first takes with a limit of an hour per track. It was a very sixties mindset. For quite a long time after that I thought that was how you made records. It took quite a long time for me to realise you could – and probably should – take longer. The guy in the studio had a Roland 303 that he didn't really know how to use, so he gave it to me. Shortly afterwards I lent it to Bob [Stanley] and Pete [Wiggs]. When they said they wanted to have a go at making an acid record, I gave it to them and told them to go to the same studio we'd used for *Jack the Tab*.

We'd never been to an acid house club, which is why *Jack the Tab* doesn't sound anything like the records that were actually getting played. The first time I went to Shoom, I took Genesis. The first person we bumped into was Andrew Weatherall, who proudly showed off his Psychic TV tattoo. That was enough to convince Gen that he was the king of acid house. He didn't quite fit in with the Shoom crowd. I remember he sent his picture in to get his membership card and he had mad staring eyes and a t-shirt with HATE written on it. I think they decided not to fast-track him.

Jack the Tab very quickly opened some mad doors. I got offered a solo deal with Warner's, who at the time had Madonna and Prince and all these massive acts. They were offering me a deal on the basis that I'd just made an acid house record with Genesis P. Orridge. No demos, nothing. Initially The Grid was me and Gen, but he didn't want to sign to a major label, so they just signed me. I was going to work with a bunch of different producers, but after going into the studio with Dave Ball the band became me and him. I started working out of an office on Kensal Road that we shared with *Boy's Own*. I don't think either us or them had ever run our own office before. I drew a bunch of cartoons for the magazine, things like the update on the old *Sniffin' Glue* 'now form a band' statement.

Acid house was deeply addictive. Quickly, we were going out every night. I didn't go to sleep on a Saturday night for about three years. Initially Tuesday was our night in, then we found an acid house party in Brixton on a Tuesday, so we went out then as well. It never really seemed to cost any money either. You never paid to get in and

you didn't end up spending any money. I was very lucky because I'd gone from Bam-Caruso to working on music with Gen, then I'd signed a deal with Warner's and I'd started writing for the *NME* about dance music. Everyone else I knew who had jobs wasn't so lucky – they suddenly didn't have jobs any more. Partying every night meant they had to give up work, or they got sacked. There was a weird limbo period where people's careers were just disappearing, but then people would start inventing their own new jobs in this new world; people would become something to do with music or with clubs or with various underworld activities. It worked itself out pretty well.

Sometime in the spring of '88 I went to the Falcon and told Jeff about Shoom. There was a country-ish thing on, something Gram Parsons-y, and I stood there at the door babbling to him about this new club, this new sound, saying he had to come. I saw Jeff as a kindred spirit and was convinced he'd get it. Acid house was 'one of those moments' you read about in hindsight, something was properly happening. It's quite rare to be involved in a scene or an event and know that it's happening right at that point, like you are part of a secret society. And also knowing that it wouldn't be a secret for very long – a few months maybe. There was a certainty that something was going to explode and that this was the very start of it. You didn't want to share the knowledge with everyone, but Jeff was definitely someone I wanted to open the door to that world for.

In the ensuing years, I always kept in touch with Jeff. When The Grid became a full-time thing Heavenly did press for the band at various points, and when that quietened down I DJed for them regularly at various versions of the Social. Music I played out always veered towards the psychedelic – I think it stayed my fallback position. Sometime at the start of the 2000s, I had a regular spot on Sean Rowley's radio show on BBC London. I was midway through a weekly A to Z of psychedelia, where I went in and played a few crazed singles on whatever letter it was that week. Pretty sure we only ever got up to L.

Title spread: Hitting no.7 in the UK album charts, the cosmic psychedelia of Temples' Sun Structures would be one of Heavenly Recordings' biggest albums of the 2010s.

Below: Producer and DJ Richard Norris saluting psychedelia's cross-pollination with dance.

One particular week, Erol Alkan was the other guest. We knew each other a bit through his club Trash. Erol was on after me, listening to my hour of weird psyche stuff. He absolutely loved the music I was playing and wanted to hear more, so I made him up a load of CDs, which he then said he really wanted to hear loud, in a club.

Quickly after that we started doing our Beyond the Wizard's Sleeve nights in east London. We'd play for seven hours back to back, one record each, as much of it off 7-inch singles as possible. We were so excited about hearing those records out loud, it was an incredible buzz. We'd also play things like 'You Doo Right' by Can in its twenty-plus minutes entirety, because we'd never heard it in full really loud. This was psychedelia as dance music. At the end of the night, we'd get fifty quid to split between us.

Beyond the Wizard's Sleeve records grew out of those nights. We were editing tracks and extending things so we could play them out. They worked so well, we started releasing them as bootlegs and then started getting asked to remix people like Peter, Bjorn and John, Midlake, Goldfrapp and The Chemical Brothers. We started making our own record, but about halfway through Erol got cold feet and we shelved it for the best part of a decade.

I'd done a remix for 'Mesmerize' by Temples under the name The Time and Space Machine and soon after they asked if Wizard's Sleeve could do something. After some time away from working together, Erol was actually keen to do it, and we both said we'd like to try to do something different from our end, not just a quick remix of a single that would come and go. Originally we wanted to take bits from the whole *Sun Structures* album and make up one single long track but, when we started working on it, it morphed into a project that took in the whole record. There's quite a lot of psych albums that have weird interludes between the tracks where things phase in and out. We were very keen to

go down that route in order to make something that really sucked you in, something immersive.

When we got the parts, we found it was a really dense record. They'd recorded it in a home studio and added layer upon layer of sound. Each part was very melodic, very hooky, and there were so many of them. Listening to the mix as it was, you'd miss a lot of it. It meant we could draw out a lot of brilliant stuff that was buried; we could make these abstract interludes and different versions of things. We pulled it apart, really. It became a bit of blueprint for how we worked on our own record afterwards. Some people get hold of parts for a remix and they scrap everything to build something new. We weren't interested in that, we wanted to reshape what had already been done. Our idea was always, 'What's the essence of the track and how can we shine a different light on it?'

Both of us wanted to make something very psychedelically tinged, using vocals and melody as much as possible. *Sun Structures* was the perfect thing to try that experiment on – it seemed like a way of forming a deeper relationship with the music. When we were putting the whole thing together, we looked to records like *Smile* by The Beach Boys, records where thematic elements would ebb and flow through the whole record. We wanted it to be seen as a whole piece.

Pretty much everything we mixed got used, apart from one track where Erol thought the original vocal line sounded like something from *Off the Wall* by Michael Jackson. That got us to work out a kind of Jacko-esque backing track that ended up on the cutting-room floor. The seventies disco feel was great, but it didn't really sit with our overall, fully psychedelic view of the record. I think its only ever outing was when I played it out at the Heavenly weekender at the Trades Club in Hebden Bridge.

Allowing someone to remix an entire album isn't something a lot of labels would do. Heavenly is a bit different, though. There's a lot of trust and

an ever-present spirit of adventure. I don't really think my relationship with Jeff and Heavenly has changed over the thirty-plus years we've been friends. You start off excitedly talking about a certain kind of record as a kid, and there you are, three decades on, making the thing for him and having the same conversations around it.

We aren't in each other's orbit all the time but there's a clear connection that's based around the ongoing search for the kind of record or night out that, when you experience it for the first time, slightly alters your mind and shifts your perception of things. It's what I was after when I was trying to track down bands for *Strange Things* . . . and when I was evangelising about Shoom. Hopefully the experience makes you think in a slightly different way. That's a relationship that's never going to stop. I know some people's enthusiasm for that eternal hunt might have waned, but for me and for Heavenly and all of our mates, that obsessive gene is still dominant. It's really not going anywhere.

A second jaunt to Paris in 2013, where a new generation of Heavenly acts performed at La Maroquinerie to coincide with France's Record Store Day. Described, perhaps not entirely seriously, by the Quietus as a 'sombre, abstinent affair'.

Opposite: Finnish pop-
banger merchants LCMDF
(Le Corps Mince De
Françoise) released Love
& Nature on Heavenly
Recordings in 2011.

Left: 'Future Me' and
'Ghandi' by LCMDF, the
latter featuring an Andrew
Weatherall remix.

Below: The fuzzy
garage-rock debut of
The Soft Pack, formerly
known as The Muslims,
was released by
Heavenly Recordings
in the UK in 2010.

If Heavenly has a spirit animal, it's Christopher Camm. Chris has been part of the Heavenly community forever. Factory Records had its own salon (FAC 98 – Swing, situated in the basement of the Haçienda). Heavenly has a hairdresser who is also a best friend, a confidant and a constant cheerleader. The chair in Chris's shop is much like a psychologist's couch. It's somewhere to ponder, to posit ideas, to test theories, to sit and think. And it's heard it all over the years, every plan from inception to hangover. And he's usually suffering that same hangover too.

A true denizen of Soho – the real Soho, not the new, gleaming version – Chris is the living embodiment of the fact that in Heavenly there's no such thing as an extended family: it's a design for life for whoever wants it. *Robin Turner*

CHRISTOPHER CAMM

I've been based in Soho since the eighties. After moving from Portsmouth I worked as a window cleaner until I got a hairdressing apprenticeship at Vidal Sassoon. In the early eighties that was a pretty cool thing for a working-class kid like me. There were very few straight hairdressers around, especially ones with backgrounds like mine.

After finishing at Sassoon and working around Soho for a bit I went to the States for a year. When I came back in early '87 London was grey. It wasn't happening at all. It was a hangover from the old Soho, from the fifties, sixties and seventies. It was like it was regurgitating itself all the time. I was working to make money to get myself back to New York when my mate Roscoe said, 'You've got to come to Shoom.' I went to one in the basement of the YMCA on Tottenham Court Road and it was a bit shit, they were trying to create a scene but it wasn't there yet. And then I went to the first one back at the Fitness Centre, everyone was on E and everything changed. Overnight, London became the best city in the world. I couldn't imagine anywhere else that you'd want to be at that point in time.

For a few years, you didn't want to leave London at the weekend in case you missed something.

There's an old story about Ronnie Scott and his old business partner Pete King. They were driving down to Brighton one weekend in King's big car and Ronnie said, 'You've got to turn around.' Pete asked why. 'I can't handle it, we're missing something. We've got to go back.' That's what it was like. Everyone knew who'd played what record at what party, who dropped what when, what pills you'd done. People seemed to have photographic memories of what had happened and people talked about it all week. You were excited all week, you couldn't wait to get out and see where the night took you. Even if you went somewhere and it was shit, you'd end up somewhere afterwards that would save your night out. People weren't staying out because they didn't want to go home, they were staying out because it was really fucking good fun. It was fun for days on end.

I met Jeff on that scene at the first Flowered Up gig at Kazoo underneath a hotel on Praed Street. I was living in Camden and I'd met Des and Liam, who I'd become friends with. They were exactly the kind of people I'd left home to get away from; when I got to know them, I felt like I'd come home. At the gig, Jeff looked completely out of place. There were all these young, baggy kids with that look – wide trousers, loose t-shirts – but his whole look was nothing like that. He had proper Levi's and this wild, big hair. The venue had no stage and Liam refused to look at the crowd, he was too nervous, and after they played, Jeff was this ball of energy, full of so much praise for it even though the singer had hidden away. That enthusiasm hasn't ever gone away thirty years later. It's infectious and addictive. That's one of the reasons why he's been one of the most constant people in my life since that night. Before I got to properly know them, people would say about Heavenly that 'they're all mad'. Where I'm from, they would be perfectly normal. That's how everyone was. They might seem mad in a sea of normal people, but where I'm from they are normal.

I really became part of the furniture at Heavenly when they moved into Soho in 1993. I was working on Berwick Street, so we were close neighbours. Soho and Heavenly are symbiotic; the place suits them so well. There's never been a signpost leading to Soho, there's not a tube station called Soho. It just is. It exists as its own thing. Much like Heavenly, really. Soho gives them energy levels that helps them just deliver something different, something better. When they were in Wardour Street and Frith Street, there was a real magic, a glint. And that's back since they've moved to Old Compton Street. When they left Soho, I felt like I'd lost a limb, even though I've been there a lot longer than them. It's where they belong physically and spiritually. It's to do with the Social too: the close proximity to that place makes it such an obvious and easy place to hang out, to put on gigs, to lose days and nights.

The old Heavenly office being where it was – above Ronnie Scott's, with Fred's around the corner, Chinese Jimmy's off Bateman St, the Arts Theatre Club next door; lots of places where you could get a late-night drink – it meant people could go in and out without anyone noticing. It made it feel like a speakeasy, even though it was a place of work. It wasn't just that it was in Soho, it was in that particular place, where there have always been lots of doors to disappear behind. They weren't all seedy, they were an amazing hive of creativity; they were conduits to happiness. I remember being in that office one time when the police walked in. It was my birthday, so I turned to Jeff and said, 'I told you I wanted a roly-poly-gram!' That defused any tension. After that, they didn't seem to mind what was going on, they were just checking if it was an illegal drinking den. Thinking about it, maybe we'd all have been richer if we had started selling cans out of there.

Whenever we'd end up in their office at night, I always thought people in the record business who'd stopped by seemed quite straight – people who didn't seem like Soho people, it was just somewhere they'd come to before they trekked off home. It seemed like they were slumming it in a rock 'n' roll way when they'd turn up. It was almost voyeuristic. Jeff and Martin and everyone there really did feel like Soho people, they fitted right in.

Where I grew up, it was very tribal. I feel I missed out on a lot of experience in my teenage years for being too aligned to one tribe. Heavenly seemed to have absorbed everything, and all those influences have affected the aesthetic of the whole thing. Meeting those guys made me look at everything in an equal light. When acid house came along, I thought we were all seeing everyone and everything in an equal light, but we weren't. Lots of the old tribal prejudices people used to have were still there, just buried a little deeper. I think I'd been very caught up in trying to be cool. It takes a bit of experience to realise that if you're a good person, you're going to be cool anyway.

Heavenly really are an inspiration. They show that you can be honest and entrepreneurial without becoming jaded by the system. I think they really do believe in magic. Maybe that's sometimes been to their detriment, through misplaced trust. Through all the madness, their first passion is still the music. Everything else spins around it – they might party but that's not the first thing. The music is always first.

Title spread: Long-time Heavenly confidant and spirit animal Chris Camm, photographed on Frith Street by Martin Kelly.

The sound of one blank generation looking at another:
London five-piece Charlie Boyer and the Voyeurs.

Across 2013 and 2014, Heavenly Recordings would
release the one-two punch of their debut Clarietta
and follow-up Rhubarb Rhubarb.

Huw Evans – H Hawkline – would join the Heavenly Recordings family to release 2014 compilation Salt Gall Box Ghouls *and 2015's* In the Pink of Condition, *and would go on to release another album of off-kilter Welsh outsider pop with* I Romanticize.

HH Live 2014
Yn Fyw

SEPTEMBER // MEDI

03 The Musician, Leicester*
06 Festival No6, Portmeirion
09 O2 Academy 2, Oxford*
10 Wedgewood Rooms, Portsmouth
11 Koko, London*
12 Gorilla, Manchester*
13 The Sage (Hall 2), Gateshead*
14 The Lemon Tree, Aberdeen*
16 Electric Circus, Edinburgh*
17 The Duchess, York*
18 Plug, Sheffield*
24 The Social, London
26 Branchage Festival, St Helier

* supporting Cate Le Bon

We'd heard the name King Gizzard and the Lizard Wizard bandied about. I mean, it's one you notice, no matter how much you've had to drink. It wasn't necessarily a name I was going to listen to. Somebody I trusted told me to get on it – James Endeacott was an early adopter, he would have been banging on about them. I listened to it and I wasn't that into it. One day, a video for a track called 'Head On/Pill' turned up. Any track with a title like that, I've got to listen to. I put it on and it was monumental. This incredible performance video, and the track just takes off. Wow. I really wanted to put it out for Record Store Day, one-sided vinyl, and a really loud cut.

I tracked down the manager – Eric, also a member of the band – and asked if we could license 'Head On/Pill'. He said we could and added that they had another album [*Oddments*] ready, which I listened to and wasn't madly into, at which point he told me they had another one coming too. Bloody hell, really? That was *I'm in Your Mind Fuzz*. Such a great title. Most people would have just stopped at mind. It was a really, really good record.

We did a licensing deal with them for a couple of records. We ended up doing nine records with them in less than four years, and we saw them go from playing the Shacklewell Arms in Dalston to headlining Alexandra Palace – all on their own brilliantly militant terms. They manage themselves, they're on their own label [Flightless]. When they left us, they didn't go to another label, they just did it on their own label. They don't need any help, they're huge and they're really brilliant and fun and exciting – King Gizzard are very like the Grateful Dead but they never had to sign to Warner Brothers. The way the Dead used to encourage people to tape shows, King Gizzard put the files out for records specifically for fans to share.

They're really unorthodox. And there's not enough unorthodox any more. That's why they're so big, because they're so unorthodox. If they don't know the right answer, they just say no. The amount of times I'd try to convince them to do live radio

sessions. They'd always ask if they could mix it, and I'd say, 'It's live. How can you do that? Just play, you're the best live band in world right now, it'll be amazing.' 'I think we'll pass on that one, Jeff.' Unless they can control how they sound and look, they're just not interested. And that's why kids love them. Mad artwork, mad sound, no compromise and – apparently – it sounds really good if you've got a massive bong on the go.
Jeff Barrett

It was incredible being witness to the rise of King Gizzard and the Lizard Wizard. One moment, everyone thought the name was too daft. Then in the blink of an eye they were headlining Green Man Festival and had teenage boys in tears as they moshed down the front.

I remember Jeff phoning the office after meeting the band in New York for the first time. 'They're cool guys; they drink beer, smoke fags and chat about records. I like them.' When they came to the UK, they played the most bonkers live show, blowing everyone's minds at the Shacklewell Arms, which was the sweatiest gig I've ever been to. I realised how mad it had got when I clocked everyone tutting at me after I'd lugged another suitcase full of copies of *Nonagon Infinity* to the post office as the mail orders piled up.

I'll never forget standing behind the bar in the Trades Club, watching our artists watching them and a mass of arms flailing in the air, crowd-surfing and stage-diving to 'Rattlesnake'. It was amazing that band, who two days later sold out Brixton Academy, were up for playing at our weekender in Hebden Bridge.

At Green Man, before they headlined the main stage, Jeff ran over to me with a access-all-areas pass, knowing I'd be frightened in the inevitable, insane mosh pit. I couldn't have been more delighted to stand side of stage, in line with two of the best drummers in the world as the band melted minds. After that show, I kept pinching myself as I stumbled around backstage, smiling with utter disbelief at just how brilliant that band with the silly name were. When I saw Jeff, I asked

him if the novelty of an AAA pass ever wore off. With a glint in his eye he said, 'Of course not, it's part of the magic.' *Katherine Cantwell (office manager)*

ERIC MOORE

Heavenly first got in touch via email in early 2014. They'd heard 'Head On/Pill' somewhere on the internet and asked if they could put it out on a loud 12-inch. We agreed and we ended up putting out twelve releases with them between 2014 and 2018.

I remember just being stoked to be going to London for the first time, let alone playing our own headline show there. The Shacklewell Arms felt massive, and it didn't worry us that all our amps and drums could barely fit on stage (I remember my kit was behind a wall and I couldn't see the crowd at all let alone anyone else in Gizz). I'll never forget Jeff shouting a round of warm pints in Nottingham that we all took a sip of and placed gently back on the bar. I don't think he understood why we knocked them back. ('We like our beer cold in Australia,' someone murmured.) I hope he wasn't too offended. The first time we got to Glastonbury (in 2015) was an eye-opener. We'd flown directly from NYC after a show and had to play three shows at the festival on the same day. On no sleep. Somehow the Heavenly team looked as if they had done the same, only twice over. We ended up playing a midnight show to about a hundred people in the Crow's Nest that included a power outage. Somehow one of Jeff's sparky mates ended up hooking into the power and got everything up and running again.

Heavenly became our de facto family in the UK and Europe. We would never have lasted half as long without them.

Top: King Gizzard and the Wizard Lizard at a packed Shacklewell Arms in 2014.

Opposite (bottom): The Australian outfit performing a landmark Brixton Academy show in 2018.

This page: Peterborough's The Wytches painting modern psychedelia black with Annabell Dream Reader in 2014 and All Your Happy Life *in 2016.*

Opposite: Jangling indie-pop from the Wirral: Hooton Tennis Club, who recorded with Bill Ryder-Jones and Edwyn Collins.

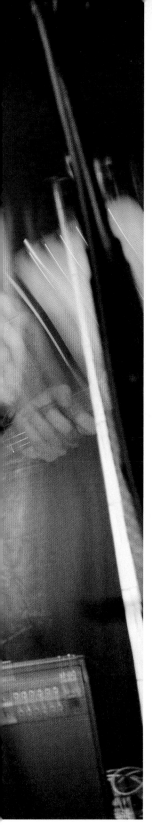

KID WAVE
GLOOM EP

KID WAVE
ALL I WANT

Opposite: Lush harmonies and dreamy, melodic pop – Heavenly Recordings would release Kid Wave's only album, Wonderlust, in 2015.

This page: A 2014 collaboration album with Mark Lanegan was the first of several records for the label by Kent singer-songwriter Duke Garwood, who released two solo records – Heavy Love and Garden of Ashes – as well as two as part of a Lanegan double-act.

The Heavenly twenty-fifth birthday weekend took place at the Trades Club in Hebden Bridge in January 2015. Prior to that, we had no real emotional attachment to the Trades. It was on our radar and we had respect for it from afar because of its position as a grassroots gig promoter in a small town in West Yorkshire. I knew Hebden Bridge was a hippie town, and I knew that there had been a strong alternative counterculture there. It still has that, but not in a Glastonbury town, crystal shops way.

In terms of bookings, the Trades was punching above its weight and it was allowing groups go to play a part of country that nobody else was really promoting in. It's hard to think of other counties that have got venues that small with bookings that big. Somewhere comparable like Totnes doesn't have a venue as good as Trades.

I first went there when Jimi Goodwin was booked to play just before his album *Odludek* came out. He was doing the BBC 6 Music Festival in Manchester and needed a couple of warm-up shows. I went and fell in love, really. It's a great, great venue with a brilliant promoter in a really lovely, really beautiful town that doesn't force itself and doesn't labour the fact. The alternative culture in Hebden seems to have sprung out of there being were so many empty buildings in the mid-1960s – warehouses that had been empty because of the declining industry there. And from the fact that the hippies discovered you could buy houses there for six pounds in 1966.

You get a real confluence of people in that town. You've got literary people who go there to visit Sylvia Plath's grave in Heptonstall; you get Ted Hughes groupies and Brontë people. You get walking people. And you get a lot of kids on drugs, a lot of misfits and weirdos. And that kind of sums up every single person that works at the Trades Club. What's not to like? And it's three quid a pint.

So Jimi played a great gig. When we were stood outside afterwards, Dave Rofe (Doves manager)

said to me, 'You should do a Heavenly night up here.' He didn't know that my mind had started to think about doing something to mark twenty-five years – and that if I have an idea like that it's never just, 'Oh, let's have a party somewhere.' It's immediately multi-dimensional in my brain. Danny and me went back up to meet Mal, the promoter, who was a lovely guy and open to our ideas. It was supposed to be a one-off but we've done four there now.

What I love most about the Trades Club is that it has influenced, inspired and given hope to local musical talent. And that's paid dividends for us because we signed The Orielles from Halifax, just further up the Calder Valley; Working Men's Club are from Todmorden, just a few miles down the road. I think it's great that you've got a venue to aspire to play in a small town like that. The kids in those bands all used to sneak into gigs when they were underage. Getting their first headline gig at the Trades is like headlining Brixton Academy for them. When I watched Working Men's Club headlining there and Sid the singer jumped into the crowd, I came away thinking that at least one of those kids is going to go away and form a group. And that gives you a lot of hope.
Jeff Barrett

MAL CAMPBELL *promoter at the Trades Club*
Jeff came to see Jimi Goodwin play a solo show at the Trades. My friend, the writer Ben Myers, was going to meet him in a pub round the corner so I thought I'd take the opportunity to plead with him for TOY to play the club. I listed the few Heavenly bands that had played already and made my case. Little did I know that I was soon going to get the whole roster.

Jeff got in touch a few months later to say he was passing through, so we had a drink and long chat about music, and then Danny and Carl came up for a night out. I think they were scoping out me and the venue. Rightly so – no one wants to work with arseholes, do they? I was shocked when Jeff asked me what I thought about having the twenty-fifth birthday at the Trades. And elated, obviously. There really wasn't a precedent for

doing something like that. Who has a weekend like that in a little northern mill town with a population of 5000?

That weekend was everything we all hoped it would be. Watching Cherry Ghost from the side of the stage for a Saturday matinee show was a revelation. Just mind-blowing. Si barely touches the strings and this sound comes out and he plays these beautiful, timeless songs that you can't believe you haven't heard before. Later on, Mark Lanegan was the busiest I've ever seen the Trades Club. Had I been any less transfixed, I would have been freaking out. He doesn't like a spotlight on him so the stage was really dark, and you could feel the audience kind of

leaning in – to the stage and the music. And, of course, he has this voice . . . it's like Mount Rushmore, or the sermon on the mount. It's lazy writing to say 'the voice of God' but you do hear the wisdom born from hard times and you feel like you want to bloody pay attention! I was just transported, as was everyone there.

The relationship with Heavenly has been a godsend to me, really. I lived in London for twenty years before I moved to Hebden and, in the beginning, felt a little like I was out in the sticks, as they say. But now it feels so vital. I was a big fan of what Roger Eagle did with Eric's in Liverpool and always thought that any venue worth its salt should cultivate a young

music scene. And it happened. Kids that were jumping up and down at gigs here formed their own groups, and two of them are now signed to Heavenly. And even younger kids see that it's achievable and that gives them even more drive with their own music. So it's blossomed before my eyes, and I can't tell you how much that means to me. It's fucking brilliant. And do you know what? All the groups help each other out. So it's not just me stroking my chin saying 'that chorus needs more work', or something. They are influencing and nurturing each other and each trying to find their own sound. It's not a scene where everyone sounds like The Orielles. They are smart, they know you have to do your own thing.

What I love about Heavenly is that they are as obsessed as I am. They are constantly banging on about new remixes, lost classic records from the early seventies, books on alcoholic explorers, anything. And they're all great dancers, the Heavenly crew. I feel they don't get enough praise for that.

Title spread: Shivering Calder Valley: the 2015 Heavenly Weekender would begin a fruitful relationship with the indie scene of Hebden Bridge and Todmorden.

Above (L–R): Wytches and H Hawkline.

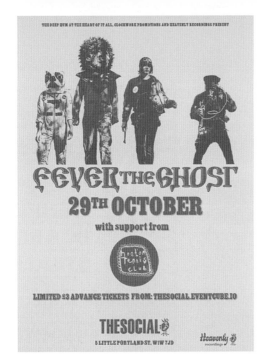

Opposite: In 2016, Martin Craft, known as M. Craft, released Blood Moon, a beautiful collection of late-night, stargazing songs. The following year, he reimagined that album as a gorgeous, ambient sister piece, Blood Moon Deconstructed.

Below: In 2015, Heavenly Recordings released the grandiose psych-pop of Zirconium Meconium by LA's Fever the Ghost.

Below: Cate Le Bon of Carmarthen meets California duo DRINKS.

Bottom (left): Hooton Tennis Club; (right) Tim Presley of DRINKS.

Opposite: Lucy Mercer of Stealing Sheep and Temples frontman James Bagshaw play the Heavenly & Friends stage at On Blackheath festival.

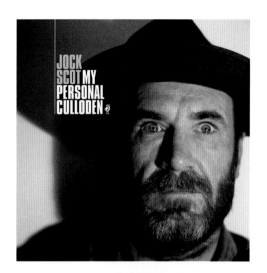

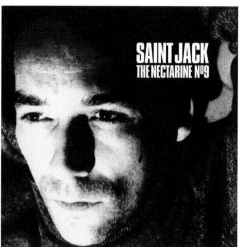

Dear Davey,
Here I am explaining, (bragging) to Tessa P. SLIT., just what she is missing, Thanks again to yoursel', Simon and Lucky Kenny, for making my stay in Glescae Toon so enjoyable and groovy. The days slipped by with nary a care, in fact, just what was needed. I got on the wrong train, "The Flying Scotsman" no less. Due to "tiredness" and was put off at Embra Waverley. I had to beg the Station Master to allow me to continue my journey without paying the £36 extra. Oscar-winning stuff. Eventually docked at 7 o'clock & this did not stop me having a bevvy with the Stargazer
CHEERS JOHN.

In 2015, Forever Heavenly reissued two lost classics – Jock Scot's 1997 poetry-meets-proto-post-rock collection *My Own Personal Culloden* and *Saint Jack* by The Nectarine No.9, originally released on Postcard in 1995.

22 Hemstal Road
[redacted]
NW6 2AS.

Dear Davey,
Here is a lovey-dovey lyric which maybe you can put a tune to or use in some way. If not, don't fret. Yesterday, this pen wouldn't write, now it's exploding everywhere. Sager was mucho impressed by Choc. 45 although he would never admit it. His wife told me she caught him dancing round the room to it at full volume. Have you got a tape of "Tiger Tiger" that you did for the radio? He needs all the encouragement thats going, the huffy bastard. Well, he is a fuckin JAMBO. I am so far in debt money now has no value or meaning. Beatnik pound plummets! I need a rich "babe" which I believe is the current term for chicks. But the last one I chatted-up, just as I was tampering with the hem of her mini-kilt, came away with an all-time classic. "I leave for Sri-Lanka in the morning." I still haven't recovered from that one. I look forward to the London gig. See you then.
Fayes brother J...

Hats off to Jock Scott. He's not afraid to do the gardening in a dress and he's brought out a full-length album, writes Damien Love

JOCK Scott is wearing shades to filter the light and a shapeless green hat that looks as though it's been thatched on to his head. He's also wearing a large red button badge that bears the legend "I am 44". "My sister gave me it – it's my birthday in September and I told her I would wear it every day until my next birthday, so it's a family obligation." He is not, however, wearing one of his old girlfriends' dresses, as, he assures me, he likes to when he's doing the garden because "you need a bit of freedom of movement."

[illegible] company executive – until he got thrown out of Stiff records for [illegible] the boss. He's travelled [illegible] Europe as Minister in [illegible] Good Times on the [illegible] bus, and he's drank [illegible] night in London lock-ins [illegible] friend Shane Mac-[illegible]

[illegible]elationships [illegible] not work out any [illegible]re. There's too [illegible] pressure in [illegible] modern world

[illegible] He's been in the Spanish [illegible] and sawed down trees [illegible] all, Jock Scott has [illegible] a poet.

[illegible] first collection, 'Where Is My Heroine?', appeared in 1993, but his conversations with the muse started much earlier, back in the Leith of the late Sixties. "I started writing poetry as an adolescent," he says. "Most people do, but I persevered with it. Everyone writes poetry – well, all the people I grew up with wrote poetry. My sister wrote poetry, my class mates wrote poetry, but they all stopped doing it, because people laugh at you. Most people stop doing it after months; after they've fell out with their girlfriend they write some poetry and that's the end of it. Or if their hamster dies or something. But I kept with it ... until I reached its present ... dizzying level of proficiency."

We're meeting to talk about Jock's latest venture, *My Personal Culloden*, a full-length album of his readings set against music provided by Edinburgh's Nectarine No.9. It's not the first time Scott and Davey Henderson's band have worked together; the questing poet appeared on their 1995 *St. Jack* album and has turned up on stage at a few of their concerts. He first encountered Henderson back during the afterbirth of punk, when the musician was the oblique driving force behind the legendary Fire Engines, a meeting he fondly recalls.

"I didn't know Davey when I lived in Edinburgh. I was living in London, '78, '79, and I came back up on a periodic visit – might have been Hogmanay or something – and went to a party on the top floor of a tenement with my carry-out after the pub. And I remember getting to the door, and there was a white card on the door that said "No Fire Engines." So, I went in, and it was all the Edinburgh Art College posse hanging out, having a great party. But there were four little guys in a corner talking to each other and starting a Scottish Bluebell matchbox, all wearing black suits and white shirts and bow ties, and I said: 'Who are these guys?' I thought it was the Beatles or something. And somebody whispered 'That's the Fire Engines. They're no meant tae be here.' I immediately wanted to meet them, so I went over and introduced myself. The Fire Engines. And they gave me this matchbox, and it was full of little blue pills. So I had a few and we were up talking all night."

For *Culloden*, the Nectarine No.9 come up with a series of fields that range from the psychotic through the wistful open range melodrama of 'Thunder Over Kilburn', into a strange kind of recurring Tom Waitsified fairground boneyard waltz. The unifying factor is the way that all the music seems to be playing on a radio somewhere in the room next to Jock Scott's mind, his words muttering and floating above or behind the music, a coincidental [illegible] noise yet apart from it. [illegible] readings are frequently hysterical, occasionally scary and, when least you expect it, downright moving. He's gifted with a Regal voice – both in terms of its kingly pace and the brand of fags he chars it up with – and reads his poems as though he had found them stashed secretly under one of his friends' beds, and was reading them to the rest of his mates while the guy was out the room.

"The recurring theme is unre-[illegible] about my problems in dealing with [illegible] I try to deal with it in a light-hearted manner, rather than a tragic sense. I mean it's 1997. [illegible] Relationships do not work out. People have got to stop kidding themselves that you [illegible] a job, get married, have children and be happy; that just does not happen any more, and people have got to get hip to that fact. They can't expect this government, religious, society imposed bullshit any longer. They've got to start thinking for themselves. Relationships cannot work out any more. There's too much pressure in the modern world for it ever to happen. Why should you live with someone for 30 years and never fuck anyone else when you're seeing people in the street that you want to every day? ... you're just repressing yourself. You've just got say, 'Look, I'm sorry doll ...'"

I point out that Scott himself seems pretty cut up when, as in so many of his poems, it happens to him. "Oh, aye," he considers. "It's never funny if you're keen on someone and they're out the door ..."

Still, as long as whoever it is leaves a nice dress for the garden and there's a typewriter handy.

❑ *My Personal Culloden is released through Postcard Recordings of Scotland.*

How many people are lucky enough in life to find themselves working with an artist who, when you say, 'Have you started thinking about your second record yet?' replies, 'Yes. And it's going to be in Cornish.' I count myself as a lucky bastard to have met Gwenno and to be working with someone who feels that they can work with our label and do that. When she told me she was making the record in Cornish it was a nice moment. My mother was Cornish and I've had a strong affinity with the county ever since I first went there.

I knew that we had a really good chance with *Le Kov* because, quality of the music aside, there was a story there. There's an intelligence, a thought process and there's a concept. All brought together by a highly articulate artist. Her concept was a unique thing. Nobody else had done it. I'm not saying nobody's made a record in the Cornish language, but nobody has made a record in the Cornish language after making a record in the Welsh language [*Y Dydd Olaf*] after having been in an English-language pop group [The Pipettes].

I've got nothing but massive respect for Gwenno. She's not a commercial artist. She's an artist, and a successful one. She pushes herself and challenges herself every step of the way. She makes art. I'm properly in awe of her. *Jeff Barrett*

GWENNO SAUNDERS

Myself and Rhys [Edwards, who produced *Y Dydd Olaf* and *Le Kov*] met Jeff when I was supporting Gruff Rhys on his *American Interior* tour. We'd done everything ourselves through Rhys's [now defunct] label Peski Records, and had come to a bit of a brick wall. We were completely DIY up to that point so it was just really fantastic to be able to share ideas with someone who was so open to them. I've had a lot of very different musical experiences in the twenty years that I've been releasing stuff, and so I was in a really good place to know what I was trying to do by that point.

I always view each project I start as a new exploration. That means going right back to the core of your being to find something new. I find the concept of where the 'idea' comes from such a magical thing. You have to wring out every single creative molecule from your being when you make an album. By the end you've exhausted yourself completely and it's quite incredible that you're able to discover a new idea again each time that seems to come out of nowhere.

In a world where music is so commodified and there's such an overwhelming sonic familiarity all around, the ability to get lost in the music and to suggest unfamiliarity feels integral to the alchemy of it. The music I make is an opportunity to suggest another reality, another way of being. There are plenty of people doing that in modern music and embracing whatever language they have. I do definitely think it's one (small) way of resisting late capitalism, and it certainly helps me to hold on to a little bit of hope that there are other ways of organising ourselves, as language has such a huge impact and influence on our lives without us even realising it.

On a personal note, using the Cornish language (Kernewek) in my music has allowed me to tap into my subconscious as it's a language of a land that I haven't had the chance to live in (yet!), as well as being the dominant language of my childhood. It exists in an isolation which allows me to cut out all the noise. I have this (completely rogue) theory that each language forms its own personality, and for me Kernewek has this free spirit because of its history – the fact that it has insisted on carrying on existing when the tide is against it, and in how it reflects the story of the people that have shaped it over the centuries.

My interest in music is in the absurd and ridiculous; in those moments where things seem to come out of nowhere that can't be predicted or controlled. But then you do a bit of research and you see that it was there all along beneath the surface, and it represents a whole other world and way of doing things. That's the fun of it, I think. With that approach in mind, it's been a joy to work with Heavenly as I always feel encouraged by Jeff to be as outlandish with my ideas as I can be!

Eaves *Joseph Lyons*

Temples *James Bagshaw*

Temples *Thomas Warmsley*

King Gizzard and the Lizard Wizard *Michael Cavanagh*

King Gizzard and the Lizard Wizard *Craig Cook*

King Gizzard and the Lizard Wizard *Eric Moore*

Fever the Ghost *Casper Indrizzo*

Fever the Ghost *Mason Rothschild*

Fever the Ghost *Nick Overhauser*

TOY *Alejandra Diez*

TOY *Maxim Barron*

TOY *Charlie Salvidge*

Temples *Samuel Toms*

Temples *Adam Smith*

King Gizzard and the Lizard Wizard *Stu Mackenzie*

King Gizzard and the Lizard Wizard *Lucas Skinner*

King Gizzard and the Lizard Wizard *Joey Walker*

King Gizzard and the Lizard Wizard *Ambrose Kenny-Smith*

Fever the Ghost *Bobby Victor*

Duke Garwood

TOY *Tom Dougal*

TOY *Dominic O'Dair*

Gwenno *Gwenno Saunders*

The Wytches *Daniel Rumsey*

The Wytches *Gianni Honey*

The Wytches *Kristian Bell*

The Voyers *Charlie Boyer*

The Voyers *Samir Eskanda*

Britain *Katie Drew*

Britain *Joey Cobb*

Kid Wave *Mattias Bhatt*

H. Hawkline *Huw Evans*

Jimi Goodwin

Hooton Tennis Club *Callum McFadden*

Hooton Tennis Club *Harry Chalmers*

Hooton Tennis Club *James Madden*

The Voyers *Danny Stead*

The Voyers *Ross Kristian*

The Voyers *Sam Davies*

Kid Wave *Lea Emmery*

Kid Wave *Harry Deacon*

Kid Wave *Serra Petale*

Stealing Sheep *Emily Lansley*

Stealing Sheep *Rebecca Hawley*

Stealing Sheep *Lucy Mercer*

Hooton Tennis Club *Ryan Murphy*

Mark Lanegan

Jock Scott

Hearing Confidence Man for the first time was an instant response to a brilliant track. That's not the hard part of what we do, really. 'Boyfriend' was a killer single – a great song with fantastic production that made me think of 'Groove is in the Heart' by Dee-Lite. Simple as that. I just thought whoever has made this record I know I am going to love. I wanted to be friends with those people. I knew they were going to be fun, and a laugh.

The track had made its way to me via a friend and an agent, Paul Buck. He'd been sent it by an Australian promoter saying, 'This is a laugh, have a listen.' When I called the manager, he told me he was aware of Heavenly but that the call had come out of the blue a little bit as the four of them had made the track and they hadn't really thought about whether they were actually going to be a group or not. They were all in different bands. I said I wanted to put it out anyway. I wanted to see people dance and I wanted to share their music with the world. When we eventually did meet, it was every bit as beautiful as I'd hoped – maybe more so. They were as naughty and as mischievous, as fun and as daft and brilliant as anyone could have ever hoped for.
Jeff Barrett

CONFIDENCE MAN
Heavenly are probably the only other people we know who are as crazy as we are. When we first came over to London and met them we only had one track out and had no idea what we were doing. They took a chance on us from right across the globe and welcomed us with open arms. We knew who they were and, right away, it was a match made in heaven. Looking at what they've done in the past, it's pretty clear they've always known the importance of fun in the world. When we met them that was when we realised just how good the match was. Actually, maybe it's such a good match it borders on the unhealthy.

Australia is pretty unique for music. That's what happens when you're cut off from the rest of the world. It makes sense that Heavenly (who are weirdos) would find something special in us left-of-centre Australians. It's a beautiful connection. Whenever we come to Britain it's always wonderful

and totally chaotic. We played Crow's Nest up at the top of the Park at Glastonbury Festival, which felt like a big and surreal moment for us. We didn't fit on the stage properly, and I remember it being absolutely packed. Clarence kept falling off the stage and a whole bunch of Heavenly folk held him up so he could keep drumming. It was beautiful teamwork, a sight to behold. We were on a slant so we kept sliding off the stage, there was hay everywhere and Sugar Bones had a swollen ankle, but he didn't give a shit. That show felt like true punk to me. I couldn't hear myself over the people screaming along to 'Boyfriend' and, as always, there was Jeff with a huge smile on his face, right in the middle. Always in it. The man gets down too. They all do. When we came back and played at the Scala there were people dancing on top of the DJ booth. Everyone in the venue was covered in sweat, it just seemed like a real party.

We didn't really have a plan when we started off, we were just making music and playing shows as a weird natural thing. We started working with Heavenly and it all started to go crazy. Now our plan is to force ourselves down the throats of all the people who don't like the music as well as the ones who are already on board. Thankfully, Heavenly have always been hugely supportive of that ambition – without them (Jeff, Danny, Kat and Daisy) we probably wouldn't be doing this. We'd have a very sexy, moderately successful cleaning business, and what a shame that would be.

If we had to sum up the Heavenly ethos in a single sentence, it would have to be: Never give up, never go home and never say no.

Love always, Janet, Sugar, Clarence and Reggie.

Don't you know they're in a band?
Sugar Bones and Janet Planet
from Confidence Man.

HEAVENLY

Friday February 13
A Heavenly night out in Nottingham
7pm - Duke Garwood
at Rough Trade, free instore with djs' Jeff Barrett and H Hawkline
9pm - H Hawkline and Hooton Tennis Club
at The Chameleon with djs' Heavenly Jukebox
For more information go to heavenlyrecordings.com

Opposite (top): We Are Nots: Memphis garage-punk four-piece Nots released two albums on Heavenly Recordings in the UK in 2015 and 2016; (bottom) Danny Lee Blackwell of Night Beats, who released three Nashville-facing records on Heavenly Recordings between 2016 and 2019.

This page: Dutch songwriter Amber Arcades' 2018 European Heartbreak would soundtrack tumultuous political years in the UK.

ALBUM LAUNCH SHOW
THE S PARROT
+ VERY SPECIAL GUESTS

SEPT 7 • VICTORIA

A xmas party

08/12/17

Below: Heavenly showcased the intimate songwriting of Detroit's Anna Burch on 2018's Quit the Curse *and 2020's* If You're Dreaming.

The Orielles.
with special guests Boy Azooga, Inland Taipan & Dreaming
Manchester deaf institute.

European union.

Above: Hailing from the proggy and experimental edges of France's pop scene, Halo Maud's ethereal songs flit between English and French language and focus on notions of freedom and power through a wild and playful lens.

Left: The Parrots formed in Madrid and quickly created an addictive fuzz-rock racket in venues around the world and on their 2016 album Los Niños Sin Miedo.

Opposite: Diego García of The Parrots takes to the floor.

I knew David Wrench as a producer and I knew he worked out of a studio in Bethesda, North Wales. A lot of bands we knew had recorded there and loved it. But, really, all you need to know is there in the Caribou records that he's worked on. They're out of this world. They're what led me to want to work with him on Temples and TOY records.

One night at Glastonbury I was DJing in the Land's End bar up in the Park and David was there having a bit of a dance. When I finished, I got talking to him and he told me he'd met this young lady called Evangeline who he'd started making music with. He described them as 'story songs', a little bit Ivor Cutler, a little bit Syd Barrett. He didn't know what it was yet but he thought they were on to something good.

A while after the festival he got in touch saying it had turned into something and he asked if he could play it to me. I went to his studio in Old Street and I met Evangeline and when he played it, it was a bit Ivor Cutler and a bit Syd Barrett and even a bit Joyce Grenfell. It was funny and odd, mad art-school business. It makes me smile. Live, Evangeline takes on all comers. She doesn't give a fuck. She just happens to look fantastic and be fantastic and have a mental way with words. She's properly unique. They both are, really. *Jeff Barrett*

DAVID WRENCH
Audiobooks began accidentally. It was meant to just be Evangeline coming to look at my new studio. I was busy so set her up on a synth so I could do some work. Then I listened to what she was doing, joined in, handed her a microphone and we recorded our first single 'Gothenburg'.

From that day onwards audiobooks sessions have been really focused. They're about getting stuff done, about switching into that creative mode. We are both busy people, so neither of us has time to waste. Why have a night out when you can write or record a new track instead? That said, I don't think making serious music and having fun are exclusive. Scott Walker said he had a lot of fun making *The Drift*. I've always taken the music really seriously. I want it to be genuinely good and have depth. But it's also great to make people smile or laugh too.

I knew Jeff from various Heavenly artists I'd worked with, and the label itself meant so many things to me, from the Manics to Saint Etienne, Beth Orton, Doves, Gwenno. Jeff has this incredible passion, love and drive. After hanging out at Glastonbury I had a pretty good hunch he'd get it.

EVANGELINE LING
Music and art are different but they can both reach a similar point of wow! The wow bit is the thing that is interesting. However, I like Andy Warhol saying 'being good in business is the most fascinating kind of art'. I guess there is an art to how one goes about things. When we record I tend to like to draw the curtains and drink a bit of whiskey before hitting the mic.

If Jeff was a character in an audiobooks song, he'd be the hero of the story; someone that followed his gut and supported a cause that everybody else thought was silly and a waste of time. He would have a good understanding of vibes – vibes in songs, people, places. He always seems to have good instinct of where it's all at.

The inhuman league: Audiobooks' Evangeline Ling live at the Social (top) and David Wrench at the Sebright Arms.

BELIEVE IN MAGIC 245

In 2017, James Endeacott recommended that Heavenly listen to the debut album by Georgia-born songwriter Mattiel, which had just been released on Burger Records. Within a year, Heavenly Recordings gave that same album its first UK release, following it up with the deadpan bluesy balladry of Satis Factory in 2019.

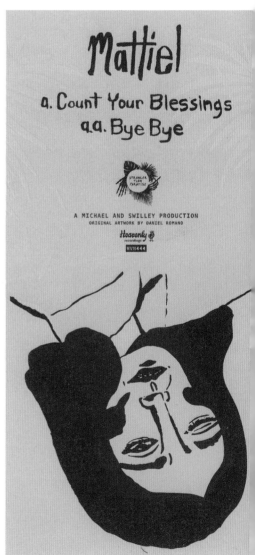

This page: A Heavenly weekend in Leeds: Hatchie and Confidence Man on stage at the Brudenell Social Club, June 2019.

Opposite (top): Taking in all points between jazz, Krautrock and world funk, Boy Azooga released their debut album 1, 2, Kung Fu! on Heavenly Recordings in 2018; (bottom) Remembering the future as if it was yesterday: Orielles' guitarist Henry Carlyle-Wade. In 2020, The Orielles released their critically acclaimed space-centric Disco Volador.

February 1994. I'd only been at Heavenly for two months when I found myself in the passenger seat of a car hurtling around Belfast at 7 a.m. trying to find a bottle of vodka. The sun was trying to rise, but the weather was so grey and smudged you wouldn't really have noticed when it did. The driver was totally deranged. I'd met him three hours previously, yet he was already my best mate in the world and I'd decided to trust him with my life. We really did need to find that vodka. It was locked in the back of someone's car, and that someone was too incapacitated to move, so we were tasked with finding it. The fact that there were multiple tanks on manoeuvre didn't seem to bother us, and they didn't seem that bothered by us. The whole night had been surreal – what difference does the British army make when you're off your nut in the room above a hairdresser's shop in Northern Ireland?

I was in Belfast for David Holmes' and Iain McCready's club night Sugar Sweet. David was managed out of the Heavenly office and I'd been given the job of taking *Select* magazine over to review the club. But that really was just the half of it. I'd met David a few times in the Heavenly office and I'd heard him DJ at Sabresonic, playing mind-bending techno music. Hearing him play in his home city was something else though. The crowd had an energy and an intensity unlike any I'd seen anywhere in England. As David himself has stated, there were 'communities [that] fucking hated each other but among them you had groups of people whose religion was music'. As clichéd as this sounds, that club was truly a church. What that made the hairdresser's shop afterwards, I'm not sure. It certainly appeared that a few of us were experiencing the Rapture. As I learnt over the following months and several trips back, that was David's life back then, and it was a riot.

When we started the Heavenly Sunday Social, Andrew Weatherall and David were the first two people we wanted to book, although diaries dictated they each played in the second month. David's set was blinding – as driven and ecstatic as his techno sets, yet painted from a completely different palette of sounds. It took northern soul away from the rarefied environment of a 100 Club all-nighter and

shoved it into a room below a pub full of drunken partygoers and made it feel like punk rock.

Working as David's press officer on his solo records, it was clear that his ambition was going to take him away from crazed nightclubs and on to somewhere else entirely. Tracks he recorded sounded like scores for unwritten movies, conjured deep images and winding storylines. His 1997 single 'My Mate Paul' always seemed to me like a sleek sibling of the sounds played during his Sunday Social set. Modish and unique, it was a talc-on-the-floor stomper that could work magic on any club soundsystem.

When David started scoring movies, one had to doff a cap. There aren't many people who can put together soundtrack albums that flow like great DJ sets – David definitely can. That move did mean those Sugar Sweet-style techno sets became a thing of the past. And I've no idea if his mates are still out hunting for vodka at sunrise. I'd be happy to join them if they are. *Robin Turner*

DAVID HOLMES

I suppose I was in the right place at the right time. Fate played a big part in everything back then. In the early 1990s I was meeting all these wonderfully creative and very influential people, and all of us shared the same passion and love for music. The first thing I heard on Heavenly was Andrew Weatherall's remix of 'Only Love Can Break Your Heart'. When I started making music, Andrew kind of took me under his wing. I started working in the studio with Jagz Kooner and Gary Burns and, after a meeting in a Soho pub with Jeff, I was introduced to Robert Linney, who worked in the Heavenly office and became my manager. In the pub, Jeff and I talked about northern soul, Dexys Midnight Runners, punk and modism. We shared a lot of the same musical history and I was immediately smitten by his enthusiasm and love of music. I remember saying to him I used to be a mod and he replied with, 'Whadya mean "used to be a mod"? You're still a mod!' I've never forgotten that. I might have been wearing different clothes and listening to different music but the mindset was exactly the same.

Jeff asked me to DJ at his wedding, where I played lots of sixties r 'n' b, soul and northern soul. That day is a bit of a blur. I remember being completely twatted, which was a regular occurrence back then. When they asked me to do a set at the Heavenly Sunday Social the following year, they wanted me to play the same kind of records I'd played at the wedding. And it was one of the greatest nights. I couldn't believe the reaction I was getting from the same records I'd played when I first started out in the mod clubs of Belfast in the early eighties. It was monumental. The thing about those parties was it was all about the music, no matter what genre it was. As long as it was quality. Those nights really opened my mind to what was possible and what I could get away with as a DJ. Everything changed after that and my sets were never the same again.

Although growing up in Belfast during the Troubles was insane, it also had benefits. There were times when I just wasn't allowed out. Being the youngest of ten kids, I had a great education in music and film, which is what I spent most of my time doing, locked in my own imagination devouring music and watching films. When I started producing music, film very naturally became a huge influence. Andrew Weatherall was also instrumental in this as he influenced me to forge my own path and not be the derivative of the derivative.

When I was making my first album *This Film's Crap Let's Slash the Seats* Jeff listened to the track 'Gone' and heard the line ' . . . and you can never go home any more' from The Shangri-Las track 'I Can Never Go Home Any More' and suggested that Sarah Cracknell sing that line on it. That was a game changer for me because, although I was a fan of the Shangri-Las, I wasn't aware of their producer Shadow Morton. That really started my education with all these legendary producers, which paved the way for Unloved.

I'd moved to LA to work on a Steven Soderbergh film called *Haywire* in 2010. That's when I met Keefus Ciancia and Jade Vincent. They invited me to play records at their weekly jam the Rotary Room at a venue called Little Temple on the corner of Santa

Monica Boulevard and Virgil Avenue. Very soon after, they asked if I wanted to record with them, and Unloved was formed. Living in LA and working in the oldest studio in town – Electro-Vox on Melrose – I was living every producer's fantasy, so for that period and in my own mind I was a modern-day Shadow Morton, Phil Spector or Jack Nitzsche, working with a twenty-first-century Wrecking Crew. From there, we started working on *Killing Eve*, which has been like winning the musical lottery.

When our first, self-financed album came out, I was told that Jeff was a fan, which was so lovely to hear. We had a bunch of offers for our second album, but there was only one choice. I'm so glad and grateful that I'm back on Heavenly. In Heavenly you feel like you're part of a family of friends and musical obsessives. That's what keeps us going: knowing that your label boss and all the Heavenly staff are into it as much as you are.

Unloved's parallel universe B-movie artwork was created by innovative designer Julian House.

'I'm the sausage man, the shadow licker . . .'

Dury duty: 2018's Prince of Tears *would be a landmark for Baxter Dury, featuring the hit 'Miami'. In 2020,* The Night Chancers *followed.*

Opposite: Like a garage band fed into a malfunctioning Game Boy, the highly eclectic CHAI would release both PINK *and* PUNK *consecutively across 2018 and 2019.*

As much as Heavenly is a record label and an office, it's also the disparate group of people who've worked in the latter, helping to create, release and promote the former. This is an erratic history of those people.

TASH LEE MCCLUNEY *(1994–1999)*
I started working at Heavenly in 1994 in the Wardour Street office. When I left in 1999 we were in Frith Street. I've always described working there as like being in school on a snowy day. Totally fucking free. I really tried to work hard when I was there but I was always so easily distracted.

ROBIN TURNER *(1994–1997/2001–2009)*
Although I'd done a few days at the end of 1993 as office cover, I started properly in the first week of January 1994. Tash started a week or two after me. She was replacing Spencer as office manager after he'd gone off on tour, drumming for Saint Etienne. When he came back, we had a Tash and a Spence. They were amazing workmates but I was never sure how much office management either of them did. Or how the office would manage without them.

CHLOE WALSH *(1995–1999)*
My only other office experience was the two years I had just spent working at Creation Records where I'd witnessed a corporate takeover, the discovery and rise of Oasis, a cocaine-induced nervous breakdown and constant office in-fighting. I'd also had one of those thick office stationery catalogues lobbed at my head while I was talking on the phone one morning, by someone who was unhappy with the quality of the packing tape available. Heavenly seemed entirely tranquil in comparison.

MARTIN KELLY *(1990–2009)*
The office was an important meeting place for a lot of people in Soho. All kinds of people used to swing by, be it bands, DJs, solo artists, journalists coming in to blag records, pop stars needing the toilet, drug dealers and mates. Paul [Kelly] was always in there, Bob Stanley would come by to use the phone, Andy Weatherall would sit and talk for ages. Paul Weller, Jason

Pierce, Johnny Marr . . . Ian McCulloch once came round on a Monday afternoon. He and Jeff had a shouting match where neither of them got a word in edgeways. Underworld's Karl Hyde used to come into the Wardour Street office a lot to go to the pub with Robin. Their office – Tomato – was just up the road on D'Arblay Street. Famously, one time he went off to the Ship to wait for Robin and a series of events unfolded that ended up as the lyrics to 'Born Slippy .NUXX'.

I'm pretty sure that Jeff and I were two of the first people to ever hear the finished version of 'Wonderwall'. We were in the office early in the morning and Noel Gallagher walked in. We'd known him for ages; Oasis played some of their first gigs after they got signed supporting Saint Etienne at the end of 1993. He'd just finished mixing the track overnight at a studio on Berwick Street and buzzed the intercom to ask if he could come up and listen to the final version on our system. I'm not sure anyone outside of the band had heard it yet. Back in Capersville days, I remember Weatherall bringing in 'Loaded' straight from the studio, definitely before the band would have heard it. I was pinned against the wall by it, it was so mind blowing what he'd done. Things like that are part of the fabric of the office, not just the records that came out or the hangovers that got started there. We acted as sounding boards for a lot of musicians who knew we were great cheerleaders.

CHLOE: Heavenly was a clubhouse. Because it was right in the middle of Soho, people would very frequently not make it home after the pubs shut. It was like we had access to a twenty-four-hour gang hut. I can only remember sleeping overnight in the office once, and that was when I was having my flat's floors varnished and couldn't go home. I was supposed to stay with a friend in Stoke Newington but wound up going out after work, then having some sort of impromptu party back in the office and crashing out on the couch. That was unusual for me, though. I usually made it back home and then I'd come in in the morning and have to clean up the empty bottles from the night before. I think everyone spent the night on that couch quite frequently – they had toothbrushes in their desk drawers. That couch was not hygienic. It looked like you could get high just sitting on it.

TASH: There was a dark-green sofa in the office. It travelled with us from Wardour Street to Frith Street. I never had to sleep on it at night – Spencer did a few times – but it definitely rested a few of my hangovers. Jeff would say to me, 'If you aren't well, don't come in.' But Heavenly was always the best place to be after one of our mad nights. I had to be there to talk about what had happened. Nothing would keep me away. After Sunday nights at the Albany, I'd be there on that sofa with a polystyrene cup full of brandy at 10 a.m. in the morning trying to sit myself upright.

ANDREW WALSH (1997–present)
I had a proper job for a couple of years working in the offices of 'Britpop accountant' Frank Dixon before he was jailed. We looked after Heavenly and I was given the task of dealing with them. The first time I met Jeff and Martin, Jeff asked if I'd mind nipping out and buying beers for the meeting. That kind of thing didn't happen in an accountants' office. When they left, I followed them down the stairs and begged them for a job. I'm not usually impulsive, but something made me know it was the right thing to do. And it was: I'm still here almost twenty-three years later. Not long after starting, I came back from a traditional long lunch to the sight of Mani sat at my desk. He'd just joined Primal Scream and I was a massive Roses fan and somewhat overawed. I tried to casually introduce myself. He said, 'Yep, I know you're Andrew. Here's a list of your messages.' He'd sat answering my phone while I was at lunch. It was just that kind of place.

TASH: Sometimes you'd walk downstairs in the office and find, say, Bobby Gillespie teaching Beth Orton how to play Bobby 'Blue' Bland's version of 'It's Not the Spotlight'. Or there'd be Martin opening up his guitar case to show her some chord sequence. That was just standard. It was a world full of creatives all eager to share what they had learnt. As Keith Richards says, 'The best thing a musician's gravestone can say is, "I passed it on."' Now you can look up any song in existence and someone's done a YouTube video of how to play it. We had to rely on our mates, who were more than happy to pass it on.

CHLOE: After Jeff had kids, he always got in early every morning. By lunchtime he'd done everything on his 'To Do' list (always an incredibly tidy, handwritten list he kept on his desk) and was quite demanding in having you accompany him to the pub. I probably worked a three-hour day at least twice a week and would sometimes argue with him about having too much to do to leave the office. 'Pub. Now,' was the response. There was an extreme sense of responsibility to the artists we worked with and we got great results for the people who hired us in the press office. We certainly weren't fucking around the whole time but it did feel like this demented little raft of fun afloat in the po-faced seriousness of an industry that was designed to make money. Any time we'd run into someone from a company like Sony at the Ship there would be a sort of friendly banter of them making fun of us for having armfuls of 12-inches and drinking pints at lunchtime, and us making fun of them for wearing a suit and making loads of money. (D'oh!)

MARTIN: I often think the office was like how people used to say Apple was on Savile Row in the late sixties. People would just walk in all the time, and a lot of them were mad. You'd be working away at your desk and you'd look up and there was a load of people you didn't recognise. You just got on with it. Sometimes Jeff wouldn't even know who they were. 'Who's that?' 'No fucking idea, mate.' It might be some random who'd walked in off the street. People knew where the label was because the address was on every release, and they'd come by to see if Beth or Sarah Cracknell or The Chemical Brothers were in. And there were times when people we half knew would just start using it as their own personal office. There was a cockney rudeboy who would come in and ask if he could make a phone call. Two hours of full-volume shouting in patois later and you knew all about the fact that he's having a really brutal custody case

with his ex-wife in Jamaica. That kind of thing wasn't usually a problem but I do remember returning from lunch one day to discover no one has noticed we'd been relieved of three or four laptops.

JEFF BARRETT *(1990–present)*
You'd often get quite random people being brought along. One of the boys from Busted turned up with a friend of ours and a conversation ensued between him and a pilled-up, similarly aged fella from 22-20s.

'What sort of music do you make, then?'

'Erm, blues rock, I guess.'

'Oh. Ah. Right.'

One night, Kelly Osbourne turned up and started asking me whether I knew if Miles Kane was coming tonight. And another, Conor Oberst and his manager Nate Krenkel popped by for a beer with two girls before a Bright Eyes gig at the Astoria. After they left, Nicky [Moore, promoter of the Social, 1999–2005] said, 'I didn't know you knew Lucy Liu.' I didn't have a clue what she was on about. I often wonder what those people thought the office actually was.

SPENCER SMITH *(1992–2009)*
There was a caff opposite the Wardour Street office called Bar Bruno. I never liked going there, but people used to send me over to get takeaways when they were too lazy to go themselves. Jeff would always insist I got him a fry-up on a proper china plate rather than a paper one, which drove them mad.

TASH: Still standing though, Bar Bruno. Despite the huge pile of missing crockery.

MARTIN: It was incredibly helpful that we had Robin and Chloe running a thriving press office out of there in the mid-nineties. It meant that when we were quiet, there would still be records going out under the Heavenly umbrella, in mailers with Heavenly releases. That might mean records by Underworld or The Dust Brothers on

Junior Boy's Own, The Charlatans on Beggars Banquet, Primal Scream on Creation, David Holmes on Go! Beat, or Death in Vegas on Concrete. Often new Heavenly artists would get a lift from being associated with those bands.

CHLOE: In my memory, Robin played 'Born Slippy' to me on my very first day. 'We're going to be working on this.' Imagine starting a new job and the very first day you're handed a stone cold classic to work on! I remember *Trailer Park* being a really huge moment for the label and for me, just personally, as a press officer. But 'Born Slippy' became this complete monster and I'm still amazed I had any involvement with it at all. I've got the platinum disc and everything. The first Chemical Brothers album was an exciting time and it was really nice to be a part of The Charlatans return to success too. I remember being in Nottingham (for a night at the Bomb maybe?) and getting a call on my brick-sized mobile on a Sunday morning to hear that *Tellin' Stories* had gone to No. 1 and just jumping around in the middle of the street.

DANNY MITCHELL *(2004–present)*
I used to work at Smithfield's, a venue near the meat market. They had a lot of big beat nights there, as well as Leftorium [the Social spin-off night that featured DJ Harvey's last London residency]. The Heavenly Jukebox was still on at Turnmills, which was just round the corner. I caught wind that Heavenly were opening a bar in the West End with the help of the guy who ran Smithfield's so I hustled for a job there. If my favourite label was opening a bar, I wanted in. It didn't disappoint. It was pretty wild behind the bar when it opened, and in front of it, especially when Jeff, Martin, Robin and the gang would descend with whoever was in town with them that day.

Many of the bands on Heavenly played acoustic gigs in there. Doves played quite soon after the bar opened, Beth Orton too. I got as involved as I could. I'd work the bar, do the door or the cloakroom and eventually I'd promote my own nights in there.

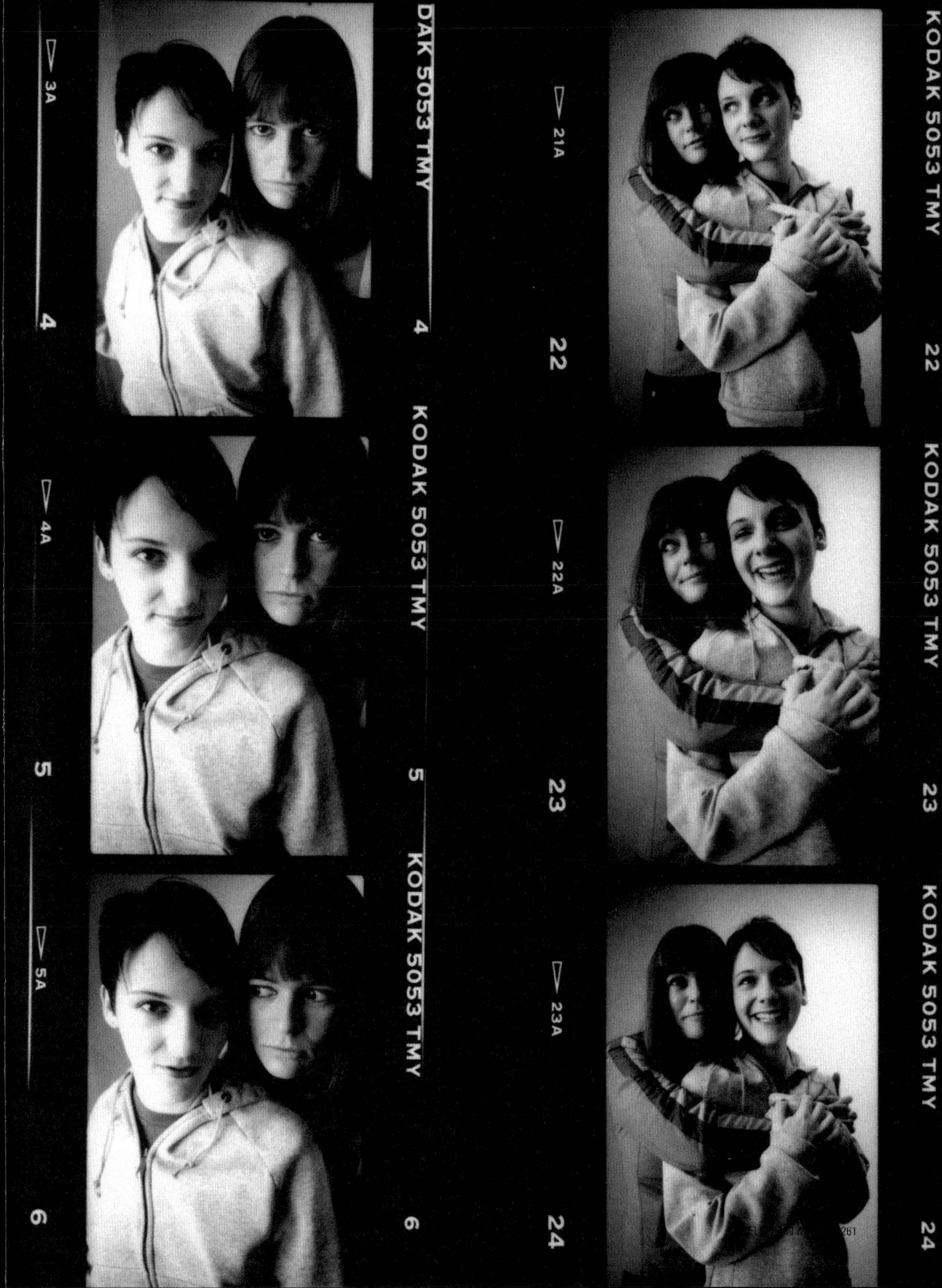
KODAK 5053 TMY
3A
4
4A
5
5A
6
21A
22
22A
23
23A
24

P.259: Spencer Smith and Chloe Walsh in the Wardour Street office, 1996.

Previous page: A 1996 photo shoot for DJs the Heavenly Birds – Heavenly's Chloe and Tash.

Above: Martin Kelly in Frith Street.

Right: Organised chaos in the office.

Next page (left): Carl Gosling and Danny Mitchell, the Heavenly Jukebox DJs; (right) Carl and Danny's corner of the office.

I was also working in a gallery just off New Oxford Street (TomTom, founded by, to quote Paul Gorman, 'British design hero' Tommy Roberts). Jeff, Martin and Nicky Moore would come in from time to time. That job ended in a full-on *Quadrophenia*-style walkout and a visit to the Social (obviously) to let off steam. I got talking to Nicky, who at that point ran the bar for Heavenly. She told me that Jeff had boxes of demos piling up in the office and he might need someone to listen to them. Looking back now that was quite surreal – a lifeline handed to me at the end of the bar in true Heavenly style. I knew what Heavenly was, I'd grown up with it since I was a kid, I was going to the gigs, partying or working at the clubs. I'd had the jukebox at the Social soundtracking all the years I worked there, which was an education in itself. I knew the music outside of the label which inspired the label.

I think Jeff was impressed that I'd made notes on every demo and didn't waste his time with too many howlers. [*Editor's note: this isn't quite true. In 1997 Tash knocked back a demo tape that featured the Beta Band's first EP with a letter that Spence had dictated to her, which rejected them simply because they couldn't spell Shepherd's Bush. This is to the office's eternal shame and the Beta Band's singer Steve Mason still refers to it to this day.*]

CARL GOSLING (promoter, the Social, 2005–present) I started working in the Heavenly office on my day off when I was working at Selectadisc, a record shop three streets away. I helped out at the Social, the sister venue and clubhouse of the label. Nicky was my boss and I did whatever was needed. Danny had started working there not too long before that and we made up a new young corner of the office by the door. One day I was busy putting CDs away into the racks at the shop when Robin and Martin came in. It was a busy Friday, the shop was packed, but the boys insisted on me going to the pub with them for a chat. I tried to explain that I couldn't just walk out in the middle of the day, but in the end I relented and walked down the road to meet them at the King of Corsica. Nicky was leaving, so they offered me the job of running the Social, programming all the music in the venue. Actually, they insisted I take it.

My first proper day at the office was the day immediately after the album launch for the first Magic Numbers album. I went to the party in Farringdon, which went on very late, and then we went back to the office. That was my first experience of the other side of my new workplace. I probably got home at 5 a.m. The next day, I struggled to get up and ended up turning up at eleven in the morning, late on my second day as a full-time member of staff. I walked in to find only Spencer there, and he was incredulous that I'd made it in. He sent me straight out to the shop to buy six cans of Red Stripe, of which he insisted I drank three.

CHLOE: I very clearly remember Jeff telling me solemnly one day, 'There's two types of people in the world, Chloe. People who take drugs and people who don't.' (Haven't been able to prove him wrong yet.) Jeff was a mentor and an amazing press officer. He could get anyone excited about anything. It was incredible to watch him. Since I'm still doing it for a living more than twenty years later I assume he taught me very well indeed. I do remember he would say that if we liked something then other people would as well. It was just our job to find them. I learnt from him the importance of knowing all the music critics' personal taste. In those days a lot of the job was listening to the music and working out exactly who you needed to champion it. Nowadays, no one answers their phones so that enthusiasm and excitement has to be conveyed via text or email. I'd much rather be able to invite people to the office to watch Jeff dance to something in front of his stereo. That was definitely the fastest route to print-media success.

ROBIN: There was always music in the office, every hour it was open. Ours and other people's, demos, remixes; mad music that Spence was making (under the name The Ooh Ooh Ah Aah Band) after he'd half taught himself to use GarageBand; Carl's heavy jungle mixtapes. All played at ear-splitting volume.

JEFF: One night, one of my oldest mates, Dave Fern, was stood there on the sofa punching the

air to a Vines tune. He turned to me and asked, 'Why haven't you ever taken me to this place before?' He'd literally been there every other week for the previous five years.

ANDREW: Over the years, Jeff blew up more speakers than Phil Spector. He'd play music at a level that obliterated any possible conversation. Once every few weeks, another speaker would pop.

MARTIN: There used to be a big pile of speakers in the corner of the office. Tannoy was the chosen make. Occasionally we'd get them re-coned but usually they'd just sit there.

ANDREW: We've got a pair of speakers in the office now that are unblowable. I've spent a fortune on them. Jeff's had a few goes but they've held out so far.

We had lots of mad ideas in the pub. What's different about Heavenly is that people would actually make the ideas happen.

MARTIN: Robin's mad pub idea was the Sunday Social. When he first brought that in, I kind of creaked: 'I can't do that any more . . . I'm too old. It sounds like hard work going out every week.' The more he explained it, and was passionate about it, the more convinced I became that it was actually a brilliant, necessary idea. Normally that wouldn't happen in a record company office. At Heavenly there's always been a support network of other nutters around you who are willing to back you up. That blur of socialising and work came with the territory, it's where the best ideas came from and got acted on. When we were in Wardour Street, Robert Linney used to call those pub ideas 'Ship talk', after the pub we used to frequent back then. Although he was taking the piss, 'Ship talk' was what kept us afloat and interested for years. Jeff has always been amazing in those situations, encouraging left-of-centre ideas and also helping friendships grow. So much of what's always made Heavenly work is that it's a group of friends, even if the friends have changed over the years.

ANDREW: When we moved to Frith Street, the rent was extortionate. Money was so tight I ended up becoming friends with the bailiff who would come round on behalf of HMRC every month. We became such good mates that I was the only person on his round that he'd allow to pay with a cheque rather than a banker's draft; allowing us more time to try to survive. It wasn't until Doves and The Magic Numbers broke we could make ends meet.

DANNY: A lot of working there was about finding your own place. To a certain extent I had to just get on and work it out myself as there wasn't exactly a set way of doing things. I mean, I started coming in more often as I didn't have my own computer or a phone at the time and I was getting deep into those boxes of demos and needed to get back to people. I asked Spence if I could commandeer the photocopier table and set it up as a desk. I got this guy who fixed the office computers who everyone just knew as 'X-Files' to fix an ancient iMac and set me up with an email address. I guess that made it official.

Carl [Gosling] had just started working in the office around the same time as me, helping Nicky before she eventually left, and he took over her job. We made our own space in the corner and had a blast. The bar was a short walk away, the office was a short walk back – work, pleasure, pleasure, work, it literally rolled into one.

MARTIN: We would all end up doing a bit of everything. We'd all have to be tour managers, do edits on tracks, we'd have to promote little gigs or do the lights at gigs. We were each doing whatever was needed in order to make stuff happen. I'm sure that still goes on there now.

ROBIN: I remember Robert giving me a DAT of a new track David Holmes had made, telling me to go to Porky's, the cutting room on Shaftsbury Avenue, and get an acetate made of it. I didn't have a clue what I was doing and managed to get the thing re-EQed, which made it totally useless for David to play out. There were a lot of things like that, where

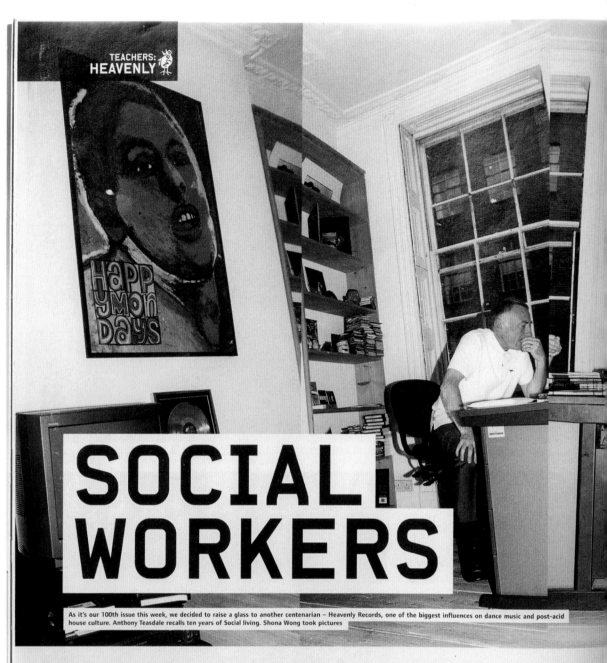

TEACHERS:
HEAVENLY

SOCIAL WORKERS

As it's our 100th issue this week, we decided to raise a glass to another centenarian – Heavenly Records, one of the biggest influences on dance music and post-acid house culture. Anthony Teasdale recalls ten years of Social living. Shona Wong took pictures

HEAVENLY RECORDS have a cool office. Not cool in the Ikea, weird shaped desk way, but cool in the picture of George Best and Shaun Ryder way; minimalism mixed with books, records, posters - all testament to over ten years of putting out cool. Based in Soho, Heavenly is the sort of record company that many of us dream of working for when we're idealistic teenagers. There are no subsidised restaurants and big boardrooms with flip charts at one end. Instead, there's a bustle about the place, a feeling that something is happening. Each room is staffed by people making phone calls, listening to music, perusing the press and the Internet while icons that range from the Stones to nameless heroes of Northern soul look down, making sure it stays that way. Just as at major labels you can feel the power of money coursing through the building, so here the energy comes from the music the label puts out.

You might wonder what a dance mag is doing covering Heavenly. After all, perhaps only a quarter of their releases have been pure dance music, with another quarter evolving

from the clubs if not for the clubs. We're here because Heavenly were teaming up Primal Scream with Andy Weatherall when no-one would go near them. We're here because of Flowered Up, that mythical bunch of scoundrels from inner London who made some of the best guitar records of the 90s then disappeared. We're also here because their club, the Heavenly Social, not only launched the careers of the Chemical Brothers, it also changed the way that many of us went out. In short, Heavenly have made more of an impact on dance music than most other dance labels put together. And as they enter their 11th year, the imprint are unleashing their 100th release, a gleaming, glittery website, that'll buck the trend of such things by actually being interesting to read and not clinically boring.

The founder of Heavenly is one Jeff Barrett, a freckle faced former record shop owner and music nut who, along with faithful partner Martin Kelly, set up the label in 1990. Before that the pair had been press officers at Creation records, pushing not only the artists on the label, but bands such as New

Order and Happy Mondays for Factory. By the end of the 80s, two groups were emerging who seemed to encapsulate the new spirit in British music that was emerging in the wake of acid house – the Mondays and the Stone Roses. "It was great 'cos we were working with some great bands – imagine doing the press on 'Bummed' (Happy Mondays' seminal second album from 1988)" said Jeff. "You had some unbelievers, but it was like a punk rock mission, 'Right you don't like it, you're a cunt,' sort of thing.'"

Martin agrees, "It's great when things like that happen 'cos you feel the ball rolling and it went from being a really small thing to being a national thing. When they did the G Mex – I didn't think they did gigs that big."

The pair decided to form Heavenly out of the ashes of an old label Sub Aqua as a 'natural progression of what was happening at the time'. As an enthusiastic clubber, Barrett, then aged 27, was seen as a perfect 'in' to others who wanted to push themselves in the music industry. Des Penny, manager of the

(L-R) Jeff, Spencer, Andrew and Martin

nascent Flowered Up was one of them, as Jeff remembers.

"There were these kids in London, they were ten years younger than the Mondays and they looked great – they were casuals, they were working class and they epitomised what was going down. London needed something and Flowered Up were it. They were kids that went to these clubs, that wore those clothes, that danced to this music."

Taking them on, the press officer nous of Martin and Jeff came into play, bagging the band both a *Melody Maker* and an NME cover before the group had even released their first single. By the very fact that they looked so good and had interesting things to say, the pair were able to get a level of publicity for the band that they hadn't earned. Yet, their first single, 'It's On' did not disappoint.

Just as Shaun Ryder's Little Hulton brogue was there for all to hear on the Monday's tunes, Flowered Up's singer Liam gave the group a signature of its own with his norf Lahhhndaaan

twang. And just as the Mondays had Bez, so Flowered Up too had that most early 90s of pop accessories – a drug addled dancer with a maraca. In their case it was Barry Mooncult, a man who spent all the band's gigs wearing a huge, foam flower round his neck. He was also responsible for one the most famous parties of that era, as Martin testifies.

"He was a glazier and through working on this job he managed to get the keys to this big fucking mansion – an Arab's mansion."

Jeff disagrees. "No, it was owned by a racehorse owner who'd done a runner on VAT and tax evasion and his house got seized by the government and for some reason they employed Barry Mooncult's glazing firm to go and fix the windows so they could put it back on the market. Anyway, he went and cut a set of keys, and before you know it Flowered Up are squatting it and having a party. They'd been running into town during the week with a set of Polaroids showing the master bedroom, which was mirrored

from floor to ceiling with a circular revolving bed. So the first day they racked it out, pushed a button and...." (makes snorting action)

Even though Flowered Up have a notoriety unequalled by any of the label's other artists, Heavenly was also the first home of the Manic St Preachers, whose angry philosophising found favour with Barratt and Kelly, even if they did move on after two singles. But it is St Etienne who are the group most closely associated with the identity of the label. Recently signed to Mantra, Martin is still their manager and their press campaign emanates from Heavenly. Jeff remembers how *Melody Maker* journalist Bob Stanley played him a track he'd made with partner Pete Wiggs.

"Bob was aware of what we were doing and he came up to me and told me he'd done a track. So I met him in a pub on a Wednesday night in Shepherd's Bush and I put a Walkman on and listened to 'Only Love Can Break Your Heart'. I thought it was absolutely fucking brilliant, totally, totally brilliant."

your job description just blurred into something completely different.

DANNY: I knew how to use Photoshop so I ended up doing countless posters and a few record sleeves. We were trying to make things work with no money, trying to be as creative as possible.

ANDREW: We made Carl tour-manage The Duke Spirit [managed by Heavenly] for a gig in Iceland on the day before the gig. He'd never done it before. 'You'll be fine, mate. Now go home and get your passport.'

DANNY: 'Keep the receipts.'

CARL: There were no rules or plans for how I was to work. I'm not 100 per cent sure Robin or Martin really knew what the job they were offering entailed. I was given a venue and told to basically do what I liked. Bring in new club nights, book bands, come up with ideas for artwork, exhibitions, screenings. Myself and Danny formed a close bond as the office new boys and quickly threw ourselves into Social life and nights. The venue was soon putting on bands three or four nights a week – full rock 'n' roll bands, sometimes four or five in one night, on a stage in a room that frankly was not made for it. But somehow it worked. We worked strange hours and had absolute freedom to come and go. But mainly we stayed right there, arriving early and leaving late, because that was where things happened.

SPENCER: I went drinking after work in Soho one night and headed back to the office to book a cab on the EMI account. Somehow, I ended up inviting a bunch of strangers who were stood outside into the office for a drink. The next thing I remember is being woken up at home by a phone call from the work-experience guy asking where I was, and why there was broken glass and blood all over the office floor. I got him to clean it up and headed into the office. When I got there, we found a handbag that one of the strangers had

left behind. We looked inside for a number for the owner and found one along with a bag of eighty pills. After much debate we did the right thing. Kept twenty pills, put sixty back then called her.

CHLOE: I'm very thankful that my time at Heavenly was pre-technology. There's not much stored in the memory banks and no one had a camera phone. I seem to be the only one who remembers Pat Kane from Hue and Cry coming in to show Robin and me the not-yet-launched *Guardian* website on the new-fangled internet. He was wearing a suit and had been carrying this massive laptop around which he couldn't get to work, so he was sweating buckets and mopping his brow after walking up the stairs in Wardour Street ('Really hot down here, innit?'). Jeff walked in, clocked us and a sweaty Pat Kane, and gave the most incredible look of 'What the FUCK are you two clowns up to now?!' He walked backwards out of our office shaking his head in disgust.

ANDREW: There was a point where our cleaner moved into the office without telling anyone. Her husband had just died and she was obviously cut up, so she ended up spending more and more time in there. Sometimes you'd come in really late for a party and she'd be asleep in the mad cupboard under the stairs that Robin worked in.

CARL: One Friday evening I was smashed, walking to the office from the Social with a DJ and his mate who'd been playing. When I got there, I couldn't work out how to open the front door on the street. It took me so long, I pissed myself. We eventually got in and I went to the toilet, where I cut my pants off with my beard scissors, forgot to pull my trousers back up and fell down the stairs, losing both shoes in the process. Somehow, they ended up in the DJ's bag and went with him back to Glasgow. I couldn't find my shoes anywhere, and the cleaner was asleep in Robin's room at the time so I stole hers. I went home and got bollocked by my girlfriend for having no pants on and wearing a pair of women's Hi-Tec trainers that clearly weren't mine.

CHLOE: By the time I left I'd worked there for a sixth of my life. I felt like if I didn't leave I might stay forever, but I couldn't think of anywhere else I'd rather work. It seemed like madness to go and work in another bit of the British music business, leave my friends to work with people who took themselves too seriously and weren't having half as much fun as we were. So I took a job in New York. Jeff was kind enough to throw me a leaving do in a pub in west London which continued for the entire weekend at various flats and was responsible for the birth of at least two children that I know of.

DANNY: When The Magic Numbers record came out, they were all over radio, their gigs were sold out everywhere and I was getting paid to travel over the country and abroad to see bands, all on EMI money. I thought that was the norm when really it had been a very long time coming.

When the EMI deal ended, the only thing we managed to retain was the name and the logo. Heavenly had to be rebuilt from the ground up. We set up an office on Portobello Road with Carl from the Social. We had literally nothing for about three months. The real kicker was that the last Doves album, *Kingdom of Rust*, came out around then and it missed out on the No. 1 spot to Lady Gaga by about twelve sales. None of us had our eye on it: we'd usually all go and buy a couple of copies, and get our mates to as a kind of good luck voodoo thing. It was tragic. Although we got thrown a lifeline by the Cooperative [later to become part of [PIAS]] we struggled. Physical sales suddenly disappeared, nothing was selling. I guess from the outside we were still perceived as a major-label indie but on the inside it was back to square one and we had to relearn what it was to be an independent label in a very challenging time.

JEFF: Sometime early in 2008 EMI was bought by a venture capitalist who immediately put the company on hold while analysing what it was he had vastly overpaid for. So Andrew and I started going fishing. Those days spent by the water inspired us to start a website that would reflect

the conversations we had when we were outside. Records, films, books and all aspects of the natural world were discussed and, not long after, with Robin's help, Caught by the River was born. At first it was just a site where we posted diary entries. It was a fanzine, presented in a different way but with the same kind of passion that those homemade, usually music-based publications were built on. Before long it developed its own language and started to promote small-scale events before eventually presenting stages at several different UK festivals.

Eventually the deal went south and the money disappeared. It left us in a perilous situation where we didn't know if we could continue. It was pretty scary, to be honest. But, in reality, it forced us to rethink ourselves and that led us to become something much closer to what we were when we started out. This was definitely helped and assisted by this website that we'd initially just thought of as a way of killing time until EMI sorted itself out, but what we created in that time became a very important factor in the future of the label.

We moved to a smaller office and scaled the operation right back. There was so much uncertainty but Caught by the River was one of the things that helped us reinvent the label and find an audience we'd lost during our years with EMI – it was us taking a DIY approach to communication. It chimed with people and it gave us a different way of thinking.

The rebirth of Heavenly applied a similar approach to how we'd run Caught by the River. We had to become a small thing. The way the business was changing meant we had to do that in order to survive. It allowed us to think differently. Thinking about small things on very little money makes you more creative. And, as with the site and with how we'd run something like the Sunday Social before, we carried a firm belief in the motto 'Don't ask, don't get.' Caught by the River introduced us to new people, and allowed us to have different

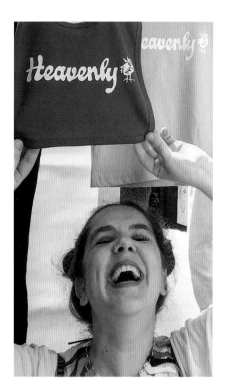

conversations and to mix things up. It created
a new energy that really fed into the label.
Different people were interested, people like
Luke Turner from the *Quietus* and the writer
Ben Myers. We'd gone from being a bunch of
mad pissheads who were putting records out
through a major to a bunch of slightly less
pissed heads talking about fishing and the great
outdoors and people like the sound recordist
Chris Watson. The *Quietus* wouldn't have been
interested in our big EMI releases but when we
signed TOY they were one of the earliest and
most vocal supporters of the band. We were still
doing what we thought we'd always done, which
was to create a platform for artists to express
themselves. Having a DIY aesthetic gave us
a new sense of identity. More importantly
for me, it kept me sane when I thought I was
losing it.

KATHERINE CANTWELL *(2013–present)*
I was pretty nervous the first time I walked into
the Heavenly office. I wasn't really sure what
an independent record label looked like. I had
it in my mind that it would be filled to the brim
with records, with great music playing loudly,
flyers strewn on the table, magazines stacked
on shelves and album sleeves and band photos
taking over every inch of the walls. That was the
dream: 219 Portobello Road didn't disappoint. You
could tell magic happened there. It felt magnetic
and it clearly had a wild energy to it . . . not least
because they were playing Daniel Avery's *Drone
Logic* incredibly loudly. I loved guitar bands, I'd
not yet heard electronic music like it. Like I'd
dreamt, there were iconic posters of Don Letts
and Dexys Midnight Runners on the walls, and
stacks of records piled everywhere. I didn't ever
want to leave. I started working one day a week
in between my university studies. I wanted to go
into music journalism but I got told by the *NME*
that my writing was OK but that my passion was
clearly in 'championing bands to anyone who was
willing to listen'. That skill of getting behind talent
and shouting from the rooftops is one I think each
record label should have. It's certainly been part
of the remit for everyone who's ever worked at
Heavenly. With Jeff leading the charge, of course.

*Opposite (clockwise): Katherine feeling Heavenly; Diva
and the Heavenly Jukebox in the Old Compton Street
office; Katherine, Daisy, Diva and Jeff enjoying some
big French ones in one of the locals.*

we have moved...

Heavenly 72 Wardour Street, London W1V 3HP Planet Earth
telephone 071 437 3350, facsimile 071 437 3317

DAISY GOODWIN *(2017–present)*
I first hung out with the Heavenly crew when
I worked for the Crow's Nest at Glastonbury,
which was run by Tony Crean – a friend of my
family and of Heavenly's. That year King Gizzard
played a mind-blowing set in the tent. The whole
thing was packed to bursting point, rocking back
and forth with hundreds of sweaty, moshing
bodies. Then suddenly the power cut out. We
were all manically running around trying to get
things up and going again. When we finally got
the power back they played about three chords
of 'Head On/Pill' and then stopped dead.
That was it – a perfect rock 'n' roll moment.
A couple of years later, when I was working
at Friendly Records in Bristol, I got a call out
of the blue from Jeff. He asked me, point
blank, if I wanted a job at the label. I couldn't
believe it. I finished off my exams and moved
to London the next day with a suitcase and
never looked back. As Jeff said to me on a
Soho rooftop later that year, 'This is the Best
Fucking Job in the World.' And he couldn't be
more right.

When you step into the Heavenly world you are
family. We've got each other's back through
thick and thin. The times I feel it the most is at
the end of an amazing festival when everyone
comes together on the last night to dance to
records Jeff is playing somewhere on-site. A
lovely weathered group of friends joining in for
one last dance. You will never feel a stronger
sense of belonging. How then do you choose
the highest of the Heavenly highs? Hard, but
this is one of mine. At End of the Road in 2018
Jeff, Diva and I were asked to be the Heavenly
Jukebox – the collective DJ name for whoever
from the office is up for playing records – at
the Cider Bus. We played for six hours straight.
For the first couple it was just happy strays and
hardcore fans. But once the headliners stopped
playing our tent was suddenly heaving, filling
up with new faces, old friends and our bands
Boy Azooga and The Orielles. It felt like a proper
scene and truly was a real moment of pure pride
for me. There's no better feeling than having a
crowd chant, 'One last song! One last song!' We

ended with Larry Levan's mix of 'Stand on the
Word'. Everyone went mad.

DIVA HARRIS *(2015–present)*
It's weirdly easy to forget, when you're in and
around it every day, that the Heavenly office
itself, the room, is beautiful and full of cool shit.
The thing that jolts me into remembering is that
sometimes, when people come over for the first
time, they want to take a picture. There is lots of
great art – and that's definitely largely down to
Danny's eye/handiwork – but also, more than that,
we work surrounded by the detritus of a thousand
mad, and mostly brilliant (I think I can say that)
ideas; the detritus of the label's history as well as
that of our personal histories and interests, lots of
them intersecting. It's hard to explain.

The Office-with-a-capital-O is just as much
everything on the walls and surfaces and
floors of the office-with-a-lower-case-o as it
is all of us. It's the various Paul Cannell birds
next to the wobbly stacks of bird books; the
glow of a neon sign across a framed portrait of
Pee-wee Herman; box files of vintage esoteric-
interest magazines about the countryside next
to a cardboard tray of poppers; a poster for a
long-ago Dexys show (with a portrait of Kevin
Rowland painted by hand by a Bollywood poster
artist), juxtaposed with the one in the loo which
says, 'I really think the Rolling Stones should
stop now.' There's the actual Heavenly Jukebox,
beautifully decorated by Pete [Fowler], which
used to stand at the end of the bar in the
Social but now, beyond fixture, is essentially a
gorgeous and very space-invasive feature light.
And while we are on the subject of not working,
the thing which most defines the Heavenly
office in my mind is the bastard soundsystem
which, in the entire five-ish years I've earned my
bread, has almost literally never once worked
as it should. What a farce.

The thing that we're all united by as people is
the same thing that unites the disparate objects
in the office; it's a cataclysm of rabid fannery, be
that of music, art, books, mags, stupid gags etc.
We are all voracious enthusiasts, bursting to tell

our mates about it, whatever it is at the time, and whether that's with our gobs or our websites or our lacquers or the walls. That's the real magic of Heavenly; for me, that explains it better than any of the thousand anecdotes about bands, or misbehaviour, or nights that were so good that someone went home wearing the cleaner's shoes. The walls make tangible that indefinable Heavenly stuff that floats around in the ether and our brains and veins and bonds us all together like some kind of blood-cult.

CARL: Heavenly has given me new ways of thinking and living. It's given me the inspiration, support, freedom and confidence to have an idea and just fucking get on and do it. It taught me to never fear asking people to do stuff, whoever they are. It taught me that good ideas can be had – no, will be had – in the pub on a Monday lunchtime. Like many other people working in the same industry, I'm blessed with a job that entails listening to a lot of music. Mine also involves working with bands and DJs and bringing people together to talk and dance. And I get to do it with a bunch of my best friends.

ROBIN: At the end of the day, the fact that Heavenly has always been such a strong community and a tight friendship group is such a beautiful thing. But it did always raise the question as to whether any of us could work anywhere else.

DANNY: I was pretty much unemployable before I started there.

MARTIN: I've found out since leaving ten years ago that I'm still unemployable.

TASH: After leaving, I learnt that I couldn't work anywhere else. Of course, I've had to but I still struggle with authority.

CARL: Work in that office never really ends, because it never really feels like work has even started in the first place.

CHLOE: It's definitely a bit like a dysfunctional family. Sometimes bickering and getting on each others' nerves; often someone having some sort of personal crisis that the whole office was aware of. The thing I'll never forget is how I would wake up every morning genuinely excited to get into the office because I was going to see five of the funniest people I'd ever met in my life. Monday mornings especially, hearing everyone recap whatever they'd been up to over the weekend was the most brilliant start to the week. I've never been able to replicate that since. I've worked in offices with great people and made incredible friends through work, but there was something about the Heavenly misfits that made it the most joyful and hilarious place. I must've laughed more in those four years than all the time since put together. I wish we'd all kept diaries but we were having far too much fun. Like they say about the sixties . . . if you can remember everything that happened at Heavenly, then you weren't really feeling Heavenly.

MARTIN: If the Heavenly office was a person, it would be Jeff Barrett. It's a reflection of who he is. Hard working, very sociable, jumps from idea to idea, hard to keep up with, keeps antisocial hours, is fun to be around and a brilliant laugh.

Bits and pieces behind Jeff's desk in Frith Street.

Jeff in the Monmouth Street office, 1992.

That voice. Starless and Bible-black. Pure soul dredged from deep, deep down at the molten core of it all. Once heard, never shaken; a sound that signifies a life lived fully, sideways in reverse, always going downtown in the wrong direction. The voice is one thing, the songs it sings open up a whole different dimension. There are desperate prayers aimed at beneficent gods and psychedelic route maps for midnight journeys straight into the heart of the strange.

That voice belongs to Mark Lanegan. A towering musical presence for the best part of four decades, there are few singers who can consistently beckon you onto their particular trip in the way Lanegan can.

Although Lanegan became a full-time Heavenly artist in 2013 with the release of the covers album *Imitations*, his relationship with Jeff began when Heavenly Songs signed his publishing for 2004's masterful *Bubblegum*. After beginning working with the label, Lanegan hit something of a purple patch as his Heavenly songs took the listener down myriad paths, from *Imitations*' worn down and wonderful take on 'You Only Live Twice' to 'Stitch It Up's clattering ram raid on 2019's *Somebody's Knocking*.

There is perhaps no more apposite a title for a Mark Lanegan record than *Straight Songs of Sorrow*. These tracks are splinters from a broken heart, love letters never sent and confession-box tales delivered by that voice as it floats over spartan acoustics and junk-shop electronics. It's absolute proof of Lanegan's status as a true one-off, the kind of performer others just think they are. *Robin Turner*

MARK LANEGAN
When I first met Jeff Barrett I don't think I even knew that he had a label. I was wilfully ignorant of many things business-related, and unintentionally ignorant of most things in general back then. I can't remember exactly where or how we met but I will never forget the impact he had on me because I was instantly taken with his balls-out enthusiasm for my music and his madcap,

rapid-fire willingness to just start throwing ideas as to what I should listen to and what I should do musically. I remember thinking 'Wow, I can't believe this dude knows who the fuck I am, and he also has an endless stream of good ideas. What the hell?'

Pretty quickly I came to realise he owned a label, one that Doves – one of my favourite new bands at the time (and still to this day) – had just made their first record for. There was no chance of me recording for Jeff, since I was in a long-term contract with Beggars Banquet/4AD at the time, yet Jeff remained my most staunch supporter and the ultimate enthusiast, telling me about cool new music, continuing to toss ideas at me whenever we were together. And never with any personal stake in it, just a pure love of the music. He eventually became one of my publishers, which I dug because it meant I would see him more often, and his zeal for life was infectious, in that I was always uplifted by his presence. Eventually free of all my other deals, the first thing I did was call Jeff on the phone and said 'Hey, Jeff, I'm finally free. Can we make records together now?' And he immediately said yes. Jeff has done things for me and given me advice that no one else had, or would, ever give. After almost thirty years in the business I had finally found a true home at Heavenly. To be working with a real record man, an astute and wily lover of music I looked up to as a kind of father figure, even though he's just a short few years older than me, has been the blessing of my life in music. The rich history of Heavenly rivals that of any label and its legacy. That should be celebrated by lovers of quality, cutting-edge music forever.

Gazing from the shore: Heavenly hero Mark Lanegan signed to the label in 2013.

THE

ORIELLES

BLUE SUITCASE
(DISCO WRIST)

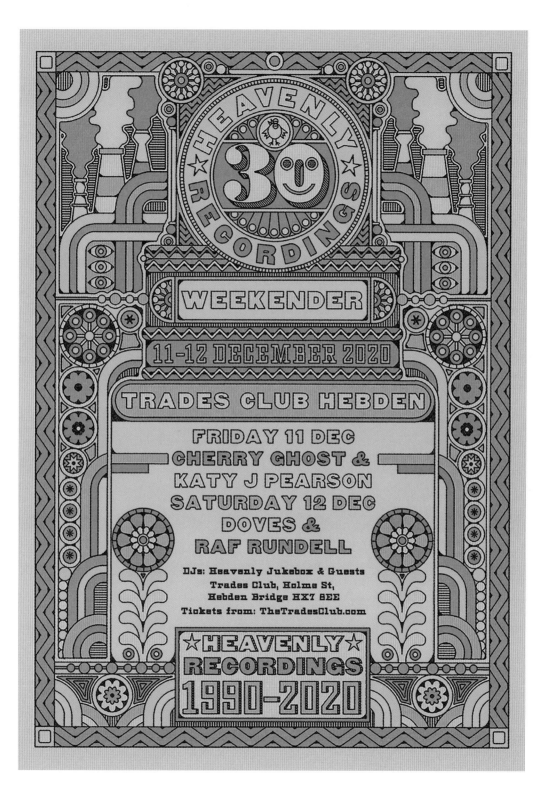

This page: Perky pop-fuzz from Dutch family Blom – having been blown away by a performance at Salford's Sounds from the Other City festival, Heavenly released Pip Blom's debut album Boat in 2019.

Opposite: Dream-pop from Down Under, Hatchie (Harriette Pilbeam) released her debut album Keepsake on Heavenly in 2019.

The last piece of this jigsaw is the first piece of the next one.

Working Men's Club are a group who fuse the energy of the dancefloor to the ecstasy of a rock 'n' roll gig, and they do it very, very well. Coming together a lifetime after Flowered Up's loose-limbed, full-pelt party (a band who similarly brought together the sounds of supposedly conflicting environments), they are a lifeline thrown from the north of England just when it needs one. Their twenty-minute, gauntlet-thrown live sets build upon a similar singular determination as shown in the early Manics gigs or in TOY's barrage of white noise or King Gizzard's all-enveloping, end-times roadshow; their steely, machine-made backbone as clipped and precise as any of the body-rockin' electro on Don Letts' second Roxy LP or the low-slung funk of Weatherall's Orielles remix.

At a point where music appears to have fractured and rearranged into algorithmic playlists, where no one knows anything but pretends they know every damn thing, and nostalgia remains the strongest currency, along comes a group to make you dance, sing . . . anything. A group to fall for, to follow, to believe in.

And, really, just how magical is that? *Robin Turner*

Working Men's Club are without doubt one of the most exciting groups that have ever landed in my life. And that precedes Heavenly. They're one of the most exciting groups I've ever worked with, I've ever liked, I've ever seen. Syd is one of the most talented kids I know. He's got a strong work ethic, a vision and a total belief. He's so beyond his years at just eighteen and a half.

We'd first heard about this new band from the Calder Valley because they were looked after by Damian Morgan, who manages The Orielles. We knew it was early so didn't bend his ear about it too much but then we saw an early press shot of the band – three kids who looked really

great, very striking. They looked like the greatest band you'd never heard. I asked Damian what was happening and he said they were putting out a one-off single on the Manchester label Melodic. He sent us 'Bad Blood' and we knew immediately we had to see them, so we got them a gig the following week at the Social. They day they played, 'Bad Blood' went on the BBC 6 Music playlist, so they were no longer under the radar. Thankfully, the Social being our bar, we didn't tell any industry people that they were playing.

That first time I watched Syd perform, I could tell that he had it. He looked great, like a young Tim Burgess or a young Billy Mackenzie. A pin-up pop kid. They hadn't been going very long – a matter of months. They obviously weren't anywhere near fully formed, and I didn't realise just how un-fully formed they were. There was something special there though. I left that show with a lot of people saying, 'Bloody hell, that was a bit good, wasn't it?' But that wasn't what I got. There was something I couldn't put my finger on, but my instincts told me there's something not just really good in there, there's something potentially really amazing.

I spent most of the night after the gig stood outside the Social drinking beer with Syd, talking and asking him questions, really listening to him. Asking him, asking him, asking him. I really liked him. He could talk, he could listen, he could articulate. He was obviously clever. His songs weren't stupid, too. I could already tell that the words were good, and that he really did care about it. I agreed to go see him again the following week, playing at the Trades Club. And I said to him, 'We're going to come up next Friday and it's your turn to ask the questions. Because I'll be honest with, you made an impression on me.'

I came home and I slept and they were on my mind. I woke up, they were still on my mind. Wendy said, 'What were they like?' And I said, 'I think I'm gonna work with them.' I just had a feeling, and you don't get that many like that.

So I went up that night, and we met and they did ask a couple of questions, but they just wanted a record deal, really. They liked our label. I know we obviously made an impression on them. Daisy came with me so it wasn't just like they were talking to granddad. We made a handshake agreement about a deal that night. Signing them was one of the smartest hunches I've ever followed.

So I lucked out with Working Men's Club. I've been lucky with so many of the groups I work with, in that I've been given the opportunity to actually do the thing I hope I've learnt how to do over the all these years – which is to be able to help a group make a record. How to help them realise what they've got. That's a job where you can't ever explain to your parents what it is you do; sometimes you can't even explain

it to yourself. That first night I watched them, I thought to myself, 'I think I know how to do this. I think I get where he's coming from.' I even came up with a producer idea that night as well, and Ross Orton has played a crucial part in their development. This was before it was all drum machine, back when the band was much more traditionally structured. There was so much going through my head, watching them do a twenty-minute set at our bar.

The week after we signed the band, Syd sent me a demo of 'Teeth', saying, 'I'm keen to know what you think of this because I'm not sure whether it's a Working Men's Club song or not.' And I thought, 'What do you mean? What is it if it's not?' So I played this heavy, primal, programmed drum thing and thought, 'Wow, OK!' Somehow I knew that he'd had that inside him but hadn't

found it until now. Of course it's a Working Men's Club song. I think my reply to him was: 'Go put that through the band filter, get that in the practice room now. I can't wait to see what that sounds like.'

One of the founding members of the group was already pursuing a singer-songwriter, Laurel Canyon-type thing outside of the group, so we knew she would eventually be leaving. The other founding member didn't want to be that electronic, he wanted it to be more of a guitar group. So straight after signing, this group fractured. And from that, I watched this seventeen-year-old kid put together this astonishing new group. Astonishing looking, astonishing sounding. He kept sending me these demos, these electronic tracks kept coming. I realised we'd just struck gold.

The thrill of working with Syd and with his band is extra special for me because thirty-plus years on from getting the buzz I got when I started out, seeing the Mary Chain and Primal Scream in the mid-eighties, then East Village and then Flowered Up at the start of this journey – the same buzz I got hearing Andrew DJ – I'm having it again. And you know what? After all this time, how good is that? I'm still believing!

But it isn't just me – Heavenly has never been just me. I just happened to start the ball rolling and I'm the one with the biggest gob. All of us feel this way, we're all daft for music. There's a lot of luck involved in the business and where I sit today, thirty years in, I feel lucky, and that's because I know that all of this can carry on after me. As David Holmes once said to me, 'Music forever!' *Jeff Barrett*

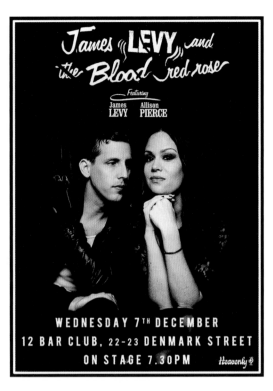

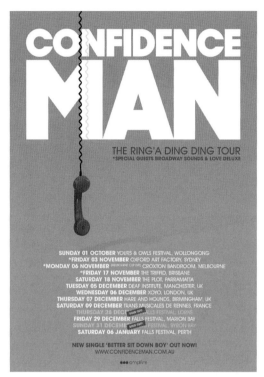

Right: 'Pearson is a rare thing in that she's emerged as a fully-formed new artist' (Music Week). Katy J. Pearson's second single 'Take Back the Radio' helped soundtrack the summer of 2020.

Opposite (bottom): Henry and Esmé from The Orielles at Stockport's Eve Studios during the summer 2019 recording of 'Come Down on Jupiter'.

This page: Henry Carlyle-Wade on stage with The Orielles.

HVNLP1

HVNLP2

HVNLP3

HVNLP4

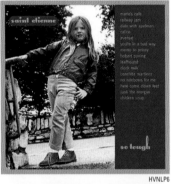

HVNLP6

HVNLP7

HVNLP8

HVNLP9

HVNLP10

HVNLP11

HVNLP12

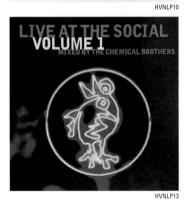

HVNLP13

HVNLP14

HVNLP15

HVNLP16

HVNLP17

HVNLP18

HVNLP19

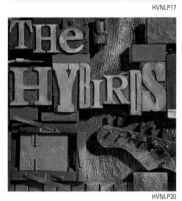

HVNLP20

HVNLP21

HVNLP22

HVNLP23

HVNLP24

HVNLP25

HVNLP26

HVNLP27

HVNLP28

HVNLP29

HVNLP30

HVNLP31

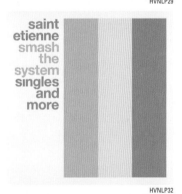

HVNLP32

HVNLP33

HVNLP34

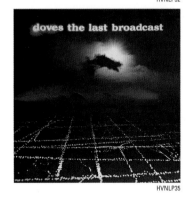

HVNLP35

HVNLP36

HVNLP37

HVNLP38

HVNLP39

HVNLP40

HVNLP41

HVNLP42

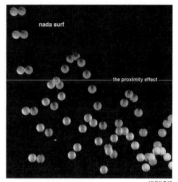

HVNLP43

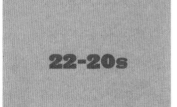

HVNLP44

HVNLP45

HVNLP46

HVNLP47

HVNLP48

HVNLP49

HVNLP50

HVNLP51

HVNLP52

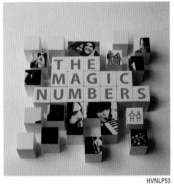
HVNLP53

HVNLP54

HVNLP55

HVNLP56

HVNLP57

HVNLP58

HVNLP59

HVNLP60

HVNLP61

HVNLP62

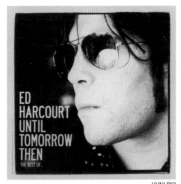

HVNLP63

HVNLP64

HVNLP65

HVNLP66

HVNLP67

HVNLP68

HVNLP69

HVNLP70

HVNLP71

HVNLP72

HVNLP73

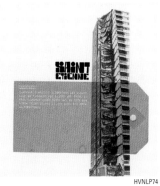

HVNLP74

HVNLP75

HVNLP76

HVNLP77

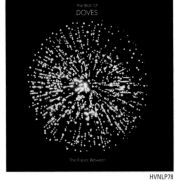

HVNLP78

HVNLP79

HVNLP80

HVNLP81

HVNLP82

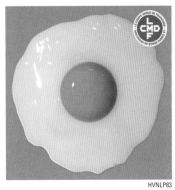

HVNLP83

HVNLP84

HVNLP85

HVNLP86

HVNLP87

HVNLP88

HVNLP89

HVNLP90

HVNLP91

HVNLP92

HVNLP93

HVNLP94

HVNLP95

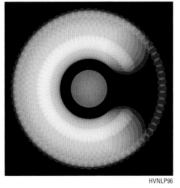

HVNLP96

HVNLP97

HVNLP98

HVNLP99

HVNLP100

HVNLP100RS

HVNLP101

HVNLP102

HVNLP103

HVNLP104

HVNLP105

HVNLP106

HVNLP107

HVNLP108

HVNLP109

HVNLP110

HVNLP111

HVNLP112

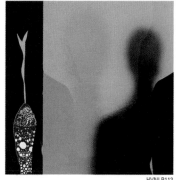

HVNLP113

HVNLP114

HVNLP115

HVNLP116

HVNLP117

HVNLP118

HVNLP119

HVNLP120

HVNLP121

HVNLP122

HVNLP123

HVNLP124

HVNLP125

HVNLP126

HVNLP127

HVNLP128

HVNLP129

HVNLP130

HVNLP131

HVNLP132

HVNLP133

HVNLP134

HVNLP135

HVNLP136

HVNLP137

HVNLP138

HVNLP139

HVNLP140

HVNLP141

HVNLP142

HVNLP143

HVNLP144

HVNLP145

HVNLP146

HVNLP147

HVNLP148

HVNLP149

HVNLP150

HVNLP151

HVNLP152

HVNLP153

HVNLP154

HVNLP155

HVNLP156

HVNLP157

HVNLP158

HVNLP159

HVNLP160

HVNLP161

HVNLP162

HVNLP162I

HVNLP163

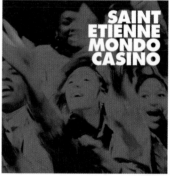

HVNLP164

HVNLP165

HVNLP166

HVNLP167

HVNLP168

HVNLP169

HVNLP170

HVNLP171

HVNLP172

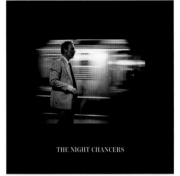

HVNLP173

HVNLP174

HVNLP175

HVNLP176

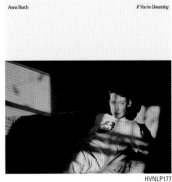

HVNLP177

HVNLP178

HVNLP179

HEAVENLY SINGLES

HVN1 – HVN100

HVN1	**Sly & Lovechild** The World According to Sly & Lovechild
HVN2	**Saint Etienne** Only Love Can Break Your Heart
HVN3	**Flowered Up** It's On
HVN4	**Saint Etienne** Kiss and Make Up
HVN5	**The Moonflowers** Get Higher
HVN6	**East Village** Circles
HVN7	**Flowered Up** Phobia
HVN8	**Manic Street Preachers** Motown Junk
HVN9	**Saint Etienne** Nothing Can Stop Us
HVN10	**Manic Street Preachers** You Love Us
HVN11	**Fabulous** Destined To Be Free/There's a Riot Going On
HVN12	**Saint Etienne** Only Love Can Break Your Heart
HVN13	**Paul Cannell** Toasted Cheese Sandwich
HVN14	**The Rockingbirds** A Good Day for You
HVN15	**Saint Etienne** Join Our Club
HVN16	**Flowered Up** Weekender
HVN17	**The Rockingbirds** Jonathan, Jonathan
HVN18	**Cannellism** An exhibition of artwork by Paul Cannell
HVN19	**Flowered Up, Saint Etienne and The Rockingbirds** The Fred EP
HVN20	**Espiritu** Francisca
HVN21	**The Rockingbirds** Gradually Learning
HVN22	**Saint Etienne** Live in Paris '92 (flexi disc)
HVN23	**Saint Etienne** Avenue
HVN24	**Espiritu** Conquistador
HVN25	**Saint Etienne** You're in a Bad Way
HVN26	**Kevin Pearce** Something Beginning With 'O' (book)
HVN27	**The Rockingbirds** Further Down the Line (promo)
HVN28	**Espiritu** Conquistador
HVN29	**Saint Etienne** Hobart Paving/Who Do You Think You Are?
HVN30	**Heavenly Bodies** merchandising catalogue
HVN31	**The Rockingbirds** Rockingbirds R Us EP
HVN32	**Socialism** Ad
HVN33	**Espiritu** Los Americanos
HVN34	**Paolo Hewitt** Heaven's Promise (book)
HVN35	**In The City** A Heavenly Night at the Hacienda
HVN36	**Saint Etienne** Xmas 93 (fanclub CD)
HVN37	**Saint Etienne** Pale Movie
HVN38	**Flowered Up** Better Life
HVN39	**Secret Knowledge** 2 Much of Nuttin
HVN40	**Saint Etienne** Like A Motorway
HVN41	**Saint Etienne** Xmas 95 (fanclub CD)
HVN42	**Saint Etienne** Hug My Soul
HVN43	**The Rockingbirds** Band of Dreams
HVN44	**The Heavenly Sunday Social**
HVN45	**Dr. Robert** The Coming of Grace
HVN46	**Monkey Mafia** Blow the Whole Joint Up
HVN47	**Northern Uproar** Rollercoaster/Rough Boys
HVN48	**Q–Tee** Gimme That Body
HVN49	**Dr. Robert** Circular Quay
HVN50	**Saint Etienne** He's on the Phone
HVN51	**Northern Uproar** From a Window/This Morning
HVN52	**Northern Uproar** Livin' It Up
HVN53	**Monkey Mafia** Work Mi Body featuring Patra
HVN54	**Northern Uproar** Town
HVN55	**Espiritu** You Send Me
HVN56	**Beth Orton** I Wish I Never Saw the Sunshine
HVN57	**Northern Uproar** Living in the Red (acetate)
HVN58	**Various Artists** High in a Basement (album sampler)
HVN59	**The Hybirds** I'm Coming Out
HVN60	**Beth Orton** She Cries Your Name
HVN61	**Espiritu** Baby I Wanna Live
HVN62	**Famous Times** Something to Believe
HVN63	**The Hybirds** The Only Ones (part two)
HVN64	**Beth Orton** Touch Me with Your Love
HVN65	**Beth Orton** Someone's Daughter
HVN66	**Espiritu** Man Don't Cry
HVN67	**Monkey Mafia** 15 Steps EP
HVN68	**Beth Orton** She Cries Your Name
HVN69	**Famous Times** The Blue Man EP
HVN70	**Northern Uproar** Any Way You Look
HVN71	**The Hybirds** Take You Down EP
HVN72	**Beth Orton** Best Bit
HVN73	**Northern Uproar** A Girl I Once Knew
HVN74	**Espiritu** You Don't Get Me
HVN75	**The Hybirds** Stranded
HVN76	**Monkey Mafia** Ward 10
HVN77	**Northern Uproar** Goodbye
HVN78	**The Hybirds** 24
HVN79	**Bronx Dogs** Madame Mars
HVN80	**The Hybirds** See Me Through/24
HVN81	**Dot Allison** I Wanna Feel the Chill
HVN82	**Beth Orton** Live as You Dream (promo)
HVN83	**The Hybirds** Peter Take Me Down
HVN84	**Monkey Mafia** Long as I Can See the Light
HVN85	**Schizoid Man** Karate Juice
HVN86	**Monkey Mafia** Healing the Nation
HVN87	**Dot Allison** Mo' Pop
HVN88	**Monkey Mafia** Work Mi Body
HVN89	**Beth Orton** Stolen Car
HVN90	**Matt Harding** 2-3-1
HVN91	**Dot Allison** Message Personnel
HVN92	**Beth Orton** Central Reservation
HVN93	**Dot Allison** Close Your Eyes
HVN94	**Bronx Dogs** Mission to Free
HVN95	**Doves** The Cedar Room
HVN96	**Doves** Catch the Sun
HVN97	**Omega** Amoeba Retro Failure
HVN98	**Doves** The Man Who Told Everything
HVN99	**Snowblind** Cut
HVN100	**heavenly100.com** (original website)

HVN101 – HVN200

HVN101	**Ed Harcourt** Something in My Eye
HVN102	**Electric Moccasins Of Doom** Kickstart
HVN103	**Snowblind** Easy Girl
HVN104	**Ed Harcourt** She Fell into My Arms
HVN105	**Culture/Tappa Zukie** Two Sevens Clash/MPLA
HVN106	**King Tubby/Junior Byles** Bag a Wire Dub/Fade Away
HVN107	**Ed Harcourt** Apple of My Eye
HVN108	**New Buffalo** 16 Beats
HVN109	**Nada Surf/Ed Harcourt** Blonde on Blonde/Jetsetter
HVN110	**Ed Harcourt** Shanghai [cancelled release]
HVN111	**Doves** There Goes the Fear
HVN112	**The Vines** Highly Evolved
HVN113	**The Vines** Get Free
HVN114	**Dog** Jerusalem
HVN115	**Beth Orton** Concrete Sky
HVN116	**Doves** Pounding
HVN117	**Dog** Bitten
HVN118	**Rebelski** Scarecrow
HVN119	**Beth Orton** Carmella
HVN120	**The Vines** Outtathaway!
HVN121	**Ed Harcourt** Still I Dream of It/The Ghosts Parade
HVN122	**Doves** Spaceface
HVN123	**Nada Surf** The Way You Wear Your Head
HVN124	**Flowered Up** Weekender
HVN125	**Beth Orton** Anywhere
HVN126	**Doves** Caught By the River
HVN127	**Ed Harcourt** All of Your Days Will Be Blessed
HVN128	**Nada Surf** Hi-Speed Soul
HVN129	**Beth Orton** Thinking About Tomorrow
HVN130	**Ed Harcourt** Watching the Sun Come Up
HVN131	**Beth Orton** Daybreaker Roots (Manuva Remix)
HVN132	**The Vines** Homesick
HVN133	**Nada Surf** Inside of Love
HVN134	**22-20s** Devil in Me
HVN135	**The Vines** F.T.
HVN136	**Saint Etienne** Come on Christmas (fanclub CD)
HVN137	**The Vines** Ride
HVN138	**22-20s** Why Don't You Do It for Me
HVN139	**The Vines** Winning Days
HVN140	**Ed Harcourt** This One's for You
HVN141	**22-20s** Shoot Your Gun
HVN142	**Don Letts** Various Artists (album sampler)

HVN143 **The Magic Numbers** Hymn for Her
HVN144 **22–20s** 22 Days
HVN145 **Doves** Black and White Town
HVN146 **Ed Harcourt** Born in the '70s
HVN147 **The Magic Numbers/Hal** Anima Sola/
Keep Love as Your Golden Rule
HVN148 **22–20s** Such a Fool
HVN149 **Ed Harcourt** Loneliness
HVN150 **Doves** Snowden
HVN151 **The Magic Numbers** Forever Lost
HVN152 **Doves** Sky Starts Falling
HVN153 **The Magic Numbers** Love Me Like You
HVN154 **The Magic Numbers** Love's a Game
HVN155 **The Magic Numbers/The Webb Brothers**
Cold Fingers/Try
HVN156 **The Magic Numbers** I See You, You See Me
HVN157 **Ed Harcourt** Visit from the Dead Dog
HVN158 **Edwyn Collins** You'll Never Know (My Love)
HVN159 **The Vines** Gross Out
HVN160 **The Vines** Anysound
HVN161 **Ed Harcourt** Revolution in the Heart
HVN162 **The Vines** Don't Listen to the Radio
HVN163 **The Magic Numbers** Take a Chance
HVN164 **The Little Ones** Lovers Who Uncover (radio promo)
HVN165 **The Magic Numbers** This Is a Song
HVN166 **The Little Ones** Oh MJ
HVN167 **Cherry Ghost** Mathematics
HVN168 **Cherry Ghost** People Help the People
HVN169 **The Little Ones** Lovers Who Uncover
HVN170 **The Magic Numbers** Undecided
HVN171 **Cherry Ghost** 4 am
HVN172 **Ed Harcourt** You Put a Spell on Me
HVN173 **Saint Etienne** This Is Tomorrow
HVN174 **Jaymay** Sea Green, See Blue
HVN175 **The Little Ones** Ordinary Song
HVN176 **The Loose Salute** Turn the Radio Up
HVN177 **Jaymay** Gray or Blue
HVN178 **The Little Ones** Morning Tide
HVN179 **Beggars** The Future
HVN180 **Edwyn Collins** Home Again
HVN181 **Jaymay** Ill Willed Person
HVN182 **Beggars** You & Me
HVN183 **Saint Etienne** Burnt Out Car
HVN184 **Forever Heavenly 18th Birthday** at the Southbank Centre
HVN185 **Saint Etienne** Method of Modern Love
HVN186 **The Loose Salute** Why We'd Fight
HVN187 **The Little Ones** Tangerine Visions
HVN188 **47 Frith Street**
HVN189 **Doves** Kingdom of Rust
HVN190 **The Rockingbirds** Man In the Moon
HVN191 **219 Portobello Road**
HVN192 **Doves** Winter Hill
HVN193 **The Ooh Ooh Ah Ahh Band** Show Me the Way to Sasparella/
Who Will Buy My Sweet Spanish Oranges (They Are Enormous)
HVN194 **The Soft Pack** Answer to Yourself
HVN195 **Fionn Regan** Protection Racket
HVN196 **The Soft Pack** C'mon
HVN197 **The Magic Numbers** The Pulse
HVN198 **Fionn Regan** Catacombs
HVN199 **The Soft Pack** More or Less
HVN200 **Chris Camm** The Heavenly Hairdresser

HVN201 – HVN300

HVN201 **Doves** Andalucia
HVN202 **Fionn Regan** Lines Written in Winter
HVN203 **Cherry Ghost** Kissing Strangers
HVN204 **The Magic Numbers** Why Did You Call?
HVN205 **Edwyn Collins** Losing Sleep
HVN206 **Cherry Ghost** Black Fang
HVN207 **Sea of Bees** The Woods
HVN208 **Edwyn Collins** (Rough Trade bonus disc)
HVN209 **Cherry Ghost** We Sleep on Stones
HVN210 **LCMDF** Gandhi
HVN211 **Edwyn Collins** Do It Again
HVN212 **Doug Paisley** No One But You
HVN213 **The Head and The Heart** Lost in My Mind

HVN214 **LCMDF** Future Me
HVN215 **Sea of Bees** Wizbot
HVN216 **James Walbourne** The Hill
HVN217 **Sea of Bees** Bee Eee Pee EP
HVN218 **Big Kids** I'm Bored
HVN219 **Edwyn Collins & The Drums** In Your Eyes
HVN220 **Trevor Moss & Hannah-Lou/James Walbourne/
Sea of Bees** Passing of Time/BBC/
The Woods (3-track EP download)
HVN221 **Trevor Moss & Hannah-Lou** Spin Me a Rhyme
HVN222 **Cherry Ghost** Only a Mother
HVN223 **Sea of Bees** Gnomes
HVN224 **Will Sergeant** Extinction
HVN225 **LCMDF** Cool and Bored
HVN226 **Trevor Moss & Hannah-Lou** Making It Count
HVN227 **The Head and the Heart** Rivers and Roads
HVN228 **Fionn Regan** For a Nightingale
HVN229 **LCMDF** Take Me to the Mountains
HVN230 **James Walbourne** Drugs and Money
HVN231 **James Levy and The Blood Red Rose** Pray to Be Free
HVN232 **The Head and the Heart** Ghosts
HVN233 **TOY** Left Myself Behind
HVN234 **Trevor Moss & Hannah-Lou** Big Water
HVN235 **Fionn Regan** List of Distractions
HVN236 **James Levy and The Blood Red Rose**
Sneak Into My Room EP
HVN237 **Saint Etienne** Xmas 11 EP
HVN238 **Saint Etienne** Tonight
HVN239 **Sea of Bees** Broke
HVN240 **Stealing Sheep** Shut Eye
HVN241 **TOY** Motoring
HVN242 **TOY** (promo EP)
HVN243 **Saint Etienne** I've Got Your Music
HVN244 **James Levy and The Blood Red Rose** Hung to Dry
HVN245 **Stealing Sheep** Genevieve
HVN246 **TOY** Dead and Gone
HVN247 **TOY** Lose My Way
HVNCB **Charlie Boyer** Ducks
HVN249 **Charlie Boyer and The Voyeurs** I Watch You
HVN250 **Temples** Shelter Song/Prisms
HVN251 **Stealing Sheep** Rearrange/Boys In The Band
HVN252 **TOY** Make It Mine
HVN253 **TOY** Left Myself Behind
HVN254 **Charlie Boyer and The Voyeurs** Things We Be
HVN255 **TOY** Heart Skips a Beat
HVN256 **Heavenly** (5-track download EP)
HVN257 **Stealing Sheep** A Real Clown/Do As You Will (RSD release)
HVN258 **TOY/The Horrors** Motoring/Moving
Further Away (RSD release)
HVN259 **Mark Lanegan and Duke Garwood** Cold Molly
(RSD release)
HVN260 **Charlie Boyer and the Voyeurs** Be Glamorous
HVN261 **Temples** Colours to Life
HVN261I **Temples** Colours to Life (Instrumental)
HVN262 **Out Cold** All I Want
HVN263 **Mark Lanegan and Duke Garwood** War Memorial
HVN264 **Heavenly summer compilation**
HVN265 **Charlie Boyer and The Voyeurs** Sister Ray
HVN266 **Out Cold** Sorrow
HVN267 **Temples** Keep in the Dark
HVN268 **Believe in Magic** (patch)
HVN269 **Heavenly** (tote bag)
HVN270 **TOY** Join the Dots
HVN271 **Charlie Boyer and The Voyeurs** Evil Mothers/
Wicked Annabella
HVN272 **TOY** Endlessly
HVN273 **TOY** Join the Dubs
HVN274 **Temples** Mesmerise
HVN275 **The Wytches** Gravedweller
HVN276 **Temples** Move with the Season
HVN277 **Jimi Goodwin** Oh! Whiskey
HVN278 **Out Cold** Synchronised
HVN279 **Temples** Live in Japan EP
HVN280 **Temples** Shelter Song/Mesmerise (promo)
HVN281 **King Gizzard and The Lizard Wizard** Head On/Pill
(picture disc)
HVN282 **Temples/Jagwa Ma** Shelter Song/Man I Need (picture disc)

HVN283 **TOY** It's Been So Long
HVN284 **Jimi Goodwin** Live Like a River
HVN285 **Saint Etienne** (book)
HVN286 **Temples** Shelter Song
HVN287 **TOY** As We Turn
HVN288 **The Wytches** Wire Frame Mattress
HVN289 **Mark Lanegan Band** No Bells on Sunday
HVN290 **Kid Wave** All I Want
HVN291 **Fever The Ghost** Crab in Honey EP
HVN292 **The Wytches** Burn out the Bruise
HVN293 **The Voyeurs** Stunners
HVN294 **Kid Wave** Gloom
HVN295 **Eaves** As Old as the Grave
HVN296 **King Gizzard and The Lizard Wizard** Cellophane
HVN297 **Jimi Goodwin** Lonely at the Drop
HVN298 **Mark Lanegan** Band
HVN299 **H. Hawkline** Moons in My Mirror
HVN300 **A Heavenly Weekend in Hebden Bridge**

HVN301 – 400

HVN301 **Hooton Tennis Club** Jasper
HVN302 **Hooton Tennis Club** Kathleen
HVN303 **Temples** Temples Live in Brooklyn EP
HVN304 **Pete Wiggs/Jimi Goodwin** We've Got the Moves/
Didsbury Girl (Tear Down Dub) [Heavenly 25]
HVN305 **Kid Wave and Ben from Childhood/Caitlin Rose**
Been Thinking About You All The Time/
Listen to Her Heart [Heavenly 25]
HVN306 **Mark Lanegan/Duke Garwood** Needle of Death/
Fresh as a Sweet Sunday Morning [Heavenly 25]
HVN307 **Stealing Sheep/The Voyeurs** Murmer Earth/
Rhubarb Rhubarb (Third Webb's Rhubarb and Custard Mix)
[Heavenly 25]
HVN308 **Fever The Ghost/Temples** Calico/Keep in the Dark
[Heavenly 25]
HVN309 **The Wytches/Hooton Tennis Club** Wasteybois/Barstool
Blues [Heavenly 25]
HVN310 **TOY & Jane Weaver/H. Hawkline** Fell from the Sun/
It's a Drag [Heavenly 25]
HVN311 **Record Store Day Box Set**
HVN312 **King Gizzard and The Lizard Wizard** Slow Jam 1
HVN313 **A Heavenly All Dayer at the Shacklewell**
HVN314 **Kid Wave** Wonderlust
HVN315 **The Voyeurs** Train to Minsk
HVN316 **Stealing Sheep** Not Real
HVN317 **Eaves** Pylons
HVN318 **DRINKS** Hermits on Holiday
HVN319 **DRINKS** Laying Down Rock
HVN320 **Kid Wave** Honey
HVN321 **Heavenly 25 at the Kazimier**
HVN322 **Hooton Tennis Club** P.O.W.E.R.F.U.L. P.I.E.R.R.E/
French Crackers
HVN323 **Fever The Ghost** 1518
HVN324 **Mark Lanegan and Beth Orton** Your Kisses Burn
HVN325 **Kid Wave** Get Outta My Mind/Honey
HVN326 **Nots** Virgin Mary/Shelf Life
HVN327 **Nots** Reactor/Televangelist (demo)
HVN327ʀ **Nots** Reactor (Mikey Young Remix)
HVN328 **Night Beats** No Cops
HVN329 **Gwenno** Patriarchaeth
HVN330 **Palehound** Molly
HVN331 **Palehound** Cinnamon
HVN332 **Stealing Sheep** Apparition
HVN333 **Danny Mitchell and Carl Gosling**
HVN334 **Amber Arcades** Turning Light
HVN335 **Amber Arcades** Patiently EP
HVN336 **Amber Arcades** Right Now
HVN337 **Gwenno** Fratolish Hiang Perpeshki
HVN338 **Night Beats** Power Child
HVN339 **Heavenly SXSW**
HVN340 **Night Beats** Celebration #1
HVN341 **Night Beats** Sunday Mourning (Jono Ma Remix)
HVN342 **The Parrots** Let's Do It Again
HVN343 **The Heavenly Jukebox**
HVN344 **A Heavenly New Year's Eve with The Parrots**
HVN345 **The Parrots** No Me Gustas Te Quiero/Let's Do It Again

HVN346 **M. Craft** Chemical Trails
HVN347 **Duke Garwood** Cold Blooded
HVN348 **The Wytches** Home Recordings
HVN349 **Hooton Tennis Club** Flying
HVN350 **M. Craft** Chemical Trails (Beyond the Wizard's
Sleeve Remix)
HVN351 **TOY** I'm Still Believing
HVN352 **TOY** Spellbound EP
HVN353 **Hooton Tennis Club** Lauren, I'm In Love!
HVN354 **M. Craft** Blood Moon (Cavern of Anti Matter People Remix)
HVN355 **Hooton Tennis Club** Katy-Anne Bellis
HVN356 **The Wytches** C-side
HVN357 **Amber Arcades** Turning Light (Justin Robertson)
HVN358 **TOY** I'm Still Believing (Cavern of Anti Matter People Remix)
HVN359 **Temples** Certainty
HVN360 **A Heavenly Weekend in Hebden Bridge**
HVN361 **Amber Arcades** Turning Light Justin Robertson
HVN362 **Temples** Strange But Not Forgotten
HVN363 **TOY** I'm Still Believing
HVN364 **Amber Arcades** Which Will
HVN365 **TOY** I'm Still Believing (single bundle)
HVN366 **TOY** Fast Silver (bundle)
HVN367 **Temples** Certainty (Radio Edit)
HVN368 **Temples** Certainty (Franz Ferdinand Remix)/
Uncertainty (Grumbling Fur Machine Remix)
HVN369 **The Wytches** Bone Weary
HVN370 **King Gizzard and The Lizard Wizard** Rattlesnake
HVN371 **Hooton Tennis Club** Bootcut Jimmy
HVN372 **Temples** Strange or Be Forgotten (Villagers Remix)
HVN373 **The Parrots** A Thousand Ways
HVN374 **Hooton Tennis Club** Oh Man Won't You Melt Me
HVN375 **TOY** Another Dimension
HVN376 **King Gizzard and The Lizard Wizard** Nuclear Fusion
HVN377 **Duke Garwood** Coldblooded
HVN378 **The Wytches** Home Recordings
HVN379 **Mark Lanegan** Beehive
HVN380 **H. Hawkline** Last Thing On Your Mind
HVN381 **King Gizzard and The Lizard Wizard** Sleepdrifter
HVN382 **Mark Lanegan** Nocturne
HVN383 **Amber Arcades** It Changes
HVN384 **The Orielles** I Only Bought It for the Bottle
HVN385 **Amber Arcades** Cannonball EP
HVN386 **Temples** Strange or Be Forgotten
(Jono Ma Remix Vocal Version)
HVN387 **Temples** Strange or Be Forgotten
(Jono Ma Remix Even Stranger Version)
HVN388 **Confidence Man** Bubblegum
HVN389 **Duke Garwood** Sal's Paradise (Padre Remix)
HVN390 **The Orielles** Sugar Tastes Like Salt
HVN391 **The Wytches** Can't Face It
HVN392 **H. Hawkline** My Mine (digital single)
HVN393 **H. Hawkline** My Mine (Radio Edit)
HVN394 **H. Hawkline** Engineers
HVN395 **Confidence Man** Bubblegum (Radio Edit)
HVN396 **Amber Arcades** Can't Say That We Tried
HVN397 **Amber Arcades** Wouldn't Even Know
HVN398 **The Orielles** Sugar Tastes Like Salt (Radio Mix)
HVN399 **Confidence Man** Bubblegum (Andrew Weatherall Remix)
HVN400 **Confidence Man** Boyfriend (Repeat)

HVN401 – 500

HVN401 **Temples** Oh the Saviour! (Radio Edit)
HVN402 **Confidence Man** Bubblegum (Jono Ma Cowbell Remix)
HVN403 **Confidence Man** Bubblegum Remixes
HVN404 **Mark Lanegan** Beehive (Andrew Weatherall Remix)
HVN405 **The Orielles** Sugar Tastes Like Salt
(Andrew Weatherall Remix)
HVN406 **The Orielles** I Only Bought It for the Bottle
HVN407 **Mark Lanegan** Still Life with Roses (Gargoyle Remixes)
HVN408 **TOY** Dream Orchestrator (TVAM Remix)
HVN409 **Saint Etienne** Magpie Eyes
HVN410 **Saint Etienne** Magpie Eyes (Confidence Man Remix)
HVN411 **Saint Etienne** Magpie Eyes (Villagers Remix)
HVN412 **Saint Etienne** Dive
HVN413 **The Heavenly Emporium**
HVN414 **58 Old Compton Street**

HVN415	**Saint Etienne** Out of My Mind
HVN416	**Confidence Man** Better Sit Down Boy
HVN417	**Boy Azooga** Loner Boogie
HVN418	**Boy Azooga** Face Behind Her Cigarette
HVN419	**The Orielles** Let Your Dogtooth Grow
HVN420	**A Heavenly Weekend in Hebden Bridge**
HVN421	**77:78** Love Said
HVN422	**The Wytches** Double World
HVN423	**Anna Burch** 2 Cool 2 Care
HVN424	**Anna Burch** Asking for a Friend
HVN425	**Anna Burch** Tea-Soaked Letter
HVN426	**Anna Burch** Quit the Curse
HVN427	**Temples** Toe Rag Sessions
HVN428	**Halo Maud** Du Pouvoir EP
HVN429	**Gwenno** Tir Ha Mor
HVN430	**The Orielles** Blue Suitcase (Disco Wrist)
HVN431	**Boy Azooga** Loner Boogie
HVN432	**Hatchie** Sure
HVN433	**Dan Stock** Take It Too Far
HVN434	**Boy Azooga** Jerry
HVN435	**Confidence Man** Don't You Know I'm in a Band
HVN436	**Halo Maud** EP
HVN437	**Hatchie** Sugar & Spice EP
HVN438	**Hatchie** Try
HVN439	**Halo Maud** Tu Sais Comme Je Suis
HVN440	**Amber Arcades** Simple Song
HVN441	**Amber Arcades** Goodnight Europe
HVN442	**Halo Maud** Wherever
HVN443	**The Parrots** Soy Peor
HVN444	**Mattiel** Count Your Blessings
HVN445	**77:78** Chilli
HVN446	**Mattiel** Bye Bye
HVN447	**audiobooks** EP
HVN448	**audiobooks** Gothenburg (Radio Edit)
HVN449	**Dan Stock** Bright Ideas
HVN450	**Heavenly Cycle Shirt**
HVN451	**Baxter Dury** Listen (video)
HVN452	**Gwenno** Eus Keus?
HVN453	**audiobooks** Hot Salt
HVN454	**Confidence Man** Out the Window
HVN455	**CHAI** N.E.O.
HVN456	**CHAI** Kitty
HVN457	**Mark Lanegan and Duke Garwood** Scarlett
HVN458	**CHAI** Boyz Seco Men
HVN459	**Night Beats** Cold Cold Heart
HVN460	**Night Beats** One Thing
HVN461	**The Parrots** Girl
HVN462	**The Parrots** My Love Is Real
HVN463	**Confidence Man** Out the Window (Greg Wilson and Che Wilson Mix/Andrew Weatherall Remix)
HVN464	**Unloved** Heartbreak
HVN465	**Unloved** Crash Boom Bang
HVN466	**Unloved** Devils Angels
HVN467	**Halo Maud** Tu Sais Comme Je Suis
HVN468	**Dan Stock** Bright Ideas
HVN469	**Unloved** Love
HVN470	**audiobooks** Friends in the Bubble Bath
HVN471	**Stealing Sheep** Show Me Your Love
HVN472	**Stealing Sheep** Jokin' Me
HVN473	**Stealing Sheep** Why Haven't I?
HVN474	**audiobooks** Mother Hen
HVN475	**Saint Etienne** Surrey
HVN476	**Night Beats** Cold Cold Heart/Watch the Throne
HVN477	**audiobooks** I Wish My Lady Sang with a Sore Throat More
HVN478	**BED** White Coats
HVN479	**audiobooks** Dance Your Life Away
HVN480	**Boy Azooga** Do the Standing Still
HVN481	**Hatchie** Adored
HVN482	**The Orielles** Bobbi's Second World
HVN483	**Dan Stock** Bright Ideas EP
HVN484	**audiobooks** Dealing With Hoarders
HVN485	**Halo Maud** Dépression au-dessus du jardin
HVN486	**Confidence Man** Santa's Coming Down the Chimney
HVN487	**Unloved/Etienne Daho** Remember
HVN488	**Saint Etienne** Saturday Boy
HVN489	**Halo Maud** Des Bras (Andy Votel Remix)
HVN490	**Anna Burch** St. Adalbert

HVN491	**Pip Blom** Daddy Issues
HVN492	**Mark Lanegan** Stitch It Up/Song to Manset
HVN493	**Unloved** Love Lost
HVN494	**The Parrots** Cigarette Burns
HVN495	**CHAI** Fashionista
HVN496	**CHAI** Curly Adventure
HVN497	**audiobooks** Friends in the Bubblebath (Radio Edit)
HVN498	**CHAI** Great Job
HVN499	**CHAI** CHOOSE GO!
HVN500	**Heavenly Bird Lightbox**

HVN 501 – 600

HVN501	**audiobooks** Friends in the Bubble Bath
HVN502	**Halo Maud** Des Bras (Andy Votel Remix)
HVN503	**Unloved** Remember (Cat's Eyes Rework)
HVN504	**audiobooks** Friends in the Bubble Bath Remixes
HVN505	**Mattiel** Keep the Change
HVN506	**Mattiel** Food For Thought
HVN507	**Unloved** Unloved Remixes
HVN508	**Hatchie** Without A Blush
HVN509	**Hatchie** Stay With Me
HVN510	**Hatchie** Obsessed
HVN511	**A Heavenly Weekend at the Brudenell Social Club**
HVN512	**Mattiel** Je Ne Me Connais Pas
HVN513	**Mildlife** How Long Does It Take?
HVN514	**CHAI** Curly Hair Adventure (Radio Edit)
HVN515	**Mildlife** How Long Does It Take
HVN516	**Hatchie** Stay With Me
HVN517	**Hatchie** Obsessed
HVN518	**audiobooks** I Wish My Lady Sang with a Sore Throat More
HVN519	**Unloved** It's Not You, It's Me
HVN520	**Working Men's Club** Teeth (7-inch)
HVN520	**Working Men's Club** Teeth (12-inch)
HVN521	**Unloved** Without Love
HVN522	**Unloved** Unloved Heart
HVN523	**Unloved** Danger (Radio Mix)
HVN524	**Working Men's Club** Whitc Rooms and People
HVN525	**Katy J Pearson** Tonight/Poison Cup
HVN526	**Pip Blom** Freckles
HVN527	**Stealing Sheep** Barracuda
HVN528	**Mark Lanegan** Night Flight To Kabul Dubplates
HVN529	**Katy J Pearson** Tonight/Poison Cup
HVN530	**The Orielles** Come Down On Jupiter
HVN531	**Confidence Man** Don't It Make You Feel Good
HVN532	**Boy Azooga** Oh, Silly Me
HVN533	**The Orielles** Disco Volador
HVN534	**Boy Azooga** Oh, Silly Me/U.F.O.
HVN535	**Baxter Dury** Slumlord
HVN536	**Baxter Dury** Carla's Got A Boyfriend
HVN537	**Baxter Dury** I'm Not Your Dog
HVN538	**Baxter Dury** Say Nothing
HVN539	**Anna Burch** Not So Bad
HVN540	**Anna Burch** Party's Over
HVN541	**Anna Burch** Tell Me What's True
HVN542	**Anna Burch** Can't Sleep
HVN543	**A Heavenly Weekend in Hebden Bridge** 30th anniversary
HVN544	**Hatchie/The Pains Of Being Pure Of Heart** Sometimes Always/Adored
HVN545	**Mattiel** Merry Christmas (I Don't Want To Fight Tonight)
HVN546	**Mark Lanegan** Skeleton Key
HVN547	**Mark Lanegan** Bleed All Over
HVN548	**Mark Lanegan** Stockholm City Blues
HVN549	**Katy J Pearson** Hey You
HVN550	**Believe In Magic** (book)
HVN551	**Confidence Man** Catch My Breath (Radio Edit)
HVN552	**Working Men's Club** Valleys
HVN552	**Working Men's Club** Valleys (Graham Massey Remixes)
HVN553	**Working Men's Club** A.A.A.A.
HVN554	**Working Men's Club** John Cooper Clarke
HVN555	**Saint Etienne** Spring/Spring (Instrumental)
HVN556	**Working Men's Club** Angel

CREDITS

ACKNOWLEDGEMENTS

Heavenly has never been about one person, or the collection of people who've worked in the office over the years. Or the hairdresser or the landlords and ladies of each of the many 'second offices'. It's always been a huge, collaborative family that's helped bands and artists grow and made club nights and gigs happen.

So a huge, eternally Heavenly thanks to the backers and the barflies, the radio pluggers and the press officers, the managers and the merchandisers, the live promoters and the gig-goers, the record buyers and the stockists, the sync squads, the marketing geniuses, the publishers, the publicans, the club runners, the DJs and the dancers, the festival bookers and all those kids who rush to the front of stage right at the start of the night.

To all of the bands who showed willing and kept the faith and to all of our friends who've listened to mad ideas and who've given good advice, whatever time of the day or night, in offices, bars, venues and fields the world over.

To everyone that's joined us on this journey and helped us to believe in magic . . . can we just say we love you all and we'll buy you a pint the next time we see you.

PHOTOGRAPHY

Alissa Anderson 178. Ame 225. Wendy Barrett 89, 99, 171 (bottom). Tom Beard 254. Hamish Brown 90, 94–5, 118–9. BullyRook 238 (top). Richard Burbridge 41. Ray Burmiston 35. Louise Chandler 270 (top left). Kiera Cullaine 208–9. Kevin Cummins 44. Tara Darby 176. Jacek Davis 230. Autumn De Wild 177. Joe Dilworth 38. Steve Double 49 (*Sounds*). Carolina Faruolo 214, 215, 245 (top). Kate Garner 107 (right). Alex Germains 190. Rich Gilligan 147 (right), Steve Glashier 218. Martin Goodacre 76 (bottom), 108–9. Daisy Goodwin 272 (top). Steve Gullick 37 (bottom), 51, 52–3, 55–7, 70, 76 (top), 79, 80–1, 134, 137, 138, 162, 164–5, 180, 189, 203 (bottom), 216, 217, 219, 250, 278. Sam Harris 112, 115, 116. Luke Hayes 31. Nick Helderman 239. Valerie Hicks 25. Nigel Hillier 220. Matti Hillig 202. Alan Horne 228–9. Sophie Hur 283. Alastair Indge 73 (top). Luke Insect 188. Martin Kelly 204, 270 (bottom), 277 (bottom). Paul Kelly cover, 1, 8, 14, 16–7, 36, 65, 71, 75, 83, 100–1, 102, 105, 117, 122 (top), 123, 124, 140–1, 146–7, 153, 157, 158–9, 160–1, 167, 168, 181, 182, 187, 199, 207, 256, 259, 261, 262, 265, 269, 270 (left), 274, 277 (top), 292–3, 309, 315, 320. Neelam Khan 242, 243 (bottom), 248–9, 290 (bottom), 291. Nigel Law 62. Mark McNulty 106. Ed Miles 196. Danny Mitchell 272 (top left and bottom). Deirdre O'Callaghan 129. Stephen Parker 26, 236, 318. Lola Pertsowski 243 (top). Piran 284, 286–7. Jenna Putnam 238 (bottom). Steve Pyke 30. Phillip Randall 290. Paul Rider 61 (*MM*). Cara Robbins 210. Glyn Roberts 132–3. Dave Rofe 10. Hamish Rosser 152, 155. Erica Rossing Oberg 224. Carla Salvatore-Pacitto 245 (bottom). Simon Sarin 192. Mary Scanlon 126. Nic Serpell Rand 226–7. Paul Slattery 86, 88. Pennie Smith 18, 32–3, 95. Brian David Stevens 232–5. Hayley Taylor 172. Neil Thompson 195, 201 (bottom), 222–3. Raymond Van Mill 282 (bottom). Simon Webb 264. Kevin Westenberg 127 (*NME*). Jamie Wdziekonski 212. David Willis 77. Andy Wilsher 148 (*NME*). Kasia Wozniak (wet plate collodion photographs) 246–7 (art direction by Louise Mason). Ebru Yildiz 241, 255.

HEAVENLY HAUNTS & HANGOUTS

Designed by Herb Lester Associates. Art director: Ben Olins. Illustrator: Danielle Simonelli

ADDITIONAL CREDITS

NME and *Melody Maker* covers used courtesy of Bandlab 14, 61, 127, 148. 'Weekender' storyboards courtesy of Wiz 66. 'Weekender' poster/flyer by Sophy Hollington 68. Andy Hackett jigsaw photo by Stefan De Bastelier 85. Beth Orton photographs courtesy of Sam Harris @samharrisphoto #samharrisphoto 112, 115–6. Doves sleeves designed by Rick Myres 131. Don Letts flyer artwork courtesy of Emma Shepherd/Eskimo 145. Magic Numbers figures created by Pete Fowler 167. Loose Salute poster designed by James Bates 176. Tin Tabernacle illustrations by Pete Fowler 179. King Gizzard and the Lizard Wizard 'Albert Hall, Manchester' by Olya Dyer 214. Heavenly and Friends 'On Blackheath' by Thomas Caslin 226. The Parrots 'Album Launch Show' by Olya Dyer 240. The Orielles 'Xmas Party' by Tim Head 241. 'A Heavenly Weekend at the Brudenell Social Club' by Sophy Hollington 248. Unloved artwork by Julian House 253. *SEVEN* magazine/*DMC*/ Shona Wong 266–7. 'A Heavenly 30 Weekender at The Trades' by Nolan Pelletier 281. DRINKS artwork courtesy of Tim Presley 303. All collage photographs by Heavenly staff and friends 317.

SPECIAL THANKS TO THE FOLLOWING FOR ARCHIVE MATERIAL
AND RESEARCH ASSISTANCE

Jeff Barrett, Sonny Barrett, Wendy Barrett, Richard Beak, Katherine Cantwell, Lora Findlay, Grant Flemming, Martyn Goodacre, Daisy Goodwin, Diva Harris, Valerie Hicks, Martin Kelly, Paul Kelly, Phil King, Danny Mitchell, Rosie Pearce, Des Penney, Dave Rofe, Hamish Rosser, Robin Turner, Andrew Walsh, Wiz, Debsey Wykes.

LYRIC CREDITS

'Shout to the Top' by The Style Council (EMI Music Publishing). 'Goin' Back' by The Byrds (Screen Gems/Columbia Music Inc). 'Promised Land' by Joe Smooth (Kassner Associated Publishers Limited). 'Tutti Frutti' by Little Richard (Sony/ATV Publishing (UK) Limited). 'Cut Your Hair' by Pavement (Domino Publishing). 'Jumping Jack Flash' by The Rolling Stones (Onward Music LTD, Westminster Music LTD, ABKCO Music Limited). 'This One's For You' by Ed Harcourt (Sony/ATV Publishing (UK) Limited). 'Lost in Music' by Sister Sledge (Warner Chappell North America Limited, Sony/ATV Music Publishing (UK) Limited). 'Come Together' (Andrew Weatherall remix) by Primal Scream (Sony/ATV Publishing (UK) Limited). 'Weekender' by Flowered Up (Copyright Control). 'Do You Believe in Magic' by The Lovin' Spoonful (BMG Rights Management (UK) Limited, EMI Music Publishing Limited). 'Girl VII' by Saint Etienne (Warner Chappell). 'Gimme That Body' by Q-Tee (Copyright Control). 'Rollercoaster' by Northern Uproar (BMG Music Publishing Limited). 'Cut' by Snowblind (Heavenly Songs). 'Blonde on Blonde' by Nada Surf (Songs As Pets/Karmacode). 'Miami' by Baxter Dury (Downtown Music Publishing).

HEAVENLY ...BELIEVE IN MAGIC

Heavenly

25

Forever Heavenly

HEAVENLY

H J V B N X

Dynamite Sounds

HEAVENLY

PURE

a Heavenly recording

HEAVENLY

POP

HEAVENLY JUKEBOX

As this book was nearing completion the dreadful news reached us that our dear friend Andrew Weatherall had died.

Andrew's name and fingerprint runs all the way through this story. He mixed our very first release, remixed our second, and it's fair to say that his recent remixes for The Orielles, audiobooks and Confidence Man are up there with his best. His DJ sets soundtracked more of our nights than we can remember, from the first Heavenly party at the Camden Underworld to half a dozen successive summers in Cornwall as resident DJ on the Caught by the River stage we booked for the Port Eliot Festival.

Andrew and I became friends after meeting on the acid house club scene a year or so before I started Heavenly. We immediately identified as fellow travellers, sharing a spirit of adventure, a sense of mischief and a code of living that fed us both. We were just two guys doing our best to dodge the squares. He had the best records and the best stories. We'd stay up late talking shit, or he would come by the office for a cup of tea and a smoke and he'd make us laugh – he could always make you laugh – and sparks were created that made things happen that neither of us could have ever guessed possible.

He touched us all with his charm, his wit and his supreme talent. He was a total inspiration. Everyone who has ever worked alongside me at Heavenly loved him dearly. He was a one-off and we'll miss him very much.

Jeff Barrett
July 2020